MW00723267

BLACKROBE IN BLUE: THE NAVAL CHAPLAINCY OF JOHN P. FOLEY, S.J.
1942–1946

Fr. John P. Foley, S.J. in January 1945, at the time he left Bethesda to report aboard
U.S.S. *Vella Gulf.*
(All photographs courtesy of John Foley and William Leonard except where noted)

Blackrobe In Blue: The Naval Chaplaincy Of John P. Foley, S.J.
1942–1946

▼

Steve O'Brien, Ph.D.

Writers Club Press

San Jose   New York   Lincoln   Shanghai

Blackrobe In Blue: The Naval Chaplaincy Of John P. Foley, S.J.
1942–1946

All Rights Reserved © 2002 by Steven E. O'Brien

No part of this book may be reproduced or transmitted in any form or by any means, graphic, electronic, or mechanical, including photocopying, recording, taping, or by any information storage retrieval system, without the permission in writing from the publisher.

Writers Club Press
an imprint of iUniverse, Inc.

For information address:
iUniverse, Inc.
5220 S. 16th St., Suite 200
Lincoln, NE 68512
www.iuniverse.com

Cover painting "Divine Services" by William F. Draper, 1943.
(Navy Art Collection)

ISBN: 0-595-22694-9

Printed in the United States of America

Dedication
For Katie, Megs, Pat & Brendan with love.

Epigraph

The Heavenly Pilot

Wilt Thou steer my frail black bark
O'er the dark broad ocean's foam?
Wilt Thou come, Lord, to my boat
Where afloat my will would roam?

Thine the mighty; Thine the small;
Thine to mark men fall like rain;
God! wilt Thou grant aid to me
Who come o'er the upheaving main?

Cormac, King-Bishop of Cashel (836–908)

CONTENTS

INTRODUCTION

This book is designed to describe the spiritual life and service life of the Catholic chaplain in the United States Navy during World War II, through the experiences of Fr. John P. Foley, S.J.

Foley was Dean of Admissions and Dean of Freshmen and Sophomores at Boston College from 1938–1941. When World War II came, Foley secured permission from the New England Provincial to serve as a chaplain in the United States Naval Reserve. During the course of the war, Foley served aboard two naval vessels. One, the U.S.S. *George Clymer* (APA-27), was an Auxiliary Personnel Attack craft which brought large numbers of Marines and Army troops within striking distance of their invasion targets. The other vessel, the U.S.S. *Vella Gulf* (CVE-111), was an escort aircraft carrier.

Foley also held an assignment at Bethesda Naval Hospital in Maryland, where he ministered to the enlisted personnel and WAVEs, as well as high-ranking government officials. Aboard the combat vessels, Foley saw fighting first in the North African campaign and later in campaigns in the Pacific Theater of Operations. At the end of the war, Father Foley toured the razed Japanese cities of Yokohama and Tokyo before returning to Boston College and resuming his academic and administrative duties.

Though World War II in general has an enormous historiography, there are huge gaps in some areas, and the chaplaincy is one of them. What exists are post-war memoirs primarily written in the 1950s in anecdotal fashion, without documentation.

For example, Fr. Joseph T. O'Callahan, another New England Jesuit and the only chaplain to win the Medal of Honor, produced a memoir in 1956 after he had suffered a major stroke. *I Was Chaplain on the Franklin* details the horrific conditions prevailing on that ship after it was bombed during the Okinawa operation in April 1945. While an honest view of his experiences during the *Franklin* disaster, there is scant material on his personal life and vocation. Most of the other memoirs left from World War II era chaplains suffer from the same problems. The comparatively few that exist can be interesting narratives but offer little introspection and even the theology often seems shallow. Criticism of the government or the military is practically non-existent. Questions about the conduct and morality of the war are scarcely broached. Essential conflicts between Church and State rarely appear.

A notable exception to the trend is *Where Thousands Fell,* published in 1995 by yet another New England Jesuit chaplain, Fr. William J. Leonard, S.J. Since most chaplains were middle-aged men in the 1940s and the few surviving are nearing the century mark, it is probable that Leonard's memoir will be the last written by a World War II chaplain.

Two invaluable reference sources exist for those researching the naval chaplaincy and twentieth century Jesuit chaplains. The first is the three volume *The History of the Chaplain Corps United States Navy* by Clifford M. Drury. Two volumes are a narrative history of the institution from 1778–1949. The third volume is a collection of vital statistics of every individual who served as a naval chaplain up to that date. The other excellent source is *Jesuits as Chaplains in the Armed Forces 1917–1960* by Gerard F. Giblin, S.J. Giblin sent surveys to the surviving Jesuit chaplains from World Wars I and II and compiled a volume of vital statistics including dates of ordination, service assignments, and decorations conferred. A few brief overviews of the army and navy chaplaincy also exist.

Academics have steered clear of the chaplaincy. While nearly every other aspect of World War II continues to be thoroughly researched and reexamined, startlingly few biographical or synthetic works exist on this subject. There are several reasons for this. Most academics tend to be either hostile or apathetic toward religion and there is no great interest in the subject. Further, in treating the Catholic chaplaincy, one would have to be thoroughly trained in two unrelated fields—naval/military history and pre-Vatican II Church history. Consequently, knowledge of the specialized language and bibliography of the two fields is essential. Another problem is access to primary sources. Church records regarding individuals are difficult to access or often nonexistent. Contrary to popular opinion, there is no informational "web" in the Catholic Church. In fact, because priests are celibate and do not have families to inherit personal papers, important documents are often discarded when they die.

John Foley's story then, is perhaps unique in that the author not only was able to conduct a series of oral history interviews shortly before Foley's death, but even more importantly, was given Foley's five hundred-plus page diary kept throughout the war, in violation of navy regulations. Published wartime diaries of enlisted men and officers are common and continue to appear on a regular basis. However, diaries of chaplains available for research are exceedingly rare. An extremely detailed document like Foley's which begins from the day he embarked for chaplain school and continues until the end of war, (excepting a brief period ashore) is unheard of.

Furthermore, the document is a true diary, not meant for publication and hence a far more honest and revealing source than most chaplain's published accounts. Foley's trenchant observations on the navy and specific officers were often highly critical, and more than once he had heated arguments with his superiors over the moral welfare of the sailors. He fully realized that the dictates of the navy often clashed with the teachings of the Church and, while committed to the war effort, steadfastly refused to compromise his principles for the duration. He likewise condemned wartime propaganda and racial epithets in regard to the Japanese, a trait he found less evident in the enlisted men than in the navy and government bureaucrats who did a sudden hypocritical turnaround the day the war ended. The diary represents a highly educated clergyman who had joined the navy to be of service to the enlisted men, but one who was not about to be co-opted by the State or swayed by war's hateful passions. John Foley was fully formed theologically and was more than capable of making his own decisions regarding the moral implications of the war.

Foley's personal story is a microcosm of the chaplaincy in general, though logically the emphasis is on the experiences of Catholics in particular. Catholics had a strong support system in the Military Ordinariate and vicar, who acted as their ecclesiastical superior while they were in the service. On the other hand, Catholic chaplains often encountered examples of prejudice on both an official and popular level, which again reminded them of the Church's ambiguous place in American society. Nevertheless, the Catholic chaplaincy proved to be a boon to the Church in America during World War II and in the immediate post-war period. The experiences of these men have been little recounted. While John Foley's service was in some ways representative of the breed, he was himself an extraordinary man whose intellect, judgment, compassion and sense of justice served him and his charges well as a Jesuit chaplain in the World War II navy.

CHAPTER I

▼

"THE SWORD OF THE SPIRIT"

Christianity has always been a profession of arms. St. Paul, writing his Epistle to the Ephesians in the year 63 after his first imprisonment in Rome, spelled out the warrior ethic of the true follower of Christ.

> Stand, therefore, having girded your loins with truth, and having put on the breastplate of justice, and having your feet shod with the readiness of the gospel of peace, in all things taking up the shield of faith, with which you may be able to quench all the fiery darts of the most wicked one. And take unto you the helmet of salvation and the sword of the spirit, that is, the word of God.1

Paul's words, spiritual in tone, apply equally to the worldly life of Christians. His lesson teaches that to follow Christ one must be willing to fight and die for the truth. In the first Gospel, Matthew recounts Christ saying as much. "Do not think that I have come to send peace upon the earth; I have come to bring a sword, not peace." And "He who finds his life will lose it, and he who loses his life for my sake, will find it.2

Christ also "marveled" at the faith of a Centurion who asked him to cure his paralyzed servant. The Centurion, not wanting the Master to be seen at a soldier's house, told him " only say the word and my servant will be healed."3 The Centurion understood the value of military discipline because he lived his life giving and taking orders. He understood, too, that Christ could effect any cure by merely ordering it to be so. Christ's admiration for the faith of the soldier, a Gentile, multiplied his contempt for the faithless Israelites.

From the time of Christ, priests have accompanied Christian soldiers into the field. Solid data from the Roman Empire is scarce on this issue, but toleration for Christianity was granted by Emperor Constantine in the Edict of Milan in 313 and it is generally held that Constantine did indeed bring along bishops and priests on campaign.4 The inclusion of these men would have been on an informal basis, and there was not yet any type of organized "corps" system for priests. Soldier-priests received their title from an incident in the fourth century life of St. Martin of Tours (c 316–397). In the bitter winter of 338–339, while serving as a Roman Circuit Officer in Amiens, he was approached by a freezing beggar. Martin had already given away his money and other possessions, but removed his *chlamys* , a heavy cloak, clove it in two, and gave one piece to the beggar. The following night he dreamed that the beggar was really Christ, wearing the half cloak, who praised Martin to a host of angels for his charity.5

St. Martin's cloak continued in military service long after his death. The cloak, in Latin *capella* , was worn by French kings on campaign. During actual battles, the *capella* was consigned to a special priest for safe-keeping. These priests, guardians of the sacred relic, were designated *capellanus* , later anglicized into "chaplain". From earliest usage, a chaplain was a priest without parochial duties, but who tended to hospitals, hospices, and military personnel. The title and office in this form continue to the present day.6

In 1118, at the beginning of the Crusades, a handful of knights took up the task of guarding the pilgrims who used the dangerous road from Jaffa to Jerusalem. These "Poor Knights" dressed in rags and took a vow of poverty, chastity, and obedience. St. Bernard was instrumental in compiling a rule for such men, outlined in a pamphlet, *In Praise of the New Knighthood.* These Templars lived as monks, wore a white hooded habit, and were subject to the strictest obedience to the Master of the Knights of the Temple.7 Being both combatants and monks, every knight was in a sense, his own chaplain. The order was also free of episcopal authority, answering only to the pope himself.8 This special dispensation was unpopular with the bishops, yet this order and several others grew and flourished during the Crusading era.

A parallel, if not exactly rival organization was that of the Order of the Hospital of St. John the Baptist. The Hospitallers had been running a lodging house *cum* hospital for pilgrims in Jerusalem since 1070. The order's religious rule developed similar to the Templars and the Hospitallers, who eventually built many imposing fortresses for the care of pilgrims, also took up arms to defend their charges and holdings. The orders may also be considered the progenitors of the "combat medic" and the founders of military medicine. Organized somewhat later were orders of Teutonic, Spanish, and Portuguese monastic knights.9

The fighting monastic orders were an aberration, (albeit a long lasting one) in the history of priests in the military. During the Crusades, priest chaplains continued to exercise their traditionally understood ministry of caring for and praying with the sick and wounded, conferring the sacraments, saying Mass, and offering prayers for a successful outcome to the army's battles. These became the standard accepted duties of military chaplains, a standard that continues to the present day.10 The understanding that the priest in service would be a non-combatant, theoretically always the rule, was well established by the end of the Crusades.

The Protestant Reformation fractured the universality of Christendom and ushered in an era of religious warfare between the nation states and provinces of states that continued to adhere to the Roman Catholic Church and those that adopted the novel Protestant sects. After Henry VIII's break with Rome, his daughter Elizabeth sought to increase England's power by fomenting rebellion in Catholic-held territories.

One target of Elizabeth and her *agents provocateur* was the Spanish Netherlands, or Flanders. The standard bearer of the Catholic forces in Flanders was Alessandro Farnese, third Duke of Parma and nephew of Philip II. Farnese was called the greatest *condottiere* of his day and many times bested the troops of William of Orange, most spectacularly at the siege of Antwerp in 1585.11 The Spanish situation in Flanders, however, was desperate, and as military governor Farnese was hard pressed to control his army of mercenaries as he attempted to put down the revolt. A biographer of the Farnese family described his many virtues and added, "He was also sincerely religious; he preferred, he said, thirty God-fearing soldiers to ten thousand infidels, believing that only faith could hold together an army of men of different nationalities."12

Because of his interest in the spiritual life of his unruly troops, Farnese worked to establish an organized chaplaincy and is credited with creating the "corps" system. This meant that chaplains were to be a permanent facet of the army's personnel, rather than *ad hoc* appendages or camp followers. As Farnese was installing chaplains in the ranks, Pope Clement VIII assented to his request for an Apostolic legate for the Low Countries. The Pope sent Louis de Berlaymont, the Archbishop of Cambrai, to serve as legate, with the duties of a "military vicar." In this instance, the hierarchy of authority was clearly established. The archbishop would be the ordinary for all of the chaplains. Individual bishops would no longer have control over their men, as long as they were in military service. In practice, day to day business was conducted by a vicar-general, assigned to the task by the archbishop.13 When Farnese initially formed his chaplain corps, he turned to a recently-formed religious order, one founded, like the Franciscans, by an ex-soldier, an order conceptualized as an elite force of soldiers for God and the Pope: the Jesuits.

Ignatius of Loyola was a Basque nobleman and warrior concerned primarily with fighting and questions of honor until a French cannonball nearly severed his left leg at the siege of Pamplona in May 1521. During his long, painful convalescence at his ancestral home he was "converted" to an unshakable, ascetic Catholicism after reading a life of Christ and a lives of the saints. He spent the next decade in study and prayer. Ignatius was ordained in 1537 along with a small group of followers whom he called the *Campagnia di Gesu*. Traditionally, the name "company" refers to a military formation and the head of this nascent order was later to be known as the General. Clearly, Ignatius' military background greatly influenced the organizational structure of the order that came to be known as the Society of Jesus.14

The Jesuits were formally approved on September 27, 1540 by Pope Paul III in the papal bull *Regimini militantis Ecclesiae* and the order continued with the work it had already begun while in formation. The Jesuits would spread the good word as missionaries in pagan and once-Catholic, now Protestant lands, and would educate youth for the one true Church. These Counter-Reformation warriors were also particularly adapted for chaplain work because the order demanded an ethos of personal sacrifice and iron discipline, both essential qualities for a military man.

In November 1587, Allesandro Farnese formed the *Missio Castrensis*, a group of twenty four Jesuits who would serve as official chaplains in his army. This *Missio Castrensis* was truly the first chaplain corps system, and was another organizational step up from the system Farnese had already emplaced. It is believed that the Jesuit mission was not subject either to the legate or to the military vicar.15

The Jesuits fulfilled the same duties regularly associated with chaplains. They counseled the troops, delivered the sacraments and tended to the wounded and dying. This latter task was a specialty of the order as well. The first generation of Jesuits spent the winter of 1537 working at two Venetian hospitals, the *Ospedale degli Incurabili* and *the Ospedale Santi Giovanni e Paolo* while waiting for a ship to Palestine.16

Even before Farnese organized the *Missio Castrensis,* Catholic priests had already accompanied Portuguese, Spanish, and French explorers across the Atlantic to the New World. After initial contact with native populations these priests were mainly involved with Indian missionary work, which was a prime objective of Queen Isabella of Spain. Some of these priests were vocal critics of the *conquistadors'* treatment of the Indians, particularly the Dominican friars Antonio de Montesinos and Bartolome de las Casas. A lesser recognized function of these priests, however, was to act as chaplains to the European soldiers and sailors who voyaged to the Americas. For example, Hernando Cortez' 1518 expedition to Mexico consisted of 508 men, 16 horses, 4 cannon and 2 chaplains. 17

At the seminal stage of the Church in America, the workers were few. In the howling wilderness of Spanish Florida, a handful of secular priests and Franciscans formed the bulwark of the Church. In 1578, two Franciscans acted as military chaplains to the garrisons at St. Augustine and Santa Elena.18 Even before this, in 1566, a tiny Jesuit band landed in Florida. The Superior of this group, Father Pedro Martinez, had already begun chaplain duty before the ships left Spain for New Spain. He went from ship to ship preaching and catechizing the foul-mouthed sailors. He instituted a series of penalties, including loss of meals and imposition of fines, for those caught uttering blasphemous oaths. In New Spain, Martinez' assistant, Father Juan Rogel, acted as chaplain to the soldiers stationed at Fort San Antonio on Charlotte Harbor.19

A few Franciscans accompanied Coronado and his horsemen in his exploration of the American West in the early 1540s. During the journey these men acted as chaplains before settling in to convert the Quivira Indians. Few of these courageous friars survived and the story was the same in Texas, New Mexico, Arizona, and California, wherever the Spanish established a foothold.20

Likewise, the French presence in North America, above the St. Lawrence River, included clergy who acted as chaplains to the small garrisons in New France. Between 1604–1605, Fr. Nicholas Aubry was the chaplain at St. Croix Island in Maine.21 The French religious presence, was, like the Spanish, primarily missionary in nature and conducted for the most part by the Jesuits. The number of French soldiers was never large and the fur traders who went to the areas of Maine and what later came to be called New York were little interested in religion.

By the mid-seventeenth century, England had already established more populous colonies further south along the Atlantic coast. Once established, the English colonists often employed their own Protestant chaplains in their many attacks on the Indians. Throughout the century the New World would be a minor sideshow in the political drama being played out in Europe between the Catholic and Protestant nations. The first segments of the Great Wars for Empire, King William's War 1689–97, Queen Anne's War 1702–13, the War of Jenkins' Ear 1739–42, and King George's War 1740–48 helped precipitate the waning of Spanish and French hegemony and the waxing of English power in America. During King George's War there were at least ten Protestant ministers acting as chaplains and serving with troops fighting against the French in Canada. A figure known as Samuel Moody of York, Maine, displayed his godly reverence after the surrender of Louisbourg by smashing the papist altar and sacred images in the French church with an ax. He also stole a silver cross and later presented it to Harvard College, no doubt as a tangible manifestation of his piety.22

Such incidents were not uncommon. Ministers serving with the English and Anglo-American forces fused British political interests with vituperative anti-Catholicism and came up with a call for holy war against the "Babylon" and "seat of Satan" of New France.23 After the last of these Great Wars for Empire, the French and Indian War 1754–63, the New World was almost completely in England's orbit and New France became Canada.

The various Protestant sects established on the eastern seaboard agreed on little except for an abiding hatred for the Church of Rome. When the Anglo colonists finally revolted against the mother country, their fury against Catholics was magnified by the 1774 Quebec Act, a British law that granted a degree of religious freedom in Canada. Despite their inferior status the tiny Catholic community in the British colonies tended to favor independence. Anti-Catholic propaganda was slightly muted during the American Revolutionary War not because of a sudden outbreak of tolerance but because the rebel cause was entirely dependent upon massive aid from Catholic France and Spain. The French fleet, which brought approximately 44,000 French troops to fight with the rebels had its own shipboard chaplains who tended to the sailors and soldiers.24

The military chaplaincy in what was to become the United States was officially established on July 29, 1775 when the Continental Congress established a pay scale for the army. From this point the military chaplaincy was a *de facto* Protestant institution, although ordination by a recognized church was not a prerequisite of the job. Duties of the office were vaguely spelled out, though the main occupation of the chaplains appeared to be the vain task of stamping out cursing and other vices enjoyed by the troopers. For the most part they were unsuccessful. Throughout the war approximately 180 men served as chaplains with approximately 180 different interpretations of what the job entailed.25 Many sought the position as a sinecure because the pay was better in the army than in their congregations. Some drew pay but never appeared in the field. Some refused to visit the sick, fearing the effects of contagion; others harangued prisoners and soldiers of different denominations.26 In total, these men were a poor lot.

During the Revolutionary War, a handful of Catholic priests did serve as chaplains in the American cause, primarily with French Canadian soldiers. Fr. Louis Eustace Lotbiniere, who served with "Congress' Own" First and Second Canadian regiments is generally considered the first Catholic chaplain in American service. Both Lotbiniere and the Catholic soldiers in his regiments were censured for joining the American Army by Lotbiniere's ecclesiastical superior, Bishop Jean-Olivier Briand of Quebec. This was understandable since from the loss of the French and Indian

War, Canada was under the ecclesiastical jurisdiction of Richard Challoner, Vicar Apostolic of the London District.27

Lotbiniere, who was over sixty years of age and wealthy at the time he joined the army sacrificed everything by doing so. He served throughout the war, mostly in the vicinity of Philadelphia and apparently continued to administer the sacraments though he was under a ban of excommunication from his bishop. He was referred to as "Chaplain Louis Lotbiniere" in congressional records and his name was also listed among the officers of the Continental Army. After the war, having lost his fortune and having been rarely paid by Congress, Lotbiniere died in poverty.28

Another French-Canadian priest, Father Pierre Huet de la Valiniere, was vociferously pro-American and supported the raising of Canadian regiments, but was not given the rank of an official chaplain. Nevertheless, he was also censured and removed from his post by Bishop Briand, who angrily called him a "perfect rebel."29 A Montreal Jesuit, Pierre Floquet, also earned Bishop Briand's displeasure by hearing the confessions of Canadian militiamen in American service. Colonel Moses Hazen, the commander of the *Bostonnais* regiments, enjoyed Father Floquet's company, and wrote that he "has assisted by giving them absolution when every priest in the country refused. He has now the name of My Chaplain."30 The title, however, was honorary; Father Floquet considered his ministrations to the soldiers simply a matter of "human respect" and he had no desire to further anger his bishop.31

When George Rogers Clark's Rangers marched from Kaskaskia to take Post Vincennes in 1778, they had along a Canadian priest, Father Pierre Gibault, who acted as chaplain. Gibault already had experience in such an apostolate, having formerly had responsibility for the Catholics in the 18th Royal Irish Regiment. Like Lotbiniere and Floquet he never received any monetary compensation for his services with the Americans, and he too felt the wrath of Bishop Briand.32

Not all American Catholics sided with the rebels, however: a few remained loyal to the crown and acted accordingly. A group of Catholic

Gaelic-speaking Scots, for example, fled from New York to Canada and took their imposing Irish priest, Fr. John MacKenna with them. Thereafter MacKenna acted as chaplain to the two British regiments the Scotsmen joined.33

Once independence was achieved and the republic began to be formed, the Continental Army ceased to function and along with it the office of military chaplain. The small Catholic population continued to exist as a barely tolerated minority in the overwhelmingly Protestant nation. Politically and economically the young United States found itself isolated from England and France who, by the late eighteenth century were once again at war with each other. Both nations viewed America with contempt and occasionally humiliated her by interfering with merchant shipping. The British acted particularly egregiously by impressing American seamen into their own service.

By 1812 President James Madison and the "War Hawks" in Congress declared war on England even though the United States was ill prepared to fight. Few military records exist from this conflict, most having been destroyed when the British burned Washington in 1814. Only a handful of men have been identified as chaplains, all of them presidential appointments, and none are believed to have been Catholic.34 Between the War of 1812 and the Mexican War, chaplains were employed to some extent as teachers at army posts stretching from Maine to the Pacific coast, but again none of these men were Catholic.35

Fr. Adam Marshall, S.J. became the first priest to serve as a United States naval chaplain, and the first of a long line of Jesuits who would serve honorably in the navy and other services. Marshall was employed principally as a schoolmaster to the midshipmen on the ship of the line *North Carolina*. He went aboard in December 1824, and sailed with her on a Mediterranean cruise. He also acted in the capacity of a chaplain to the Catholic sailors, but his naval career was brief. Father Marshall died of consumption aboard the *North Carolina* and was buried at sea on September 20, 1825. 36

Catholic service in wartime counted for little with the Protestant majority in the United States. After a brief respite during the revolution anti-Catholicism had returned and continued to increase and by the 1830s nativist hysteria began to manifest itself in murderous attacks. During the ensuing decade, churches and convents were burned down across New England. In 1844 in Philadelphia, Protestant fanatics burned down two Catholic churches, a Sisters of Charity convent, a seminary and an entire Irish neighborhood. The same year in New York, nativist gangs led by Mayor James Harper threatened to put all of the city's Catholic churches to the torch, but Bishop John Hughes had already dealt with such thugs and had a policy of posting armed guards at his churches. He warned, "If a single Catholic church is burned in New York, the city will become a second Moscow," meaning he would send out his own men to torch the financial district.37 The nativist mobs backed off.

Paradoxically, it was Bishop Hughes who became instrumental in the reappearance of Catholic chaplains in the United States Army. When President James K. Polk ordered American troops to invade Mexico in 1846, several Mexican prelates had some success in convincing their people that the latest invasion by the Yanqui was in fact nothing less than a "Protestant Crusade" against Holy Mother Church. In the past, a president probably would not have considered Catholic sensibilities, but the changing demography of the United States dictated a prudent course. By the mid 1840s there was a massive influx of Irish Catholic immigrants to America. This first great wave of immigration fanned the flames of nativist hysteria to white heat, but because it was a task assigned to society's pariahs, the Irish also began filling the enlisted ranks of the army to an unprecedented degree. It is estimated that as many as one quarter of the enlisted men who served in the Mexican War were Irish Catholics.38 Furthermore, American troops did gleefully engage in rape, murder, and pillage against Mexican civilians, and desecration of Catholic churches was common, particularly by Southern volunteer troops.39

To ease Mexican tensions and to placate Catholic troops, President Polk decided to send a few priests to Mexico, ostensibly to act as chaplains, but actually to act as goodwill ambassadors to the Mexican clergy. On May 19, 1846, Polk summoned Bishop Hughes to the White House for a meeting. In his diary, Polk wrote that he asked Hughes to send priests with the army to give "assurance to the Catholic clergy in Mexico that under our Constitution their religion and church property would be secure, and that so far from being violated, both would be protected by our army, and in this way to avoid their active hostility about the impending war."[40]

In this inauspicious way, the Catholic chaplaincy in the United States Army was truly begun. In point of fact, the president had no authority to appoint military chaplains, but he could by law hire civilian employees to perform the duties of a chaplain.[41] "Dagger John" Hughes probably did not entertain much hope of convincing the Mexican clergy that American intentions were either honorable or benign, but he was a pragmatist in his own way and could see the possibilities opening up for members of the Catholic clergy in the American Army. Hughes did not send secular priests, but instead turned to the Jesuit Provincial at Georgetown, Rev. Peter Verhaegen, who released two of his men for service, Fr. John McElroy, S.J. and Fr. Anthony Rey, S.J.[42]

The need for priests in the army at this time was desperate. Catholic soldiers were often forced by their commanding officers to attend Protestant services which were not uncommonly hysterical tirades against the Church. Soldiers were subject to arrest and corporal punishment if they failed to comply.[43] When news of the priests' appointments was made public, the nativists howled but Polk refused to relent.

In Mexico, Father Rey traveled with Zachary Taylor's troops, fulfilled his priestly duties as chaplain, and was present at the historic battle of Monterey. Because of Father McElroy's advanced age (sixty-four) and physical infirmities, he remained as the hospital chaplain at a base camp for over a year. Father Rey had the sad distinction of being the first

Catholic chaplain killed on active duty; murdered by bandits while on a religious mission. Father McElroy returned to the United States with mixed feelings about the success of his service and saddened by Rey's tragic loss. McElroy, however, lived for another thirty years and founded Boston College in 1863.44

After the Mexican War, the office of chaplaincy reverted to a status of "post chaplain," which entailed serving as a schoolmaster, rather than carrying out religious duties. Few of the men who filled these posts were formerly ordained in any religious denomination, and in reality most of them were profane rabble.45 Only three priests were appointed post chaplains during this inter-war period, between 1850–1859, Fathers Ignacio Ramirez, Michael Sheehan, and Peter DeSmet, S.J.46 were accorded official recognition as army chaplains which had been denied Father McElroy and the martyred Father Rey.

As the Civil War approached, the tiny United States Army had a total of thirty post chaplains. When actual fighting commenced in the spring of 1861, the state volunteer regiments mobilized in the emergency were in need of their own chaplains. The War Department issued a directive authorizing a regimental commander to appoint a chaplain on the vote of field officers and company commanders. The men were required to be regularly ordained Christian ministers and were to be allowed the pay and rank of cavalry captains.47

The regimental appointment system was highly unsatisfactory from a Catholic viewpoint. The army officer ranks were overwhelmingly Protestant, and these men would never vote to appoint a Catholic priest as chaplain even if many of their enlisted men were of that religion. Regiments composed of Irish or German immigrants, however, were a different matter. Ethnic regiments were raised during the Civil War to induce the immigrants who were commonly discriminated against to join the Union war effort. One of the obvious advantages of joining an ethnic regiment was the chance of having a priest chaplain rather than a minister.48

Approximately forty Catholic chaplains served officially with the Union forces during the Civil War, and about twenty-eight with the Confederacy. An untold number also acted in an unofficial capacity. Even President Abraham Lincoln recruited chaplains. In October 1861 he wrote to Fr. Francis E. Boyle of Washington, D.C. requesting that he accept an appointment as hospital chaplain in that city. Thirteen priests did serve in that capacity during the war.49 One difficulty that arose with the priest chaplains was that of ecclesiastical authority when the priest was traveling with the army. At that time there was no centralized church structure which would oversee priests serving with the military. Consequently, priests were required initially to request faculties from the bishops in each diocese to which the army moved. This was a cumbersome system which proved to be nearly impossible to adhere to in practice. Pope Pius IX, made aware of the situation, granted permission for both Union and Confederate chaplains to exercise faculties beyond their own dioceses for the duration of the war.50

At this time the role and duties of a chaplain were largely undefined. Apart from an expected Sunday service, they had few official duties but took on many unofficial ones. This "handyman" role endeared them to the troops, but in this and in future wars other officers tended to dump unwanted duties onto the chaplain, who came to be seen as an all-around "morale officer." During the Civil War priest chaplains began to get the reputation of being particularly eager to suffer the life and on occasion the death of a soldier, right along with their men. In his memoirs, Father William Corby, C.S.C., of the 88th New York Infantry gloated over the fact that ministers were snubbed by the enlisted men and held in contempt by the officers, but that priests were constantly busy delivering sacraments to the men and were usually treated respectfully even by Protestant officers. 51

After the war a number of the chaplains went on to bigger, if not better duty. Bernard McQuaide, an unofficial chaplain, subsequently became the bishop of Rochester. John Ireland became the first archbishop of St. Paul.

Lawrence McMahon, who served with the 28th Massachusetts (Irish) Regiment was elevated to the See of Hartford in 1879. Father Corby went from the battlefield back to scholastic life. He became the "second founder" of Notre Dame and served as its president before becoming the United States' C.S.C Provincial General.52

In the post-Civil War period the size of the United States Army was cut drastically and the number of chaplains in service consequently declined as well. While the Civil War regimental chaplains were all released from duty, a small number of priests did join the regular army and served at various posts. In the United States Navy, the chaplaincy had been even less inclusive of Catholics than the army. Apart from the unofficial service of Father Marshall seventy-three years earlier, only two other priests had served in the navy; Fr. Charles Henry Parks and Fr. William Ironsides Reaney, commissioned in 1888 and 1892 respectively. Father Reaney came by his unusual middle name honestly—he had been born on the frigate U.S.S. *Constitution*.53

The United States again went to war, this time with Spain, after the suspicious explosion of the armored cruiser U.S.S. *Maine* on February 15, 1898 in Havana Harbor. The chaplain of the *Maine* happened to be Fr. John P. Chidwick, formerly of St. Stephen's parish in New York but since March 1895, the chaplain of that ill-fated vessel.54

Father Chidwick's tour of duty was quite uneventful until that disastrous night. He was a poor sailor and spent much of his time rehearsing the ship's choir to the accompaniment of a small organ that he had purchased. The atmosphere in Cuba was tense, however, and when the ship docked in Havana he advised his men to make an Act of Contrition every night with their prayers. He warned that death could come at anytime, and that Catholics, particularly servicemen, must always be prepared to face it. When the blast occurred, Chidwick was in his cabin reading. He immediately made his way to the deck, which was engulfed in smoke and flames. He called out absolution to the injured men scattered about the deck and then sailed around the burning ship in a lifeboat searching for survivors. Two days later Chidwick presided over the burial of the first group of bodies recovered. The bishop of Havana provided the lots in Colon Cemetery. Chidwick was later the celebrant at two more funerals for *Maine* victims; once when those buried in Cuba were reinterred in Arlington National Cemetery and years later when the ruined hulk of the vessel was refloated, towed out to sea, and sunk for the final time with the bodies of those who had gone down with her. In his later years Chidwick served as Chaplain-in-Chief of the United Spanish War Veterans.55

During the war with Spain, twelve priests held commissions in the regular army or navy and nine served with state volunteer regiments. The war itself was generally popular with American Catholics and clergy. All but one of the bishops, the fiery anti-imperialist John Lancaster Spalding, went along with the war, even though the Jingoes who had been greatly responsible for it often revived the theme of smashing papist Spain for the purity of the Anglo-Protestant world. The institution of the chaplaincy still presented ecclesiastical problems for Catholics. The apostolic see had already granted the Archbishop of New York special faculties which he could delegate to chaplains in 1888, but it was not until 1890 that a commission of archbishops was formed to recruit priests for the military. Soon, the commission began appointing priests to act as liaisons with the federal government to deal with chaplains' affairs.56

Within two decades, America was once again at war, in a greater war than the world had ever known. As the United States made preparations to participate in World War I, a far greater number of chaplains than had ever been required for the services were now recruited. The government instituted a quota system concerning the numerical breakdown of religions and sects represented in the chaplaincy. Catholics were allotted approximately thirty-eight percent in the army, but no more than twenty-five percent in the navy. To facilitate recruiting and to coordinate the many Catholic activities begun during the emergency, a group of bishops formed the National Catholic War Council. The NCWC eventually metamorphosised into the National Conference of Catholic Bishops.

Thus the exigencies of wartime spurred episcopal organization in the United States.57

By the time the Great War ended, 1,023 Catholic chaplains were on duty, either in the army or navy or as unofficial chaplains paid by the Knights of Columbus. The question of canonical authority, which had been very vague since the Middle Ages, was finally settled at this time by Pope Benedict XV. The Holy See resolved to appoint a bishop from each country to serve as Pastor for Military Affairs. This *Ordinarius Castrensis* would exercise authority over all military chaplains, wherever they were serving. The Auxiliary Bishop of New York, Patrick J. Hayes, was chosen as the first American Military Vicar with headquarters in New York City and with five additional regimental vicariates. The K of C priests remained under traditional ecclesiastical authority. 58

The service record of the chaplains in the Civil War, the Spanish American War and World War I was exemplary but the job was not without a cost. The last American officer to die in the war was a Catholic chaplain, Fr. William F. Davitt, who was killed by an artillery shell an hour before the armistice on November 11, 1918.59 These chaplains and many others continued the tradition of front line service that had become a hallmark of Catholic chaplains. The vital importance of the sacrament of Extreme Unction to every Roman Catholic necessitated the presence of the priest right on the battlefield, not at some rear echelon post. The chaplain made a celebrity by the press was not one of the combat casualties, but Fr. Francis P. Duffy, the flamboyant chaplain of the fabled New York Volunteer Regiment, "The Fighting 69th." Duffy was an unlikely type to be characterized as a war hero. He had earlier taught philosophy at Dunwoodie Seminary and between 1905–1908 published the theological journal the *New York Review*.

When the United States became embroiled in World War I, Duffy helped organize the 69th and went overseas with the regiment when its number was changed to the 165th Infantry, part of the 42nd "Rainbow Division."60 Due to his penchant for battlefield heroics, Duffy was highly decorated and seemed to personify the fearless spirit of the Catholic chaplain. Upon his death, he was immortalized in bronze with helmet and military uniform and this statue stands today in the heart of Times Square.

In March 1919, Military Vicar Bishop Hayes was elevated to Cardinal Archbishop of the New York See. The next man to fill the spot as Vicar General and Chancellor of the Military Ordinariate was Monsignor George J. Waring, who had been a military chaplain since 1904 and during the war had been Bishop Hayes' right hand as the administrator of the *Diocese Castrensis*.61

In the 1920s both the number of Catholic servicemen and Catholic chaplains plummeted. With the onset of the Great Depression and a brief respite from war, the small peacetime army had little need for a large contingent of chaplains. The depression years did, however, create an unusual hybrid chaplain vocation. In 1933, the Civilian Conservation Corps was organized by the Roosevelt administration to put young men to work, primarily in rural settings, to keep them out of the depressed civilian job market. The C.C.C. camps were run along military lines, including the services of Reserve chaplains who would usually travel from camp to camp in the manner of circuit riders. The Catholic chaplains would say Mass, distribute Communion, hear confessions and afterward send a postcard to the boys' parents, informing them that their son was fulfilling his duty to the Church. In part, the cards read, "Every opportunity is given the members of the Civilian Conservation Corps to practice their religion, even when away from home, and I know you will be pleased to learn that your son is trying to live up to his religious practices in a faithful, manly way." 62

The army did reorganize the office of the chaplain along with what it thought were more modern military parameters with the National Defense Act of 1920. This act provided for a Chief of Chaplains to serve for four years with the rank, pay, and allowances of a colonel. This rank was raised to general in World War II. Without specifically stating it, the National Defense Act created the "Chaplain Corps."63 Paradoxically the United States Army adopted a system first broached by Farnese's *Missio*

Castrensis back in 1587, illustrating that the Church's organizational acumen remained undiminished by the passage of time.

The first five Chiefs of the Army Chaplain Corps were all Protestants, but in 1937 Fr. William R. Arnold was appointed Chief. Arnold had been an army chaplain since 1913, so he was thoroughly familiar with the problems and responsibilities of the work. It was Arnold's fate to be army Chief of Chaplains during the most trying times of the nation's military history. Though the post was intended to be strictly a four-year appointment, Arnold was reappointed in 1941, and also became the first Chief of Chaplains to be promoted to general, first as a brigadier and then as a major general.64

After World War I almost the entire contingent of Catholic chaplains was demobilized, and the priests returned to their home parishes, universities, or other civilian duties. This accorded with the traditional pattern. American bishops usually looked upon military service as a temporary annoyance or, at best, an added mission duty for an already overtaxed clerical community. Unlike ministers, who could view the chaplaincy as a welcome economic opportunity, Catholic chaplains' military service away from their respective dioceses presented a hardship to those who remained at home. As a consequence, Catholics tended to be underrepresented in the chaplaincy, even after "official" discrimination had ceased by World War I. Though Catholics were allotted a quota of thirty-eight percent, only about thirty percent of the chaplains in the First World War were Catholic.65

The atmosphere in the navy chaplaincy in the inter-war period was similar to that prevailing in the army. When hostilities ceased in 1918, almost all of the Catholic naval chaplains were expected to report to their dioceses or religious communities as soon as possible. Even if a priest wanted to remain in the navy, and even if he received permission from his ecclesiastical superior to do so, there were very few billets available. Promotion to higher rank, which theoretically reflected an individual's efficiency and time in service, were frozen until 1924 and 1925. At that time there were promotions across the board, but the number of priests on duty in the navy remained minuscule. On December 7, 1941, the day America was thrust into the Second World War, there were twenty-three Catholic chaplains in the regular navy and thirty-seven in the reserves, as opposed to eighty-two Protestants in the regulars and forty-nine in the Reserves, with one Jewish chaplain in the reserves as well. This indicates that Catholics, at approximately twenty-two percent, were underrepresented in the regulars, but were overrepresented in the reserves at about forty-two and a half percent. In sum, Catholics comprised about thirty-one percent of the total of navy chaplains on duty at the time of Pearl Harbor.66

In retrospect, the Christian Church accepted the concept of priest traveling with armies to serve as military pastors from an early period, though objections were voiced intermittently by those who felt that the Church was in effect endorsing killing and warfare. Traditionally, priests who acted as chaplains had no official status in military tables of organization until Alessandro Farnese organized the *Missio Castrensis* for his forces in the Spanish Netherlands in the sixteenth century. The Anglo-Protestants who prevailed over the French and Spanish in the New World established their own chaplaincy but apart from a few French Canadian priests who served in the revolution, Catholics were proscribed until the Mexican War. At that time two priests served unofficially and at least as far as the government was concerned, in a diplomatic, rather than religious capacity.

During the Civil War a relatively greater number of priests served in the armed forces but the bureaucratic structure of the chaplaincy still discriminated against Catholics, and the priest-to-Catholic-soldier ratio in the Union Army was absurdly low. By World War I, Catholics were allotted a quota of chaplains approximately commensurate with their representation in the military ranks. Due to the difficulty of staffing the Church, which had just officially emerged from the "missionary" stage, however, the full quota was not met. What was apparent was the trend, recognizable since the Civil War, for the Catholic chaplain to be an extreme risk-taker in combat situations. Yet on the eve of the Second World War, few could have imagined what role American Catholic chaplains would play in the coming maelstrom.

Notes: Chapter 1

1 Eph. 6:10–18 (Douay Version).

2 Matthew 10:34, 39 (Douay Version).

3 Matthew 8:5–13 (Douay Version).

4 *A Brief History of the Catholic Chaplaincy and the Archdiocese For the Military Services, USA,* (Washington, D.C.: Archives of the Archdiocese for the Military Services, n.d.),9. The primary source for this belief comes from the Roman historian Eusebius, who also claimed that Constantine brought along tents specifically for worship. Centuries later breakdown "traveling chapels" would reappear for military services.

5 Mary Caroline Watt, *St. Martin of Tours* (London: Sands & Co., 1928) 98,99.

6 Dom Aidan Henry Germain, *Catholic Military and Naval Chaplains 1776–1917* (Washington, D.C.: Catholic University, 1929), iii. In Medieval times and well into the Modern period the title chaplain also applied to the personal priest of noble families.

7 Demond Seward, *The Monks of War: The Military Religious Orders* (London: Penguin Books, 1972), 30–32. An old standard on the Crusades is Hilaire Belloc, *The Crusades: The World's Debate* (Milwaukee: The Bruce Publishing Co., 1937).

8 Seward, *The Monks of War*, 35.

9 Ibid., 30,37. Templars and Hospitallers who contracted skin diseases, common in the Middle East, were required to leave their order and join the Order of Hospitallers of St. Lazarus, an outfit devoted to the care of lepers. The St. Lazarus Hospitallers built a series of hospitals in many lands for this purpose. See Gerard A. Lee, "The Military and Hospitaller Order of St. Lazarus of Jerusalem," *Irish Ecclesiastical Record* CX (1968):

372–380. The bibliography of military orders is comprehensive. A particularly interesting volume focusing on the medicinal, rather than the military aspect of the religious knights is Edgar Erskine Hume, *Medical Work of the Knights Hospitallers of Saint John of Jerusalem* (Baltimore: The Johns Hopkins Press, 1940). The book is also well illustrated with photographs of then-extant *Hospitaller* structures throughout the world.

10 Though the military orders were eventually destroyed as fighting units by envious national monarchs, a few of these orders continue to exist as elite Catholic fraternal and charitable institutions. The image of Christian Crusaders was carried over into the name of the largest Catholic fraternal organization, the Knights of Columbus, a group with no actual military antecedent.

11 Giovanna R. Solari, *The House of Farnese* (Garden City: Doubleday & Co., 1968). Farnese also visited wounded soldiers and saw to it that they had medical treatment, a rare attitude for an aristocratic commander to have in that age.

12 Ibid., 69,70.

13 John Mortimer Smith, *The Military Ordinariate of the United States of America, Canon Law Studies #443* (Washington, D.C.: The Catholic University of America, 1966), 40,41. *A Brief History*, 11,12.

14 The bibliography of the history of the Society of Jesus is beyond copious. An excellent biography which stresses Ignatius' soldierly outlook is Pere Paul Dudon, S.J., *St. Ignatius of Loyola* (Milwaukee: The Bruce Publishing Co., 1949). More recent authors tend to downplay this perspective. John W. O'Malley, S.J., *The First Jesuits* (Cambridge: Harvard University Press, 1993) believes that the commonly used Italian word *campagnia* designated any type of group or association, and that no military inference can be drawn. Given Ignatius' military background, however, it seems unlikely that the word company was chosen by accident or without the realization of its martial implication.

15 Smith, *The Military Ordinariate*, 44,45.

16 O'Malley, *The First Jesuits,* 33. Rene Fulop-Miller, *The Jesuits: A History of the Society of Jesus* (New York: Capricorn Books, 1963), 68. The Jesuits' nursing work had a two-fold purpose: first to aid the sick, but also to test their own mettle. Fulop-Miller reports that, "they chose just those labors which were most calculated to produce loathing and horror." Those labors included sharing beds with lepers, cleaning utensils and bedclothes and preparing dead bodies for burial. Francis Xavier once scraped the pus out of a man's abscess and put the foul matter in his mouth to prove his commitment.

17 Edwin Scott Gaustad, *A Religious History of America* (New York: Harper & Row, 1966), 10.

18 John Tracy Ellis, *Catholics in Colonial America* (Baltimore: Helicon Press, 1965), 38.

19 Michael Kenny, S.J. *The Romance of the Floridas: The Finding and the Founding* (New York: The Bruce Publishing Co., 1934), 175, 191. Martinez was murdered by Indians at San Juan of Alimacani, Florida, October 6, 1566, thus making him the first Jesuit martyr of the Americas.

20 Ellis, *Catholics in Colonial America,* 49.

21 James Hennesey, *American Catholics: A History of the Roman Catholic Community in the United States* (New York: Oxford University Press, 1981), 23.

22 Roy J. Honeywell, *Chaplains of the United States,* (Washington, D.C.: U.S. Government Printing Office, 1958) 20,21.

23 Ibid., 27,28.

24 Hennesey, *American Catholics,* 63.

25 Honeywell, *Chaplains of the United States,* 30,31,37.

26 Charles Royster, *A Revolutionary People at War: The Continental Army and the American Character, 1775–1783* (New York: W.W. Norton & Co., 1979), 165–167.

27 In 1783, Bishop Challoner wrote to the Congregation of *Propaganda de Fide* endorsing a bishopric which would encompass the English colonies in America. No action was taken at that time and when

American independence was declared, the authority of the London bishop over American Catholics ended as well. Even if Challoner's authority had waned, Briand surely believed that French Catholics in Canada and the small Catholic population in America would suffer less under the British than under the Anglo-Americans. See John Tracy Ellis, ed., *Documents of American Catholic History* (Milwaukee: The Bruce Publishing Co.., 1956), 129. Ellis, *Catholics in Colonial America,* 343, 388, 389. Challoner was most famous for an "updated" revision of the Rheims-Douay Bible, which appeared in 1750.

28 Germain, *Catholic Military and Naval Chaplains 1776–1917,* 1–10; Ellis, *Catholics in Colonial America,* 142; John Tracy Ellis, ed., *Documents of American Catholic History 1493–1865,* vol.1 (Wilmington, Delaware: Michael Glazier, 1987), 376.

29 Germain, *Catholic Chaplains,* 11.

30 Ibid., 12.

31 Ibid., 13.

32 Ibid., 18; Hennesey, *American Catholics,* 67.

33 Hennesey, *American Catholics,* 67. An overview of Roman Catholic chaplains in British service has recently been published. Father John MacKenna is mentioned very briefly. See Tom Johnstone and James Hagerty, *The Cross on the Sword: Catholic Chaplains in the Forces* (London: Geoffrey Chapman, 1996), 1.

34 *A Brief History of the Catholic Chaplaincy and the Archdiocese for the Military Services, U.S.A.* (Washington, D.C.: Archives of the Archdiocese for the Military Services, n.d.), 13. Traditionally, Catholic historians have asserted that there may have been priests in attendance at the Battle of New Orleans, in light of the fact that a number of nuns were on the battlefield.

35 Honeywell, *Chaplains,* 79,80.

36 *Woodstock Letters: A Record of Current Events and Historical Notes Connected with the Colleges and Missions of the Society of Jesus* LXX (1941): 466. Father Marshall left a diary of his year aboard the *North Carolina,* which was deposited in the New York Archives of the Maryland-New York

Province of the Society of Jesus. A truncated version was published in 1943. See Joseph T. Durkin, S.J., *Journal of Father Adam Marshall 1824–1825* (Scranton: University of Scranton Press, 1943).

37 Richard Shaw, *Dagger John: The Unquiet Life and Times of Archbishop John Hughes of New York* (New York: Paulist Press, 1977), 194–197. See also Oscar Handlin, *Boston's Immigrants* (New York: Athenaeum, 1975), 187–189. Robert Leckie, *American and Catholic: A Narrative of their role in American History* (New York: Doubleday & Co., 1970), 107–109. The burning of the Ursuline convent in Charlestown, Massachusetts is well documented and often analyzed. A recent treatment is Jeanne Hamilton, O.S.U., "The Nunnery As Menace: The Burning of the Charlestown Convent, 1834," *U.S. Catholic Historian,* vol, 14 #1 (Winter 1996): 35–65. The definitive history of the violence in Charlestown and the New England church burnings of the period is Robert H . Lord, John E. Sexton and Edward T. Harrington, *History of the Archdiocese of Boston in the Various Stages of its Development: 1604–1943* 3 vols. (New York: Sheed and Ward, 1944) passim. An updating of the same tumultuous diocese is Thomas H. O'Connor, *Boston Catholics: A History of the Church and Its People* (Boston: Northeastern University Press, 1998). For in-depth analyses of the longevity and nature of American anti-Catholicism and nativism, see the two older standards John Higham, *Strangers in the Land: Patterns of American Nativism, 1860–1925* (New York: Athenaeum, 1955; reprint ed., Westport, Connecticut: Greenwood Press, 1981) and Ray Allen Billington, *The Protestant Crusade 1800–1860: A Study of the Origins of American Nativism* (New York: Macmillan Co., 1938; reprint ed., Chicago: Quadrangle Books, 1964).

38 Robert Ryal Miller, *Shamrock and Sword: The Saint Patrick's Battalion in the U.S.-Mexican War* (Norman, Oklahoma: University of Oklahoma Press, 1989), 156.

39 Sister Blanche Marie McEniry, *American Catholics in the War with Mexico* (Washington, D.C.: Catholic University of America, 1937), 47,

passim; Miller, *Shamrock and Sword,* passim; Jack Bauer, *The Mexican War 1846–1848* (New York: Macmillan Publishing Co., 1974), 83–89.

40 James K. Polk, *The Diary of James K. Polk During His Presidency, 1845–1849,* ed Milo Milton Quaife (Chicago: A.C. McClurg & Co., 1910) 408,409.

41 *Woodstock Letters* XV (1886): 200.

42 *Woodstock Letters* XV (1886): 198. Esmerelda Boyle, *Father John Mcelroy: The Irish Priest* (n.c.: Thomas McGill & Co., 1878), 9–20.

43 McEniry, *American Catholics in the War with Mexico,* 127–129. For a first person account of the hatred and contempt some American officers felt for the Catholic Church, see Samuel Ryan Curtis, *Mexico Under Fire: Being the Diary of Samuel Ryan Curtis 3rd Ohio Volunteer Regiment During the American Military Occupation of Northern Mexico 1846–1847,* ed. Joseph E. Chance (Fort Worth: Texas Christian University Press, 1994), 30, 84,85.

44 *Woodstock Letters* XV-XVIII: passim. Aslso see Charles F. Donovan, S.J., *A History of Boston College from the Beginnings to 1990* (Chestnut Hill: The University Press of Boston College, 1990). McElroy was sixty-four years of age when he went to Mexico, could not mount a horse, and had to be conveyed by wagon.

45 Honeywell, *Chaplains,* 84.

46 Germain, *Catholic Chaplains,* 40,41. Germain also lists a Reverend Samuel H. Milley as a Catholic chaplain, but another source, *American Army Chaplaincy: A Brief History* (Washington, D.C.: Chief of Chaplains, U.S. Army, 1946), 23. indicates that Samuel "Willey" was a Presbyterian. Nineteenth-century military records did not always indicate a chaplain's religion, so in lieu of other corroborating evidence such as church records, a degree of confusion exists over the faith of some individuals.

47 Honeywell, *Chaplains,* 104,105. These issues and others regarding the chaplaincy continued to be debated by Congress throughout the Civil War. See also Rollin W. Quimby, "The Chaplains' Predicament," *Civil War History* 8 (1962): 26–27; Rollin W. Quimby, "Congress and the Civil

War Chaplaincy," *Civil War History* 10 (1964); 249–250; Bell Irvin Wiley, "Holy Joes of the Sixties: A Study of Civil War Chaplains," *Huntington Library Quarterly* (1953), vol. 16, 287–304.

48 The history of the Irish experience in the Civil War is experiencing a Renaissance of sorts. In the past decade some worthwhile diaries and memoirs have been published including Peter Welsh, *Irish Green and Union Blue: The Civil War Letters of Peter Welsh* edited by Lawrence F. Kohl with Margaret Cosse Richard (New York: Fordham University Press, 1986). Welsh's touching letters to his fretting wife back in New York City detail his love of the Union, the rightness of its cause, and the parallels between the southern slave power and English oppression of the Irish. Also of note is William J.K. Beaudot and Lance J. Herdegen, *An Irishman in the Iron Brigade* (New York: Fordham University Press, 1993). These are the post-war memoirs of James P. "Mickey" Sullivan, an extraordinary fellow who survived four years of fighting in a non-Irish regiment.

49 *A Brief History,* 15; Lincoln's letter appears in *The War of the Rebellion—Official Records of the Union and the Confederate Armies,* Series III. vol. 1, 721; George M. Anderson, S.J., in "Bernadine Wiget, S.J. and the St. Aloysius Civil War Hospital in Washington D.C.," *Catholic Historical Review* 76 (October 1990): 734–764, asserts that churches were sometimes taken over by the government and converted into hospitals for military use. On occasion the pastors were employed as salaried hospital chaplains in recompense. See also the dissertation by Charles Borromeo Pfab, S.M. "American Hospital Chaplains During the Civil War 1861–1865: (Ph.D. dissertation, Catholic University of America Library, 1955). The medical history of the Civil War cannot be understood without an acknowledgment of the role of the nursing sisters who cared for men that secular male and female nurses would not touch. See Ellen Ryan Jolly, *Nuns of the Battlefield* (Providence: the Providence Visitor Press, 1927); Sister Mary Denis Maher, *To Bind Up the Wounds: Catholic Sister Nurses in the U.S. Civil War* (Westport, Connecticut: Greenwood Press, 1989).

50 *A Brief History*, 15.

51 William Corby, C.S.C., *Memoirs of Chaplain Life: Three Years with the Irish Brigade in the Army of the Potomac* (Chicago: La Monte, O'Donnell Printers, 1893; reprint ed., Lawrence Frederick Kohl, New York: Fordham University Press, 1992), 54, 55. Other chaplains reported the same types of behavior. See *Woodstock Letters* XIV (1885): 376,377.

52 James P. Shannon, ed., "Archbishop Ireland's Experiences as a Civil War Chaplain," *Catholic Historical Review* XXXIX (October 1953): 298–305; James H. O'Donnell, *History of the Diocese of Hartford* (Boston: D.H. Hived Co., 1900), 171.

53 *A Brief History*, 16.

54 Harry T. Cook, *"Remember the Maine!" An Historical Narrative of the Battleship Maine as told by its Chaplain the Right Reverend Monsignor John P. Chidwick* (Winchester, VA: Winchester Printers and Stationers, 1935), no pagination.

55 Cook, *Remember the Maine!"*, passim. Chidwick served on various ships until he resigned from the navy in 1903. In 1909, Archbishop Farley of New York appointed him to head St. Joseph's Theological Seminary at Dunwoodie. Pope Pius X made him a domestic prelate in 1916. *America* (August 7, 1909): 473.

56 *A Brief History*, 17.

57 Ordinariate of Army and Navy Chaplains, *United States Catholic Chaplains in the World War* (New York: The Chauncey Holt Co., 1924) xiv, xv. For the formation of the NCWC consult Michael Williams, *American Catholics in the War: National Catholic War Council 1917–1921* (New York: The MacMillan Co., 1921).

58 Ordinariate, *United States Catholic Chaplains*, xv, xvi; *A Brief History*, 18. In addition to providing priests to soldiers and sailors who did not have official chaplains, the Knights also stocked camp libraries, provided athletic equipment, and staged entertainment of various sorts. On one occasion, the Knights provided free tickets to six entire performances of the Barnum and Bailey circus in Madison Square Garden for the Navy's

Atlantic Squadron. Maurice Francis Egan and John B. Kennedy, *The Knights of Columbus in Peace and War,* vol. 1. (New Haven: Knights of Columbus, 1920), 274.

59 Jospeh S. Kinneen, S.J., ed., *Holy Cross College Service Record War of 1917* (Worcester: Harrigan Press, 1920) 17, 87.

60 Ordinariate, *The United States Catholic Chaplains,* 82,83; Francis P. Duffy, *Father Duffy's Story: A Tale of Humor and Heroism, of Life and Death with the Fighting Sixty-Ninth* (New York: George H. Doran Co., 1919), 14. Father Duffy was practically worshipped by the Doughboys in his division. One man wrote, "He was always with the men, on or off the battlefield. Everybody, every man in the regiment, loved Father Duffy." Albert M. Ettinger and A. Churchill Ettinger, *A Doughboy with the Fighting Sixty-Ninth* (Shippensburg, Pennsylvania: White Mane Publishing Co., 1992), 72.

61 Ordinariate, *United States Catholic Chaplains,* xxiii.

62 Honeywell, *Chaplains,* 210–212; A postcard in the author's collection is signed by "Rev John L. Clancy, S.J., 1st Lt. Chaplain Res. U.S.A."

63 Honeywell, *Chaplains.* 201; Office of the Chief of Chaplains, *American Army Chaplaincy* (Washington, D.C.: The Chaplains' Association, 1946), 40.

64 Office of the Chief of Chaplains, *American Army Chaplaincy,* 41.

65 Smith, *The Military Ordinariate,* 105.

66 Clifford M. Drury, *The History of the Chaplain Corps United States Navy 1939–1949,* vol. II (Washington, D.C.: U.S. Government Printing Office Bureau of Naval Personnel, 1950), 2,3.

CHAPTER 2

▼

"A Very Special Vocation"

The surprise attack on American naval forces at Pearl Harbor on the morning of December 7, 1941 by the warplanes of the Japanese Empire did what no amount of President Franklin D. Roosevelt's maneuvering could do to get the United States into the war against the Axis powers and prevent the collapse of Great Britain. The United States Congress declared war on Japan the next day, and three days later, when Germany and Italy declared war on the United States, Congress recognized a state of war with those nations as well. Now committed to a two-front war on opposite ends of the earth, the United States faced the daunting task of raising huge numbers of army, navy and Marine Corps personnel to fight the first truly global war.

The chaplaincies of both the army and navy would need to grow to unprecedented size to accommodate the tremendous number of men who would fight in the American services during World War II. And it would be the responsibility of Bishop John O'Hara, C.S.C. to confront this difficult task. Until his death in 1938, Cardinal Patrick J. Hayes of New York was still the Military Vicar of the American armed forces. After Pope Pius XII appointed Francis J. Spellman as Archbishop of New York to replace Hayes, he also named Spellman the new Military Vicar to oversee the Military Ordinariate of the United States. Spellman was now Ordinary of an unusual number of American Catholics, both in his position as Archbishop of New York as well as bishop to all American servicemen.

Though the position of Military Vicar had been associated with New York from the Ordinariate's inception during the World War, and even earlier when the New York Archbishop was authorized to grant chaplain faculties in 1888, there was no reason that the Ordinariate had to remain in New York. After the World War I there was some discussion that the Military Ordinariate should be relocated to Washington and that it should have its own individual bishop as vicar. This change was not effected until 1985.1

Spellman understood that he could not master the Byzantine infrastructure of the New York Archdiocese if he was distracted by the day to day administration of the Military Ordinariate. The solution was to appoint a capable bureaucrat to serve as "Military Delegate," a man who was efficient but would not challenge Spellman as a rival once he became acclimated to the job. Spellman chose Fr. John O'Hara, C.S.C., the President of Notre Dame University. Spellman had the United States Apostolic Delegate Archbishop Amletto Cicognani approach O'Hara with the "offer" of the Military Delegate post, which brought with it the rank of auxiliary bishop. O'Hara's biographer believes that he had already declined bishoprics in Latin America and in the United States. Apparently O'Hara declined this post as well, but was informed by the Apostolic Delegate that refusing the post was not an option. He was being ordered, not asked.2

The reluctant Bishop-elect O'Hara would serve throughout World War II as Military Delegate. O'Hara's position *vis a vis* Spellman would be somewhat akin to that of Monsignor George Waring to Cardinal Hayes. As Vicar-General and Chancellor of the Military Ordinariate, Waring had actually run the Ordinariate for Hayes during and after World War I.

O'Hara, however, as auxiliary bishop, would have most of the faculties employed by the Military Vicar himself. Spellman would also convince Pope Pius XII to expand the authority and jurisdiction of the Military Vicar to include all servicemen and women, their families, civilians living on military reservations, all religious attached to military hospitals and of course, all priests on duty as chaplains with the armed forces.3

Months before Pearl Harbor, in February 1941, Military Delegate Bishop O'Hara sent his first circular letter to the American bishops asking them to release some of their men from parish work to the military chaplaincy. When O'Hara took over as Delegate, *The Official Catholic Directory* of 1940 listed a total of 367 chaplains serving in some military capacity, only nineteen of whom were on duty in the navy. The rest were scattered among the army and veterans' hospitals or were on auxiliary or reserve status. O'Hara's and Spellman's problem was how to get the bishops to give up any of their men for an unspecified period of time, for, considering the nature of the military apostalate, it was likely that some of these men would never return. O'Hara wrote:

> This office will be pleased to receive recommendations from Your Excellency of priests eligible for the service who might be interested. I need hardly say that a very special vocation is required for the lonesome life of a Chaplain in peace time. Naturally, not so many priests are adapted to it, but those who find the life an attractive field for zeal, can do a world of good.4

There was enough response from the dioceses and also from religious orders that on Pearl Harbor day Spellman was able to issue a statement to the effect that five hundred chaplains were on duty at that time.5 Both Spellman and O'Hara had spent a year of intense campaigning to achieve this goal, and still Catholic chaplains continued to be underrepresented with respect to Catholic servicemen. Further, Protestant sects were continually oversubscribed so that Catholic slots often went to them. Spellman went so far as to offer release to any priest in the New York diocese for the Military Ordinariate.6

But on the first day of war the Catholic chaplaincy was already reduced in strength by one. Fr. Aloysius Herman Schmitt, a priest from the diocese of Dubuque had been a naval chaplain since June 1939 and by 1941 was serving aboard the battleship *Oklahoma*. When the Japanese attacked Pearl Harbor on December 7, the *Oklahoma* was hit with four torpedoes and immediately began listing to port. Schmitt started to help the sailors in the compartment with him escape through a porthole. When all of the men were out, he began to follow, but when more sailors entered the compartment below him seeking a means of escape, he lowered himself down to push them through. Though the sailors insisted he try again to escape, the ship continued to roll and the priest disappeared under the black water. He was the first of eighty-seven Catholic chaplains to die in World War II.7

After the disaster at Pearl Harbor, there was a surge of volunteering for the chaplaincy among Catholic priests, though some Bishops still had a degree of reluctance to let their men go. The same situation prevailed with the religious orders, including the largest, the Society of Jesus. The Jesuits had a long history of naval service as well as military service, a history that harked back nearly to the period of the original *Missio Castrensis*. In 1623 Spanish admiral Ambrose Spinola asked the provincial of the Belgian and Flemish Jesuits to provide chaplains for his fleet. The rector of the Dunkerque College was to act as navy Chief of Chaplains. The Jesuits were the preferred choice for the Spanish Army and Navy, and continued to remain so until the order's suppression in 1696.8

As in the Old World, the history of the Jesuits in America was a rocky one. Along with the Franciscans, the Jesuits had founded Christianity in America during the Spanish-French epoch. The man who would become the first American bishop in 1789, John Carroll, was a member of the Society from 1762 until 1773, when the Society was suppressed worldwide by Pope Clement XIV.9 But the papal rescript *Dominus ac Redemptor* was negated in various countries by Pope Pius VII's *Catholicae Fidei* in 1801. By 1805, the order was restored in the United States when five of the ten living ex-Jesuits repeated the vows which once again made them Jesuits.10

While Catholicism in general was unpopular in America in the nineteenth century, the Jesuits were often singled out for particular odium in keeping with Anglo tradition. Furthermore, the navy, even more than the army, was thoroughly Protestant (Episcopal) in tradition. Despite all of this, American Jesuit naval service dates from Father Adam Marshall's cruise in 1825. Only two served in the navy in World War I, Edward P. Duffy and John J. Laherty.11 In the inter-war period, no Jesuits were in the navy, not even on reserve status, but in 1940, two Jesuits managed to get permission from their provincials to go on active duty in the navy. Both had extraordinary experiences in the service.

Fr. Joseph O'Callahan was a brilliant mathematician who taught at Weston and Boston College in the 1930s before being transferred to Holy Cross. There he taught math and physics, and by 1940 he had founded a math library and was head of the math department. An intense individual, Father O'Callahan should have had a fruitful if pedestrian career as an academic. Instead he joined the navy in August 1940. Much to his chagrin, he initially found himself back in a classroom teaching calculus at the Pensacola Naval Air Station. In May 1942, after the United States had been at war for over five months, he received the assignment he had been waiting for: he became chaplain of the aircraft carrier *Ranger*. In March 1945 he was transferred to the carrier *Franklin*. On March 19, off of Okinawa, the *Franklin* was hit by two Japanese bombs and began to burn uncontrollably. On his own initiative, O'Callahan organized fire fighting crews, jettisoned hot shells and provided spiritual support to the panicked crew. The *Franklin* survived, albeit as the most badly damaged ship salvaged during the war. On January 23, 1946, O'Callahan was awarded the Medal of Honor for his actions aboard the *Franklin* . He was the only chaplain to receive the nation's highest military decoration in World War

II and the first since the Civil War, when qualifications for conferral were far less stringent.12

Fr. Charles O'Neill of the New York Province was commissioned a lieutenant in the navy in November 1940. For the first two years of the war he was assigned to the *President Hayes*, an auxiliary personnel attack transport. During this period he participated in the crucial Solomon Islands campaign to wrest Guadalcanal and Tulagi from Japanese hands. Later in the war he served aboard an aircraft carrier the *Lake Champlain*. Unlike almost all of the other Jesuits, O'Neill remained in the navy after the war and had assignments with various naval and Marine Corps units until he reverted to inactive status in 1953. He did, however, remain active in the reserves and by 1954 he had been promoted to the rank of captain.13

O'Callahan and O'Neill were the pathfinders but they were soon joined by more of their brother Jesuits in 1941. Even after Pearl Harbor, however, Jesuits who had a desire to join the service sometimes met with resistance from their provincial. There was ample reason for the provincials' reluctance. Even more than secular priests, there was a tremendous amount of time and money invested in every man who wore the black habit of the Society of Jesus. In the early decades of the twentieth century and right up until the dislocations of the Vatican II era in the 1960s, Jesuit formation was relatively unchanged from the model laid out by Ignatius centuries before.

First, the course was long, ordinarily lasting fifteen years from entry into the order to full membership. The program was divided into six stages. The first stage, called the novitiate, consisted of two years of canon law study. In this period the novice would also take the perpetual vows of poverty, chastity, and obedience. The second stage was the juniorate which entailed two years of study in classical languages, literature and history. The philosophate was three years of philosophy, mathematics, and science. The fourth stage was called regency. At this time the men were sent to various Jesuit high schools for a three year period of teaching. Next came the theologate, a four year period of theological studies, with some practice of priestly ministry. The candidate was ordained after the third year, but his Jesuit formation was still not complete. The final stage was tertianship, a one year return to the life of a novice.14

As with so many aspects of life in America, the coming of the Second World War caused considerable upset in the Jesuit order. Many of the not so young Jesuit fathers sought permission to join the armed forces as chaplains though most were already occupied with full-time jobs as teachers, professors or administrators at Jesuit colleges and high schools. One of these men was John Patrick Foley, S.J. of the New England Province. When the war broke out, Foley was wearing two hats as Dean of Freshmen and Sophomores and Dean of Admissions at Boston College. Foley's career as a naval chaplain took him from Casablanca to Balboa, from Bougainville, Efate, Guadalcanal and Tulagi to Eniwetok, Guam, Tinian and Saipan. And then as the holocaust ended he saw the ruins of Okinawa, Kyushu, Yokohama and Tokyo before returning to Chestnut Hill.

John Foley's odyssey began in Motherwell, Scotland on June 6, 1904, where he was born at an uncle's house. His parents Frank and Catherine were Irish immigrants who had both settled in Boston at an early age. His mother came from Lisdoonvarna, Galway, and his father from Leitrim. The couple returned to Ireland and then went on to Scotland, where John arrived. More than ninety years later he would recall his early days, "My parents spoke so often of the beauty of Boston that I pleaded with them to take me there. And they did. I was six weeks old."15

The Foleys were typically devout Irish American Catholics. Both Frank and Catherine were daily communicants until the growing clan prevented Catherine from attending. Eventually there were eight Foley children who grew up with the same devotion to the Church. The oldest, John, unlike many future priests, never served as an altar boy. Instead he was a paperboy in his Somerville neighborhood. He had to be out with papers at five a.m. so there was no way he could serve a daily Mass. But in a sense his future was already set. Intellectual and quick-witted, Foley attended

Boston College High School, another rite of passage for so many working class Irish American boys in the early twentieth century. At B.C. High Foley was on the track team and was quarterback of the football team, but he was painfully thin and had no aspirations for any kind of an athletic career.16

What began to happen at B.C. High was a crystallization of the vague ideas he had had for some time. He came under the influence of the young Jesuit scholastics who taught there and soon understood that he wanted to be a Jesuit priest. The scholastics were in their regency and about twenty-five to twenty-seven years old. These men would sometimes tell the boys what it meant to be a Jesuit. Most of the students welcomed these digressions simply as a break from Homer or Cicero, but a few felt a calling in the scholastics' words. A classmate of Foley's went on to the Passionists, but when Foley was told by one of the scholastics that he would make a pretty good Jesuit, he was sold.17

The next step for John Foley was telling his parents of his decision. Though many Catholic families would have been delighted to have a priest in the family, there were practical matters to consider. The oldest children were usually expected to go out and work as soon as possible, to supplement the family income. Thus a priest in a working class family meant a relative hardship for everyone, especially if he was the oldest boy.

Foley's mother was ironing clothes on Memorial Day, 1923, when he told her of his decision to join the Jesuits. She asked him how long it would take. He told her thirteen years before ordination. She said, "I'll never see your ordination, talk to your father." His father was more encouraging. He said, "John, I won't stand in your way. I won't stand between you and God if God is calling."18

John Foley's resolve and his parents' permission were not the only requirements for his entering the Society of Jesus. The order itself had to approve the young applicant, and rejections, in those days of plentiful vocations, were common. The first stop was a stiff physical examination. The prospective Jesuit was expected to be in reasonably good physical condition with no serious medical problems. Though the life of a priest in a parish or in an academic setting is not extremely demanding physically, there was still duty on foreign missions, which could be taxing and which could entail years of service with poor food and shelter.

When Foley was examined the doctor noted that he had a heart murmur. This was a potentially disqualifying defect. Unknown to him, he was accepted into the Jesuits on a provisional basis and under intense scrutiny. He officially entered the Society of Jesus on August 14, 1923 and was sent to the Jesuit house of studies "Shadowbrook" in Lenox, Massachusetts for the two years of novitiate.19

Shadowbrook itself had an odd and interesting history. Originally the grounds were part of the estate of Samuel G. Ward, a wealthy Bostonian. In 1893 a mansion was built on the property by Anson Phelps Stokes, a prominent Stockbridge Episcopalian. After passing through the hands of another owner, the building and property were purchased by the redoubtable Scottish robber baron, Andrew Carnegie, who lived there from 1917 until his death two years later. By 1922 it had been acquired by the Jesuits. Fr. John H. Fisher, S.J. developed it into a house of studies for young Jesuits in the novitiate and juniorate stages of their formation. The building and grounds of Shadowbrook in the rustic surroundings of the Berkshires were an ideal location for study, prayer and contemplation and served the Jesuit community until the tragic night of March 10, 1956, when the house burned to the ground in the night, killing three priests and one Brother.20

Foley entered Shadowbrook with thirty other novices that summer and began his studies. The novice master called him in just prior to Christmas to tell him that they were keeping him. He was flabbergasted, but stammered a thank you. Another candidate named Foley was dismissed, but John was now in, if he could complete the fifteen year course. In 1925, when his two years of novitiate were up, he moved to the two-year juniorate stage, also at Shadowbrook. In 1927 he was one of the two men in his class chosen to study at Heythrop College in England for the philosophy stage, which lasted until 1930. At that time he received an undergraduate degree in languages and philology. Foley was fortunate in his quick facility for languages. In Jesuit houses in those days much mundane conversation, as well as school work, was carried on in Latin. Others struggled, but Foley was proficient enough that he was sent to teach Classics and Greek literature in the original languages at Holy Cross for the regency stage, from 1930–1933.21

The next stage of Jesuit formation was theology. For this Foley was sent to the Society's home in Weston. The New England Province of the Society of Jesus had only been independent of the New York Province since 1926, though it had already established Weston as a house of studies for scholastics in 1922. The mansion sitting on a 120 acre site was known as the Grant Walker estate. It was purchased from Mabel Shaw Walker, a grand-niece of Fr. Joseph Coolidge Shaw, S.J., a proper Bostonian who had gone from Unitarianism to the Catholic priesthood and then into the Jesuits in 1850. Though he died six months after entering the Society, Shaw anticipated that a Jesuit University would one day be established in Boston and so bequeathed his 1,700 volume library to the future Boston College, founded in 1863.22

Once established, Weston quickly became known as an important center for theological and philosophical study. In 1929 the Commonwealth of Massachusetts allowed the school to grant civil degrees and in 1932 the Holy See granted it the right to confer ecclesiastical degrees. It was here in this vibrant intellectual atmosphere where John Foley went in 1933 and where he studied advanced theology for four years.23

In 1935 he produced an essay as a requirement for the Master of Arts degree. Entitled "Herodotus—The Forgotten and Libelled Historian," the paper was not a masterpiece and reflected the flowery prose still common at the time. There is a surfeit of adjectives and Foley's thesis, which is a repudiation of Herodotus' many famous detractors and critics belies the "forgotten" aspect of the paper's title. Nevertheless, Foley made a strong case for Herodotus' virtues as an historian and also displayed his abilities with Greek translation.24

It was at Weston too where John Foley was ordained a priest of the Roman Catholic Church on June 2, 1936. The bishop who presided at the ordination ceremony was Most Rev. Thomas A. Emmett, S.J., D.D., the Titular Bishop of Tuscamia and Vicar Apostolic of Jamaica. Foley was now a priest in good standing but he was not yet a full-fledged Jesuit. That rigorous course would continue. In 1937, he went to Pomfret, Connecticut for the final one year stage of Jesuit formation called tertianship. This was to be a return to the life of a novice fourteen years earlier, emphasizing prayer and penance.25

Foley had enjoyed every year of the course and had no regrets about his decision to enter the priesthood or the Jesuits, but the final examination turned out to be a nerve-wracking trial. Foley was given a sheet in Latin of philosophical and theological theses which he had studied at the beginning of the course many years before. The test was a two hour oral examination whereby four "sharpshooters" would fire questions at him from the sheet of theses. The rector of the seminary at Weston was present as well, so the pressure was intense. Foley sailed through the examination.26

Foley was then sent to Boston College where he taught Greek and English literature from 1938 to 1940. In 1940 he took his final vows to become a full member of the Society of Jesus, seventeen years after entering the Society as a novice. Then, as "punishment for his sins", as he put it, he was made Dean of Admissions and Dean of Freshmen and Sophomores. Like most Americans, Foley had little intimation that war was so near. He was totally immersed in the duties and obligations of his work as dean. But there were ominous signs despite the government's effort to keep the undeclared Atlantic naval war a secret in that year prior to Pearl Harbor. Foley visited the Boston Navy Yard and saw a ship there that had been torpedoed and learned about other ships which had been lost in convoy.27

Franklin Roosevelt's actions also pointed the way the nation was heading. When running for his third term in 1940, he made campaign stops at armament facilities and busied himself with the destroyers-for-bases deal with the British. For various reasons, Roosevelt should have been vulnerable at that time. His domestic program as well as his foreign policies had come under increasing criticism, and many people were fed up with the plethora of New Deal "alphabet soup" agencies. Others feared Roosevelt's apparent reluctance to ever step down and his blissful disregard of George Washington's tradition of two terms only. The Republicans failed to capitalize on his weaknesses, however. Rather than run conservative Robert Taft, they nominated former Democrat Wendell Wilkie who, like Roosevelt, was an open interventionist. With little to choose from, Roosevelt was reelected. Many years after the war, Foley recalled the famous speech Roosevelt made in Boston during the campaign, "He said not one of your boys will ever fight abroad...he was lying through his teeth."28

When war broke out, Foley wanted to join up immediately but the situation was delicate. He had great responsibilities at Boston College and permission to go sailing off to war would not come easily. The first step, he knew, would be the hardest; he would have to secure permission from the New England Jesuit Provincial, Rev. James H. Dolan, S.J. Dolan was a legendary figure in the Province. He was deliberate, ponderous, and seemingly knew everything. When Foley approached him for permission, Dolan told him bluntly that he did not believe he could pass the physical examination to get into the service. Foley decided then to approach the problem in a Jesuitical way.29

A few days later he went to a doctor he knew next to the Boston Garden on Causeway Street who gave him a quick physical and an okay. Foley went back to Dolan and said "Father, I was in here the other day and you said I couldn't pass the physical. I passed the physical." Shocked, Dolan said, "Who gave you permission?" Foley replied, "I presumed the permission and I'm telling you now." The Jesuits had a rule that if they presumed permission for anything, they would tell their superiors afterward. Dolan told him he would have to get permission from Fr. William Murphy, the President of Boston College. Murphy was skeptical and told him to go and see Fr. John Long, who was Foley's direct superior as Dean of Arts and Sciences. Father Long told him, "I'm thinking of going in myself. Go."30

The next step was to get permission from the Military Ordinariate in New York. Foley made it clear that he wanted to go into the navy and was determined to serve aboard a warship. He had no desire for a stateside or shore-based station and he also had definite ideas against the army. Years later he recalled his feelings, "having learned to swim in salt water at eight years old and liking the ocean and living next door to it and having taken a voyage I knew all about it at six weeks old. I had salt in my veins. It had to be the navy."31

The Military Ordinariate had other plans. When Foley received permission to join up, he was instructed to go to the army. He wrote back and told them that a mistake had been made. He was volunteering for the navy. The Ordinariate, apparently understanding the type of man they were dealing with, wrote back giving him permission to join the navy. Foley went to a navy recruiter and this time took a full rigorous physical which he passed with no trouble at all. John Patrick Foley of the Society of Jesus was now chaplain with the rank of lieutenant (junior grade) in the naval reserve of the United States Navy for the duration of the war.32

Foley then made his final preparations to leave. His responsibilities as dean were turned over to Fr. Michael Pierce. He went to a uniform store in Boston and had a blue uniform tailored. From Bishop Richard Cushing he received a gift that all World War II-era Catholic chaplains treasured. One day Foley was helping out at a diocesan church when Cushing asked him if he had a Mass kit. The Mass kits were suitcases containing a consecrated chalice and all of the other holy objects necessary to conduct Mass in the field or in a confined shipboard space. Cushing told him that he had one for him but when Foley was leaving he did not want to seem greedy so started to walk out without it. Cushing stopped him and bellowed in his gravelly voice. "Take it now John or the next guy comes in will pick it up!" Foley thanked Cushing and left with the Mass kit, which he used throughout the war and even into the 1990s, when he occasionally said Mass in private houses.33

On Wednesday, April 15, 1942, Foley bade farewell to his family and caught the midnight train out of Boston's South Station. The train was heading for Philadelphia, the first stop on his trip to Norfolk, Virginia, and the U.S. Navy Chaplain School.34

Notes: Chapter 2

1 Robert I. Gannon, S.J. *The Cardinal Spellman Story* (Garden City, N.Y.: Doubleday & Co., Inc, 1962), 180; Interview with Auxiliary Bishop of Boston, Merrimack Region, Most Rev. John J. McNamara, Lawrence, Massachusetts, October 15, 1996. McNamara was Navy Chief of Chaplains from 1983–1988.

2 Gannon, *Cardinal Spellman,* 180, 181; Thomas T. McAvoy, C.S.C., *Father O'Hara of Notre Dame: The Cardinal Archbishop of Philadelphia* (Notre Dame, Indiana: University of Notre Dame Press, 1967), 195. John Mortimer Smith, in *The Military Ordinariate,* , 140, notes that it was in 1939 that the Roman Congregations changed the terms associated with the chaplaincy from Military Ordinary *(ordinarius castrensis)* and Military Ordinariate *(ordinariatus castrensis)* to Military Vicar *(vicarius castrensis)* and Military Vicariate *(vicariatus castrensis).* Both sets of terms remained in common usage through World War II and were used interchangeably. In 1943 Bishop William McCarty C.SS.R., Provincial of the Redemptorists, was appointed as a second Military Delegate. See *The Priest Goes to War* (New York: The Society for the Propagation of the Faith, 1945).

3 Ordinariate, *United States Catholic Chaplains in the World War,* xxiii; " Military Faculties, laid down by the Sacred Consistorial Congregation for

the Military Ordinariate of the United States of America," *Ecclesiastical Review* 107 (July 1942): 29. English text.

4 McAvoy, *Father O'Hara,* 204, 207, 208.

5.Gannon, *Cardinal Spellman,* 189; Another source, Charles O'Brien, "John F. O'Hara, C.S.C., Military Delegate (1939–1945)," *Records of the Catholic Historical Society of Philadelphia* LXIV (1953), 25, indicates that Spellman's figure is inflated. The Vicariate numbered only 463 chaplains when war was declared.

6McAvoy, *Father O'Hara,* 230.

7As with many war stories that relate the last moments of a doomed hero, the Schmitt story has various discrepancies which show up in each published retelling. An early version appeared in William A. Maguire, *The Captain Wears a Cross* (New York: The Macmillan Co., 1943), 111–114. The official navy version, Drury, *The History of the Chaplain Corps: United States Navy,* vol.II, 22, follows McGuire's account closely. The account by Walter Karig and Welbourn Kelley, *Battle Report: Pearl Harbor to Coral Sea* (New York: Farrar & Rinehart, Inc., 1944), 68 claims that he was hung up by a "handsomely bound" breviary in a hip pocket, and when he backed into the ship to remove it, the other trapped sailors entered the room, whereupon he helped them until he was overwhelmed. Yet another version, published the same year as Karig and Kelley's, Dorothy Fremont Grant, *War is my Parish* (Milwaukee: The Bruce Publishing Co., 1944), 34, claims that Schmitt's breviary was later returned to the Military Ordinariate by another navy chaplain, Father Edward Lynch, O.M.I. There is confusion also whether Schmitt had not yet said Mass that morning or whether he had just finished.

8.Smith, *The Military Ordinariate,* 46, 47. "For the Record," *Jesuit Missions* (November 1945): 250, reports that the first treatise on naval tactics was written by a Jesuit, Father le Hoste, in 1697 and as of 1945, Jesuits had written one hundred works on navigation, naval architecture, shipbuilidng and military science and tactics.

9 William V. Bangert, S.J., *A History of the Society of Jesus* (St. Louis: The Institute of Jesuit Sources, 1972: reprint ed., 1986), 393–398, 404. The suppression drove the individual Jesuits into other positions in the Church. Only a handful left the priesthood and some, like Carroll, actually benefited by moving up into bishoprics and archbishoprics. Two others in the United States were named bishops by the Holy Father: Leonard Neale and Lorenz Grassl.

10 Bangert, *A History of the Society of Jesus,* 425.

11 Gerard F. Giblin, S.J. , *Jesuits as Chaplains in the Armed Forces 1917–1960* (Woodstock, Maryland: Woodstock College Press, 1961), 26,28.

12 Richard J. Dowling, S.J., "Father Joseph Timothy O'Callahan, S.J." 1–4, and a vital statistics data sheet, both found in the O'Callahan Papers, Archives of the College of the Holy Cross, Worcester, Massachusetts. Though disabled by repeated severe strokes stemming at least partly from his heroic actions, O'Callahan completed his memoirs (actually little more than an account of that fateful day on the *Franklin)* in the mid-1950s. See Joseph T. O'Callahan, *I Was Chaplain on the Franklin* (New York: The Macmillan Co., 1956). That same year a Hollywood movie based on his life appeared, entitled "Battle Stations." He was so debilitated in his last years that he needed special ecclesiastical permission to offer Mass sitting down. He died March 18, 1964. There is a large blow up photograph of O'Callahan at the Holy Cross Science Library but little else to commemorate the school's most distinguished professor. His Medal of Honor lies nearly forgotten in a vertical file in the archives.

13 Giblin, *Jesuits as Chaplains,* 86, 87, 143.

14 Joseph M. Becker, S.J., *The Re-Formed Jesuits: A History of Changes in Jesuit Formation During the Decade 1965–1975* (San Francisco: Ignatius Press, 1992) 13, 388, 289, passim. This volume, as its title suggests, is a description of the major changes in the Jesuit course stemming from the chaotic period directly after the Second Vatican Council. Becker, a Jesuit himself, makes it clear that he is just presenting the data, "what happened,"

and he refuses to draw any conclusions as to the results. Less tenuous observers of the Jesuits and the Church in general in the post-Conciliar period have witnessed, as one sign of decay, the almost total dearth of vocations. Becker notes that the number of Jesuit scholastics dropped from 10,594 in 1960 to 3,770 in 1975. More than twenty years later, vocations in the Jesuits and other liberal orders continue on a downward spiral while traditional orders of priests and nuns are inundated with young applicants.

15 Interview with John P. Foley, S.J., Chestnut Hill, Massachusetts, March 3, 1995.

16 Ibid.

17 Ibid.

18 Ibid. Contrary to her dire prediction, Catherine Foley lived to see John's ordination and for many years afterward, dying at the age of eighty-one.

19 Ibid; *Golden Jubilee in the Society of Jesus 1923–1973*, Archives of the New England Province, Society of Jesus.

20 Vincent A. Lapomarda, *The Jesuit Heritage in New England* (Worcester: The Jesuits of the Holy Cross College, 1977), 142-144. The Jesuits, buoyed by the strength and growing numbers of American Catholics in the 1950s, rebuilt a larger Shadowbrook which opened in 1958. They could not anticipate the disastrous effects of Vatican II a scant decade later. By the mid 1960s, discipline at Shadowbrook had collapsed, centuries-old traditions such as periods of silence and wearing of clericals had been dropped and the young men were more involved in political activism than priestly formation. Predictably, numbers dropped so drastically that Shadowbrook had to be abandoned in 1970. See Becker, *The Re-Formed Jesuits*, 223, 224, 303–306.

21 Foley interview, March 3, 1995.

22 James L. Burke, S.J., *Jesuit Province of New England: The Formative Years* (Boston: New England Province of the Society of Jesus, 1976), 33–39; Charles F. Donovan, S.J., "First Light," *Boston College Magazine* (Fall 1994): 36–41. Father Donovan, University Historian of Boston

College believed that the reason Shaw left his impressive book collection to a Jesuit university that was not yet established rather than Georgetown or Fordham was simply because he had great affection for and pride in his hometown. Certainly the Shaws had a blue-blooded Brahmin pedigree, yet Joseph's mother and father as well as many family members and Protestant friends attended his ordination.

23 Lapomarda, *Jesuit Heritage,* 89. As with Shadowbrook, Weston was destroyed as an institute of learning in the wake of Vatican II. Bowing to the demands of some faculty members and the scholastics themselves, in 1969 the theologate was moved to Cambridge, Massachusetts to be closer to Protestant divinity schools. See Becker, *The Re-Formed Jesuits,* 124, 125.

24 John P. Foley, "An Essay on Herodotus—The Forgotten and Libeled Historian," Archives of the New England Province, Society of Jesus. In contrast, Foley's diary, by its nature a less formal document, is eminently profound on important matters and often tongue in cheek when appropriate.

25 David R. Dunigan, S.J. *A History of Boston College* (Milwaukee: The Bruce Publishing Co., 1947), 334; Becker, *The Re-Formed Jesuits,* 389.

26 Foley interview, March 3, 1995.

27 Ibid.

28 Ibid.

29 Ibid.

30 Ibid. As events transpired, Father Long would remain a military chaplain far longer than almost all of the World War II Jesuit chaplains. He was appointed to the army in July 1942 and spent two years at Mitchell Field on Long Island. In the last year of the war he served with the 5th Air Force in the Southwest Pacific and the Philippines and then in Japan through most of 1946, when he was deactivated. He was recalled to the army within a year and served with air units in South Dakota, Puerto Rico, The Panama Canal Zone, Texas, French Morocco, and Maine. He again reverted to inactive status in May 1956 with the rank of lieutenant colonel. See Giblin, *Jesuits as Chaplains,* 70.

31 Foley interview, March 3, 1995.

32 Though both the army and navy had a dearth of Catholic chaplains, there was a tendency for the Ordinariate to channel applicants toward the Army, where the perceived need was greater. Of the fifty-four Jesuits from the New England Province who served during World War II, sixteen were navy and another, Fr. Paul Murphy, went from the Maritime Service to the navy, making a total of seventeen. Two others from the province also served in the Maritime Service. See Giblin, *Jesuits as Chaplains,* 146, 147. There is a discrepancy over the date of Foley's commissioning. His commission, signed by Secretary of the Navy Frank Knox dates his appointment from the twentieth of February, 1942. The official navy chaplain history gives the date as the twenty-second of February, 1942. See Drury, *The History of the Chaplain Corps: United States Navy,* vol III, 95.

33 Interview with Fr. John P. Foley, S.J., Chestnut Hill, Massachusetts, March 17, 1995; Interview with Fr. John P. Foley, S.J., Chestnut Hill, Massachusetts, March 10, 1995. A nearly identical Mass kit story is related by one of Foley's fellow Jesuit chaplains from the New England Province in William J. Leonard, S.J., *Where Thousands Fell* (Kansas City: Sheed & Ward, 1995) 3,4. The Mass kits were donated by the parishioners of Cushing's Newton parish. In Father Leonard's version, Cushing raised the chalice to consecrate it and when he rasped, "*Adjutorium nostrum in nomine Domini,*" he set the pigeons to flight outside of his open window. Leonard remembered Cushing fondly and saw him as one of the few bishops who was wholly committed to sending off priests to serve as military chaplains. "He took a very, very, vivid interest in the chaplains and regarded the chaplaincy during the war as *the* apostolic opportunity of the twentieth century and...I think he was right." Interview with Fr. William J. Leonard, S.J., Chestnut Hill, Massachusetts, September 27, 1995. On this subject see also "Aren't All Catholic Chaplains from Boston?" *The Pilot,* 27 October 1995, 43.

34 John P. Foley, diary, April 15, 1942. Copy in Author's collection.

Chapter 3

▼

"Chaplains in Training"

At 7:30 a.m. on April 16, Father Foley's train pulled into Philadelphia. Since he had a few hours to kill before his connection to Norfolk he went to the oldest church in Philadelphia, St. Joseph's in Willling's Alley and was allowed to celebrate Mass by Father O'Hara, S.J. By 11 o'clock he was back on a train heading south. He had no sooner settled into his seat when he was accosted by a man who was already inebriated at that early hour of the day and who forced him to hear his life story, punctuated by war whoops and refrains from "Deep in the Heart of Texas." A conductor arrived to escort the man away while Foley began writing in a notebook. The man shouted, "Look at that, writing about me! He'll use me in a sermon. That is what he'll say, 'My dear brethren, once I was riding on a train down to Norfolk from Philly and on that train was a man who was a drunkard. He had been dissipating for three days.'"[1]

Foley did record the story of the drunk, but not for use in a sermon. From his first day out of Boston until the end of the war (with a few exceptions) Foley kept a detailed diary in which he recorded seemingly everything he saw and experienced in the navy. Neither officers nor enlisted men were supposed to keep diaries for the reason that if captured they could be a great intelligence coup for the enemy, but combatants have been keeping diaries since the advent of warfare and for the duration Foley assiduously—one might say religiously—attended to his journal.

Navy bureaucrats realized that the service was rife with diarists despite the security risks. In October 1942, six months after Foley had started his own *magnum opus* , Secretary of the Navy Frank Knox circulated this order regarding diaries:

THE KEEPING OF PERSONAL DIARIES BY PERSON-
NEL OF THE NAVY IS HEREBY PROHIBITED FOR
THE DURATION OF THE WAR X PERSONNEL HAV-
ING DIARIES IN THEIR POSSESSION ARE
DIRECTED TO DESTROY THEM IMMEDIATELY X
DIARIES AS USED IN THIS DISPATCH INCLUDES
ANY PRIVATE NOTES OR MEMORANDA OF ANY
DESCRIPTION WHATSOEVER WHICH INDICATES
IN ANY MANNER THE LOCATION OR ACTIVITIES
OF PERSONNEL SHIPS AIRCRAFT OR EQUIPMENT
OF THE ARMED FORCES OF THE UNITED STATES
OR OF ANY NATION ALLIED WITH THE UNITED
STATES IN THE PRESENT WAR2

Foley's interests were encyclopedic. Predictably he recorded his own movements and experiences but he was also a keen observer of the behavior of the officers and enlisted men, both Catholic and non-Catholic. He had great devotion to the skippers who led by example and was unsparing in his judgment of those he felt were advancing their careers on the backs of their men. As the Jesuits of old, he had a sense of wonderment at the exotic, and was fascinated by pretty flowers and colorful wildlife. He duly noted the temperatures, rainfall, geography, and even the racial characteristics and traditions of the natives of the lands that he visited. The diary in a small way was a latter-day Jesuit Relations and over the course of the war he sometimes felt that the lot of a Jesuit chaplain in the navy was little different from the North American martyrs amongst the Hurons. He may have even remembered a famous missive sent from St. John de Brebeuf in 1635 to Quebec regarding the arduous nature of apostolic work with the tribe and compared it to his own shipboard parish.

> Do not volunteer to help in any work unless you intend to continue it until the end. Do not begin to paddle unless you have made up your mind to keep at it all day. Be quite sure that the savage will retain the first impression that you make on him, and impart his feelings to his friends and acquaintances...You have to be an Indian. Bend your shoulders to the same burdens they bear, and you will be recognized as a great man; otherwise not...You are responsible for fair and foul weather, and if you do not bring rain when there is a drought you may be tomahawked for your ill-success...Finally, if, after contemplating the sufferings that are prepared for you, you are ready to say: '*Amplius Domine ,*' Still more O Lord, then be sure that you will be rewarded with consolations to such a degree that you will be compelled to say: Enough, O Lord, Enough!3

All of that was ahead of Foley as his train brought him to Cape Charles, Delaware, where he boarded the ship *Virginia Lee* for the short journey down to Norfolk. He got a room at the Hotel Monticello for $3.00 a night and considering the accommodations, he felt overcharged. But he once again met a gracious pastor, Father Blackburn of St. Mary's Church, who allowed him to say 8:00 a.m. Mass the next morning. After Mass, he was off to the Naval Operating Base and reported to Comm. Clinton A. Neyman and Lt. John F. Robinson.4

The navy chaplain school itself was a new concept. During World War I and up to early 1942, there was no set course of indoctrination for clergymen entering the navy chaplaincy. The standard treatment was simply apprenticing a new man to an older chaplain for a few months, then reassigning him with whatever knowledge he had picked up. Furthermore, there were few printed materials to act as training guides. Due to the relatively great expansion of the chaplaincy in 1940–1941, indoctrination classes were organized at four of the larger naval training centers. The first class (designated class A) at the Naval Training Station, Naval Operating Base at Norfolk was conducted by Northern Baptist Chaplain Neyman out of his own home.5

Obviously a more professionally organized system needed to be introduced. The Chief of the Navy Chaplain Corps was Presbyterian Capt. Robert D. Workman, who had been developing the concept of an indoctrination school for all newly-commissioned chaplains. Permission from the Chief of the Bureau of Navigation was secured and Neyman was appointed as Officer in Charge of the school, which would indeed be located at the Norfolk Naval Operating Base. Because Neyman reported on February 28, 1942, this is the "official" date of the founding of the school. By this time Class B was already underway.6

Neyman was given two assistants to act as faculty and also to help administer the school. The first, Lt. Comm. Thomas Knox was a diocesan priest from Savannah who had been a regular navy chaplain since 1932. Knox arrived at the school on February 28, the same date as Neyman, but it was only a temporary assignment and he had left by April 1. Knox was replaced by Comm. Stanton W. Salibury, a Presbyterian, who became the executive officer. Neyman's other assistant was Lt. John F. Robinson, a New York priest who had also been regular navy since 1936. Robinson checked in on March 3, 1942. 7

The day Foley arrived at the school, April 17, Robinson gave a warm-up lecture to the students. He made an attempt at navy humor when he told them, "Admiral Pratt states that all men eventually reach the metallic age—get silver in their hair, gold in their teeth and lead in their stern." Foley's Class E was not slated to start officially until April 20 so he still had a couple of days to get acclimated. An aspect of life in the South that northerner Foley picked up on immediately was racial segregation. After Robinson's talk, Foley went to lunch in the Officer's Mess and bought a $5.00 book of food tickets. He noticed that all of the workers were black. It was his first intimation of the caste system in the South but it was not his last. 8

That same day there was a flurry of excitement at Norfolk. For some unknown reason a German U-boat surfaced near shore and was blown out of the water by shore batteries. Only five German survivors were brought ashore. One of the priests in Class C, Wilbur F.X. Wheeler, attended to them and told Foley that they were "just boys."10 Though the U-boat threat to America had caused a degree of panic and hysteria in coastal cities, by this time in 1942 the Germans were resolutely losing the Battle of the Atlantic and losses in the U-boat service were enormous.11

Due to the hurried and improvised nature of the founding of the school, facilities were not optimal at Norfolk. Classrooms were set up in the old, cramped Catholic chapel building. Classes were conducted while renovations were carried out and amid the noise of construction and the 100 degree temperatures of the Virginia summer, few could concentrate on the lecture material.12 Furthermore, there was no room for the chaplains at the bachelors' quarters so they had to find their own accommodations. The brotherhood of Jesuits came to Foley's rescue again in an unusual way. It so happened that the sister of Father Delihant, S.J., whose parish was St. Ignatius in New York City, owned a large house in Norfolk. The lady, Mrs. Cecilia Taylor, was a grandmother, lived alone, and was glad to have Foley as a boarder for company while he was attending the school. His diary entry upon seeing the house and grounds reflected his interest in the botanical landscape of spring in the South. This same interest in flora and fauna would continue when he shipped out to the tropical isles of the Pacific. He wrote,

There are eight rooms in the house, gave me the best upstairs. Corner house—white with green blinds—Entrance, flanked by rows of irises—Side facing the street, large porch trellised with long lavender cones of wisteria—Hedge around property, banks of irises behind it, large lawn, three maples and dogwood in blossom—Flower garden, rosebushes, tulips, etc.—Backyard—oak tree, sitting set under it—Mrs. Taylor sewing there—next door, rhododendrons, wisteria, azaleas, gardenias, tulips, lilacs. In parlor, lovely white irises in vase—in hall, just inside door, vase of two shades of purple—lilacs and irises.13

Settled into this attractive home, Foley started out on Monday, April 20, for his first day of chaplain school which began with a lecture by Chaplain Neyman followed by physical drill. Though he was once a fair athlete at B.C. High, those years were well behind him now and calisthenics would not be a favorite part of the curriculum. To top off his first day, Foley nearly blacked out when given an anti-tetanus inoculation.14

Apart from the difficulties of the first day, Foley thoroughly enjoyed his time at the chaplain school. Many non-Catholics, particularly those who were married and living a comfortable civilian life, found it difficult to adjust to the navy discipline and regulated lifestyle. The chaplain-students were given navy haircuts and forced to keep uniform, shoes, and personal effects in order. They were taught to salute and respond to superior officers with a brisk "aye, aye, sir."15 This emphasis on obedience and personal discipline was a new hardship to some, but Jesuits such as Foley had been living much tougher regimented lives for nearly twenty years. Indeed, to the Jesuits of the 1940s, military service represented a slackening of discipline and much freer lifestyle than that experienced in Jesuit houses. Likewise, obedience to designated authority was an old story to the priests, particularly those who came from religious orders.16

A year later, another Jesuit at the chaplain school, Samuel Hill Ray, was asked his opinion of the curriculum by Chaplain Neyman. He answered,

> All very well, but not more strict than the training of the Jesuit Order. For instance, when we are in our early training, a Brother comes around each morning to awaken us young fellows and says very piously in Latin, 'Let us bless the Lord,' and we all answer in Latin, more or less piously, struggling to wake up, 'Thank God.' Now here a chief comes around and says, 'Hit the deck,' and we answer, 'What the...?' The words differ, but the spirit is the same.17

The chaplain school was not a seminary or divinity school. The navy was not in the business of training men to be clerics but training clerics to be navy men. There were some basic parameters that had to be met before a man could be certified as a chaplain in the navy. Candidates were required to have at least four years of university schooling and a bachelor's degree. They were also required to have an additional three years in a theological seminary and a divinity degree.18 Jesuits met these academic qualifications with about a decade of schooling and theology to spare.

In addition to the lessons in keeping uniform and orderly, the chaplains were taught how to deal with fellow officers, navy terminology and regulations, the proper way to conduct funerals including burial at sea, weddings, and how to rig for church. They were also given instructions in how to deal with servicemen of faiths other than their own.19 Catholic chaplains could deal adequately with Protestant and Jewish men, often leading them in prayer services but the situation was difficult for Catholic men who did not have a chaplain of their own faith. Non-Catholic chaplains could not confer the sacraments, particularly the celebration of Mass and that of confession. Even worse, a non-Catholic chaplain could not administer Last Rites-Penance, Holy Viaticum, and Extreme Unction for a dying man. The situation for Catholics in the service, therefore, was often less than optimum. Even if a non-Catholic chaplain was not hostile to the Church, he was of little use in matters of faith, when a chaplain was really needed.

There was a list of official duties a navy chaplain was expected to perform, codified in the regulations of September 8, 1939. Most importantly the chaplain was expected to perform divine services aboard his own ship or shore station and, when applicable, other ships, stations, and naval hospitals. He was expected to facilitate services for those of other faiths, form voluntary prayer groups, teach classes in religious instruction, and visit the sick as often as possible. He was required to keep a record of all marriages, funerals, and baptisms he performed and he was to visit or write letters to the families of men who were sick or had become casualties. Chaplains were forbidden to be involved in the business of a ship's store or post exchange or to be a treasurer of any fund.20

In practice, chaplains were also expected to be the "morale officer" on board ship and even at shore bases. As such they had to procure and run films, edit and publish ship's newspapers, take charge of the ship'slibrary, organize athletic competitions, and even sell government insurance to the men. If a man did not have the fortitude to refuse at least some of these non-religious jobs, the other officers tended to dump every onerous duty on him.

Bishop O'Hara was acutely aware of the way in which chaplains were burdened with excessive duties, and was determined that his men would not be used as lackeys by the secular officers. He was also sensitive to the fact that some of these officers would not be happy having a priest aboard, and feared the men sliding into indifferentism and loneliness. In a letter written to a navy chaplain prior to the war, O'Hara suggested ways to combat these problems.

> ...I would like you to remember always that your primary obligation is to the Church and your sole purpose is the administration of the spiritual needs of the sailors. We will

expect you to be just as exact in these matters while you are in the Navy, as you were in your own parish. You should always be very tactful in dealing with officers, and I am sure you will thereby get cooperation. You must avoid, in particular, any participation in union services of the ministers and their religious sects.

It would be advisable for you when you are in port to become acquainted with the local clergy for two reasons: 1) a chaplain in the Navy is very much alone and being in groups of mixed religions, will need the companionship of other priests and the consolation that will come from that association; 2) there may be times when you might have to call upon the local clergy to help you in your work and an attitude of friendliness will always make them cooperative.21

As far as was possible, the navy chaplain school did try to discourage religious disputes among its diverse student body. Before being reassigned, Father Knox suggested a school slogan, "Cooperation Without Compromise."22 This slogan was adopted and remains the Navy chaplaincy's motto today. Foley was a thoroughly orthodox priest and there was little danger of him drifting into heterodoxy though he got along well with Protestant and Jewish chaplains. On occasion, religious differences even prompted humor. One day Presbyterian Salisbury said to Catholic Robinson, "Converted a boy to the true Church today." "What Church?" "Yours, of course."23

As beautiful as he found the South, Foley continued to be disturbed by racial segregation and was witness to several incidents that made a lasting impression on him. Once when he was standing next to a sentry at the entrance to the base, Foley saw a black man come running along showing his pass to exit. The Marine sentry stopped him and said, "See those railroad tracks? Go back to them and walk out. Nobody runs out of here."

The man meekly turned without a word, did what he was told and as soon as he was out of the gate bolted again.24

Foley himself became involved in a few racial incidents while riding on buses in Charleston, South Carolina. One time a black soldier was pushed from a seat in the front to the back. Foley told the driver, "Good enough to stop a bullet but not to ride up front in a bus." The driver did not appreciate his observation.25 Another day he was returning to the Navy Yard from the city with two young white men sitting behind him. A drunken black man boarded the bus and sat beside him. Foley did not object but the two behind him shouted, "Push him off Captain! Hey, nigger, don't you know where you belong? Get down in the back of this bus!" There were about eight more blacks in the bus and as the white men got off at their stop, one of them punched one of the blacks. At the next stop the whole bunch jumped off and headed for the white men.26

Even in the Spring of 1942, everyone in the navy was still buzzing over who "lost" Pearl Harbor. Chaplain Salisbury was on Oahu December 7 and believed that the Americans were used to seeing planes flying in off the *Enterprise*, so that was why the Japanese were able to come in scot free.27 Salisbury told the men of the retired Admiral Taussig. Taussig had a run-in with a young Assistant Secretary of the Navy during World War I. The assistant came off second best but later became President. Taussig prophesied that war with Japan was inevitable and for his prescience Roosevelt cashiered him.

As part of their training, the chaplains were also sent out in the field to work with enlisted men at the various bases in the area. Some of the chaplains had never flown and were fearful of these low-level flights. Rev. James Kelly, despite his Celtic name, was a Baptist from Memphis and none too keen on flying. Boarding a transport plane he turned to Foley and remarked, "Wall, Ah can appreciate now the celibacy of the clergy. You don't have to worry about your wife and child."28 The Catholic chaplains were more fortunate as well in the composition of their congregation. While Foley was visiting a Marine barracks with another chaplain, the commanding officer told them, "I want to prepare whichever one of you gentlemen is the Protestant for a poor attendance tomorrow. Catholic boys turn out but not the Protestants." Methodist Rev. John Weise replied, "Well, I guess I can take it."29

The Catholics had a tremendous gift in the universality of the Church and were well aware of it. Non-Catholics, too, understood that the Latin liturgy was what held the Church together for centuries in the face of innumerable threats. In Foley's class the Catholics attended Protestant services and the Protestants attended Mass on occasion to see how the competition ran their services. After one of these services Methodist Paul Edgar remarked to Foley that he was as much mystified by that Protestant service as by the Catholic. He said his was entirely different, "It is ridiculous when you think of it. There we were, Protestant ministers of every denomination each with his own brand of service, whereas no matter where you go, you priests always and everywhere have the same Mass."30 Little did either of them know that in another twenty years the Church would jettison universal Latin and embrace the vernacular, thus prompting a balkanization of the liturgy. But in the 1940s the Church was strong, and Catholic chaplains knew that wherever they went—from Alaska to Guadalcanal, from Berlin to Tokyo, there would be a priest to meet them and a common faith and language to share in the mystery of the Mass.

At times Catholic theology ran headlong into the spirit of the day. A young navy psychiatrist was brought in to lecture the chaplains on the true nature of man. His theories did not impress the Jesuits in the room. The psychiatrist reduced the human personality to the resultant of two determining factors—"constitutional" i.e. heredity and environment. Foley questioned him, "Any room allowed for the exercise of free will in that analysis?" Reply—"I don't know what you mean by free will." Foley retorted, "Choice of two alternatives—to walk or ride in a car." The psychiatrist had not expected to defend his position and tried to ignore Foley but another New England Jesuit, Fr. Michael Doody, pressed him for an answer. A Methodist minister, Will-Mathis Dunn jumped in also. The psychiatrist finally admitted that free will existed in practice but not in "theory."31

Doctrinal disputes did crop up occasionally between Catholics and Protestants as well as between Protestants and Protestants. A member of Foley's class, Southern Baptist Kermit Combs from West Virginia, one day asserted that since the body is the temple of the Holy Ghost and liquor is poison, then anybody who drinks liquor of any kind is polluting the temple of the Holy Spirit. Episcopalian Benjamin Brown countered with his position that all creatures were created by God either directly or indirectly. Liquor was one of His creatures, therefore it could not be evil in itself. Foley agreed that this was good sound doctrine and inquired of Combs how he could explain the miracle of Cana when the Lord changed water into wine at the wedding breakfast. Combs replied that he wasn't there and that there was only a little liquor in the work performed by Christ. Brown then said that his position was ruined if there was *any* alcoholic content to the wine. Combs replied that in his church's communion service, the difficulty was avoided by using grape juice.32

Foley and the others continued to travel around the area to minister to the men in training. This pastoral work was the reason he joined the navy and was the only thing he wanted to do in the service. He considered the military a type of mission ground. His May 2 diary entry described a flight to another barracks.

> 11:30 Took off in Douglas Transport plane for Cherry Point, North Carolina. Glorious sun-drenched morning. With a roar, our giant silver plane soared up and we are on out way to our destination—3500 feet below is a crazy quilt of farm land, river woods and doll houses. James River on our left carrying fussy little tugs on its bosom. Tugs chugging along tried to make up in braggadocio what they lacked in size as they warped an aircraft carrier into her berth. Soon we were sailing through the Alps in the sky. Some were dark

mountains at the base and at top crested with snow. Occasionally, a tuft of cotton would sail by, boastfully, on its own after cutting its mother's apron strings. Then a proud craft would move along majestically, obviously an old timer. Far below, white strips of yellow adhesive tape criss cross the face of the country. Occasionally they would meet and little black bugs came to a stop at their juncture. Body of water we are passing over now is Albermarle Sound, enlisted man informs Chaplain Weise and me.

Soon we have left that behind and we are flying over Pamlico River. Now a haze obscures the ground, misty reminder of forest fires that carelessness or sabotage have lighted in these Carolina woods. 33

Foley was impressed by what he saw in the Catholic sailors. One Sunday morning Chaplain Robinson called him up and told him to get out to the battleship *North Carolina*, anchored off Hampton Roads, to celebrate Mass. He hopped the seven o'clock boat from Pier 2 which was bringing a liberty party back to the ship. The hot sun glinted off the bulk of the battlewagon and the whole scene reminded him of Castle Island back home in Boston. Once aboard he heard confessions and then said Mass in one of the mess compartments. There were about 130 men present. As he surveyed his one-time flock he thought "flags took the place of stained glass windows and a whitewashed overhead for a beautiful ceiling but I am sure that our Lord was immensely pleased with the shining faces of those splendid young men."34

The chaplain was pleased too, by the zeal of the Catholics on board. Since the ship did not have a Catholic chaplain, one of the sailors ran two classes—one for boys who wanted to learn how to serve Mass and the other for non-Catholics who had questions about the Catholic Church. The term used for such activities was "Catholic Action." It was not unusual in

those days to find these unsung apostles among Catholic laymen, and conversions to the Church were high throughout the war. Often times these
lay apostles were educated men, graduates of Catholic universities such as
Boston College. One of these men aboard the *North Carolina*, Bill Kelly,
B.C. '40, escorted Foley around the ship after Mass.35 Foley found the vessel an imposing weapon, more than ready to take the measure of the
enemy, and he felt confident of America's ability to successfully prosecute
this war.

In other circumstances, however, much of what the young sailors told
Foley about their experiences disturbed him. It seemed that those in
charge of running the war were distinguished chiefly by their cowardice
and stupidity. When visiting a group of survivors brought in from a torpedoed ship, he was told by the one Catholic among them that the ten
American sailors were members of a gun crew aboard the British steamer
Irma , which was sent to the bottom on Good Friday, 350 miles off the
coast of South Africa. The men drifted in the water for hours until they
were picked up. What embittered them about the incident was the fact
that a British Corvette was with them at the time of the torpedoing, but
sped away from the area and did not return to look for survivors for four
hours.36

Another time Foley went aboard the *Wakefield*, a 30,000 ton transport
which was formerly the luxury liner *Manhattan*. The ship had just
returned from a five and a half month's voyage to Singapore where it had
dropped off 4,500 Canadians and Englishmen to the doomed Crown
Colony. As a young sailor put it, "We delivered them safely to the Japs."
The ship was attacked and took five direct bomb hits, causing thirty fatal-
ities and more wounded.37

There was in fact plenty of bad news and little good from the war front
through the spring of 1942 while Foley and his comrades were ensconced
in the chaplain school. Pearl Harbor had been a disaster all right, a dis-
graceful humiliation that had been years in the making. As it happened,
the Japanese failed to totally decimate the sleeping armada at Pearl. Most

of the battleships were refloated and refitted to fight again and the essential aircraft carriers, which would carry the burden of the fighting across the vast Pacific, were fortunately missing from Pearl on December 7. Also the Japanese neglected to destroy the base's fuel storage capability and repair facilities. Apart from the 2,400 killed, the primary casualties of the attack were American confidence and non-interventionism, and the reputations of Pearl's naval commander, Adm. Husband E. Kimmel, and army commander Gen. Walter C. Short, who were both demoted and scapegoated for the fiasco. Both went to their graves in disgrace.38

Even if the Roosevelt administration did withhold vital information regarding the date and nature of the Japanese attack, Pearl was hardly the fortress of the Pacific that it should have been. Garrison life in the 1930s was tedium for enlisted men and a series of parties for officers. Marine Corps legend and professional Cassandra, Lewis B. "Chesty" Puller, warned as early as 1926 that Pearl was in a disastrous state of un-readiness. Little was done between then and 1941 from both the army and navy standpoints to improve security.39

The destruction of the Pacific fleet was the necessary prerequisite for Japan's first major strike outside of the Asian mainland: the reduction of the American garrison in the Philippines. The conquest of the Philippines would be another step in the establishment of Japan's "Greater East Asia Co—Prosperity Sphere." In reality, the Japanese were set to enthrone themselves as new masters of Asia once the white devils had been expelled.

If the state of readiness in the Philippines was in a lamentable state compared to that of Pearl Harbor, there was also far less excuse for the debacle that occurred there. Ten and a half hours after the Japanese struck Pearl Harbor, they hit several airfields collectively known as Clark Field in Manila, and destroyed half the force of B-17s and American P-40s on the ground. Another squadron of P-40s unknowingly flew into the Japanese hornet's nest and were likewise annihilated. Though the information that Pearl Harbor had been attacked was hours old, there was such bungling at Gen. Douglas MacArthur's headquarters that the planes were left as sitting ducks for the Japanese bombers. With the majority of the islands' air power in ruins, the American forces could not hope to stem the Japanese invasion. By December 22 the Japanese had landed in force and were triumphantly pushing the American and Filipino troops down the archipelago. Guam and Wake Island too had fallen after a task force meant to relieve besieged Wake turned back without firing a shot.40

The rapid deterioration of the American position in the Pacific would not have been a surprise to any experienced observer prior to the war. As both anti-imperialists and imperialist *par excelence* Theodore Roosevelt had noted decades earlier, the Philippines represented America's "Heel of Achilles" in the Pacific. This notion was discounted by MacArthur who for some years had been the well-paid "Field Marshall" of the Army of the Philippine Commonwealth and friend of Pres. Manuel Quezon. Using his considerable political influence, MacArthur convinced Washington that he could effectively defend most of the archipelago, provided he was supplied with a large enough contingent of troops and the latest weapons, including the much-vaunted B-17s, which were envisioned to be deployed as anti-shipping bombers.41

The vast hordes of defenders never materialized. The Philippine Army itself was an illusion. The small garrison of U.S. Army Regulars was buttressed by the Philippine Scouts, indigenous personnel commanded by American officers. By 1941, draftees were also dribbling in from the states. For the most part the troops were armed with World War I era uniforms, equipment, helmets and rifles. Coastal defense batteries were likewise antiquated. Some guns and fixed mortars had been mounted in the nineteenth century, quaint relics of the Spanish era.42

MacArthur's unrealizable strategy to hold the invader on the beaches of Luzon actually helped doom the defenders, since supplies and ammunition were lost in the first wave. Manila was abandoned without a fight before the end of December, though the American and Filipino forces fought stubbornly in their withdrawal to Bataan.43

The administration had in fact already written off the Philippines, since a relief effort would have drawn resources away from the Churchill-Roosevelt policy of "Europe First." The beleaguered defenders of Bataan and the people of the Philippines fell victim both to the bayonets of the Japanese and the cruel realities of Anglo-American politics. At Roosevelt's behest, MacArthur fled the islands for Australia on March 11, leaving the onus of defeat on Lt. Gen. Jonathan M. Wainwright, who suffered in a prison camp in Mukden until the end of the war. By the middle of May, Corregidor had fallen and the Philippines were effectively conquered. For his abject failure in command, MacArthur was decorated with the Medal of Honor by the president and deified by the American press as the "Lion of Luzon."44

The record of Japanese barbarism during the occupation of the Philippines beggars description. About 20,000 Americans of all service branches were captured. Of the thirty-seven chaplains imprisoned, twenty-one were Catholic, mostly army chaplains who were serving either with the regular army or Philippine Scouts. The Philippines were a mission of the Jesuits' New York Province, and nine of these men marched into captivity with their charges. A tenth, Fr. John J. Dugan, was from the New England Province, a friend of John Foley's, and one of the few priests who survived internment by the Japanese. After thirty-four months in captivity, he was rescued when his prison camp was liberated by Army Rangers.45 The day he was captured he knew that the prisoners were in for a dreadful ordeal. "The Japs requisitioned the hospital's Buick. I got in with the two officers and the driver started off at a terrific clip. It was then that I got my first closeup of things to come. There was a body ahead of us in the road—the body of a Filipino soldier. The driver made no attempt to avoid it. With a thump and quick swerve he drove right over it."46

The one Catholic navy chaplain captured was Fr. Francis Joseph McManus of Ohio, who had been in the service since 1936. McManus was the chaplain of the *Canopus*, originally the commercial vessel *Santa Leonora*, which was taken over by the Navy in 1921 to be converted into a submarine tender. McManus went aboard in March of 1940. The *Canopus* was a slow, third-string vessel, but indispensable to keep the submarine force in the islands operating. In December, operating out of Cavite, she was attacked twice by Japanese bombers and just barely escaped being hit. With other force withdrawals, she relocated to Marivales Bay on Bataan. There on December 29, she was again hit by bombs which caused numerous casualties when the ammunition magazine exploded and set the ship on fire. McManus rushed to the blazing compartments, helped drag the living to safety, and administered Last Rites to the dying.47

For the next few months McManus served not only the men aboard the stricken *Canopus*, but also the Catholic personnel on "The Rock," Corregidor. The *Canopus* was scuttled in early April. McManus was captured when Corregidor fell in May and was sent to the notorious Japanese Military Prison Camp No. 1, at Cabanatuan, where he was quartered with Dugan. Although conditions at the camp were abysmal, McManus and the other priests found attendance to religion among the Catholic men to be quite good, and there were daily Masses and rosaries. This was a comfort because starvation, torture, and abuse were the order of the day. It was estimated that between forty and fifty men perished daily.48 Though the priests never stooped to eating rats, other vermin were fair game. In a post-captivity memoir, Dugan recalled one repast with McManus.

> Fr. McManus said, "We're going to have a delicacy."
> "What is it?" I asked him when the dish was brought on. Its
> basis was the usual rice, but there were bits of meat mixed with
> it. "You try it," was the only answer I got, so I went ahead. It was
> really good; about like chicken. I noticed, though, that Fr.
> McManus himself was eating not very rapidly and with a sort of
> experimental air. "Well, what was it?" I demanded after I'd
> cleaned up the meal. "Snake," he said. It was down so

it was all right then. Somebody had brought it in from the wood detail.49

McManus was praised effusively by other Catholic and Protestant chaplains and the many men he served. He often volunteered to work in the place of sick men and some felt he was the most outstanding chaplain in the camp. By the fall of 1944 the Japanese began shipping prisoners to Japan, anticipating the fall of the Philippines. The transshipment of these men in what came to be known as "hell ships" is another example of brutality beyond the pale. The unmarked ships were typically bombed and strafed by American planes and the prisoners, jammed in fetid holds, were deliberately killed by a lack of water. After unendurable sufferings, McManus succumbed on January 22, 1945. He was awarded the Purple Heart and Silver Star posthumously.50 Overall, the fate of the chaplains in Japanese captivity mirrored the treatment of all of the prisoners in the Philippines.

MacArthur's counterpart in the navy was a different breed. Adm. Chester W. Nimitz had served in many different staff and command billets since his graduation from the Naval Academy in 1905. He was particularly knowledgeable about the engineering and proper use of submarines, a weapon that he would deploy with devastating effect in the war with Japan. At the time of Pearl Harbor he was running the Navy's Bureau of Navigation. In the aftermath of the disaster Nimitz was tapped by Roosevelt and Secretary of the Navy Frank Knox to go to Pearl and take command of what was left of the Pacific fleet. His unenviable task was to refloat the shattered vessels and to rebuild morale, which could not have been lower. Even many career men had lost their perspective and became convinced that the "little iron men" of Nippon were invincible.51

Early in 1942 Nimitz was given extraordinary responsibility as both Commander in Chief Pacific (CINCPAC) and overall Commander in Chief of the Pacific Ocean Areas (CINCPOA). Though subordinate to Admiral Ernest J. King, the Chief of Naval Operations (CNO) Nimitz effectively directed the war in the North, South and Central Pacific. Due to Roosevelt's willingness to appease MacArthur, the hero of the Philippines was given command of the Southwest Pacific area, including naval units. This division of command was another major blunder, which caused not only operational problems but encouraged competition between the two Pacific area commanders for the scant resources allotted from the first-priority European theatre.52

Nimitz's first priority in early 1942 was to stop the Japanese from any further expansion west and to plan for some offensive operations to begin to drive them back from their conquered territories. This was a tall order. Most of America's battleships were out of action, some permanently, others for months to come. On January 11, the *Saratoga* was torpedoed, thus reducing the total carrier force in the Pacific to three vessels—the *Enterprise*, *Yorktown*, and *Lexington*.

Disaster followed disaster. On February 27, while ferrying planes from Australia to Java, seaplane tender *Langley* was sunk by aerial bombardment. The death of the *Langley* was a particularly bitter blow. It had been America's first aircraft carrier when commissioned in 1921 and was thus an historic ship. And with the *Langley* went its chaplain, Fr. John J. McGarrity, a diocesan priest from Philadelphia who had joined the navy in May 1941. He went aboard in January 1942 and was credited by its former commander with improving the ship's serious morale problems. McGarrity and most of the crew were picked up by a tanker but when that vessel was itself sunk, the priest was lost. The navy disengeniously declared him "missing" and carried him on its rolls as such until December 15, 1945 when he was finally "presumed dead."53 From the time of the *Langley's* sinking Bishop O'Hara had tried to elicit some news from the Navy Department regarding McGarrity but was given no information. The terrible uncertainty of his "missing" status was almost worse than the final outcome but the bishop sent around a circular letter to all of his chaplains to pray for each other and their welfare, whether they were *"in via vel in patria."* 54

The few bright spots of the period came when Nimitz ordered carrier strikes on targets in the Marshall and Gilbert islands in early February. In March there were successful strikes on the north coast of Papua.55 A purely symbolic victory was achieved in mid-April when Lt. Col. Jimmy Doolittle and his tiny group of Army B-25s bombed Japan by flying off the *Hornet.56*

From December 1941 when Pearl Harbor was struck to the late spring of 1942 when Foley's chaplain school was in session, the navy had been expanding at a frantic pace. The chaplaincy was always a neglected and difficult procurement and the Norfolk chaplain school was overtaxed and understaffed from its inception. In fact while Foley's class E was being conducted, the two previous classes, C and D, were still in session as well. And the next three classes, F, G, and a large thirty man class sent to Fort Schuyler, the Bronx, New York under Chaplain Salisbury had all begun before Foley's class was due to graduate on June 12. The Fort Schuyler class schedule was so accelerated that even though it began ten days after Foley's had, it concluded on the same day.57

It was also while Foley's class was in session that the navy had its first significant victories. On May 7 and 8, in the battle of the Coral Sea, naval forces under Adm. Frank Jack Fletcher managed to turn a Japanese force away from Port Moresby. The battle itself was a strategic American success since it halted the invasion of Australia, but from a tactical standpoint the Americans suffered greater losses with the carriers *Lexington* sunk and the *Yorktown* badly damaged, in exchange for the destruction of one small Japanese carrier.58

The Japanese were stopped again, due to American daring and superior intelligence less than a month later at Midway. The complex Japanese plan included air strikes on Dutch Harbor in the Aleutians and the occupation of two of the archipelago's frozen outcroppings, Attu and Kiska. These actions were meant to divert the main American fleet away from the main target of the Midway Islands, but the plan was detected and countered. Four first class Japanese carriers went to the bottom and most of the planes that belonged to them.59 For the Americans it was a tremendous victory. From this point the Japanese would be retreating, not advancing, but the war had a long time to go and would only increase in savagery.

It was on the same day that the Battle of Midway began that the first of Foley's class learned of their assignment. Congregationalist Donald Sterling, Baptist Kelly and Fr. Charles Covert were to stay at the Norfolk Operating Base as chaplains. Foley and the rest of his group remained in an agony of expectation, wondering where their billets would be. Foley, for one, knew exactly what he wanted: shipboard duty aboard a combat vessel. He wanted to be with young sailors when they were in danger of death and to offer the solace of Mass and the Eucharist. That was why he joined the navy and that was what he intended to do, come what may. After hearing of the first three shore-based assignments, he began plotting a strategy to avoid such a fate if he also was denied a ship. He confided to his diary, "May the Lord deliver me from being an office boy for some senior chaplain. Close immediate contact with the men is what I wish and opportunities to administer the sacrament."60

Foley had to wait a few more days to learn his fate. Over the weekend of June 6 and 7 he was sent to fill in for the Catholic chaplain at Portsmouth, who was on retreat. He was busy for the two days hearing confessions and celebrating several Masses, two of which had over two hundred attendance. After one of these Masses he was hailed by a Holy Cross graduate, Bill Dunn from Troy, New York, another of the innumerable Boston College and Holy Cross men he would meet in the service. Dunn remarked that Foley must have been in the navy for some time judging from the sermon he delivered. "What do you mean?" asked Foley. Dunn told him that he used expressions only a real navy man would use, such as "lashed ourselves to our ideals," "everything squared away, etc."61 It was true that Foley was absorbing rapidly "navy culture." After decades in the Jesuits, Foley was now living in another all-male environment, one that had differing goals surely, but also one that was strikingly similar in traditions, discipline, and behavioral code. Even when he returned to

Jesuit academia and for the rest of his long life, Foley "treated" himself by continuing to use many salty words and phrases in his everyday speech.

On Monday, June 8, Foley got the news he had been waiting for for months. He got his ship. That night he wrote, "LEARNED TODAY AT 1100 THAT I WAS ASSIGNED TO THE USS GEORGE CLYMER A.P.A.—ATTACK NAVAL TRANSPORT. News means that I am going to the far off places of the globe—with American boys. May God always be with us as we go down to the sea in our ship."62

Officially, all that was left for Class E was the graduation ceremony on Friday, June 12. The graduates were Protestants Benjamin Brown, Paul Edgar, Glyn Jones, James Kelly, William Lumpkin, Ansgar Sovik, and Donald Sterling. The Catholics were Frs. Charles Covert, John Foley, Frederick Gallagher, Frederick Gehring, and Henry "Cy" Rotrige. The contingent was heavy with members of religious orders. Foley and Gallagher were both Jesuits from the New England Province though Gallagher had been a Holy Cross professor while Foley as a B.C. man. Gallagher was also one of the older chaplains to come into the service, having been born in 1898. Despite his age, Gallagher volunteered for and served in several billets with the Marines. Gehring was a Vincentian who had spent some years as a missionary in China. He would later become the most famous of the "Padres of Guadalcanal." Foley and he would cross paths again in the Pacific Theatre. Covert and Rotrige were diocesan priests from New Jersey and Missouri respectively. Two other men who had started with Class E, Kermit Combs and William Cowan, resigned from the navy.63

Foley still had the weekend of June 13 and 14 at Norfolk before being detached on Monday, June 15, 1942. But before he even heard a shot fired in anger aboard a warship, he almost became a casualty himself. On Saturday he and "Freddy" Gallagher set out for one last drive around the base. Gallagher lost his way and mistakenly took a road leading to the airport. Three guards stepped out to the road, leveled their weapons at the stunned priests and challenged, "Who goes there?" Foley finally found his voice and replied weakly, "Officers." They were told to "Advance and give the countersign." Since they were ignorant of that, they sat in silence until one of the guards approached with his pistol raised. He smiled when they told him they were just two priests who had lost their bearings and he set them on their course again.64

After being detached on Monday, Foley and Gallagher set sail up the Chesapeake Bay bound for Washington. There Foley took the Colonial for Boston, which pulled into South Station at 8:15 p.m. He had leave until June 25, when he was due to go aboard the *Clymer* at Charleston. The nine days passed quickly and it was soon time to depart. This was the adventure—the vocation—he had prayed for, a fast ship going in harm's way. Yet as he kissed his mother and sisters good-bye and boarded the train for Charleston, he wondered when he would be with them again.

Notes: Chapter 3

1 Foley diary, April 16, 1942.

2 Document reproduced in "Guadalcanal Echoes" (August/September 1997), 24.

3 T.J. Campbell, S.J. *Pioneer Priests of North America 1642–1710,* vol. II, (New York: The America Press, 1914), 104–107. The work of the Jesuits in New France and New England from the turn of the seventeenth century to the close of the eighteenth was copiously recorded in letters and journals. Between 1896 and 1901, the secretary of the State Historical Society of Wisconsin, Reuben Gold Thwaites, published these sources in a 73 volume set entitled *Jesuit Relations and Allied Documents.* As such it remains one of the most significant ethnographic studies in the Western World.

4 Foley diary, April 16,17, 1942.

5 Drury, *History of the Chaplain Corps United States Navy* , vol. II, 56; vol. III, 203. Several of the Catholic chaplains from Class A, which ran from February 2 to March 5 and Class B, which ran from February 23 to

April 14, 1942 were involved in some of the toughest actions of the war. In Class A, Fr. James J. Donnelly of Philadelphia was chaplain on the U.S.S. *Edward Rutledge* when it was torpedoed and sunk on November 12, 1942 during the North African campaign. Jesuit Fr. Daniel J. Burke served aboard the U.S.S. *Philadelphia* from June 1942 to January 1945 during which time he participated in landings in North Africa, Sicily, Anzio, Salerno and Southern France. See Drury, *History of the Chaplain Corps United States Navy*, vol. II, 181; vol. III, 41; Giblin, *Jesuits as Chaplains* , 39. Of all the World War II classes, B was the most Catholic. Twelve of the eighteen men were priests. Two of the priests from Class B, Francis W. Kelly of Philadelphia and Thomas S. Reardon of New Jersey were immortalized in the quintessential World War II classic by Richard Tregaskis, *Guadalcanal Diary* (New York: Random House, 1943), 3, 21,22. In the popular film version of this book, the chaplain is one of the main characters but is named "Father Donnelly" and appears to be a composite of the real-life Kelly and Reardon. Kelly was later decorated with the Legion of Merit for services with the Marines at the bloody battle of Tarawa in November 1943. Drury, *History of the Chaplain Corps United States Navy*, vol.II, 161. Another priest from Class B enjoys a legendary status in the Marine Corps. Paul J. Redmond, O.P., from Connecticut was an enlisted man in the Naval Reserve in World War I, was ordained a Dominican in 1930 and earned a doctorate at Columbia in 1931. After chaplain school he volunteered for service with the Marines and served most spectacularly with the 1st and 4th Marine Raiders. He received the Legion of Merit for action in the New Georgia campaign in July 1943 and the Bronze Star for heroic achievement against the enemy on Guam in the summer of 1944. Apart from his military duty he was at various times a biology professor at Catholic University, National Director of the Holy Name Society and editor of its journal, Director of Catholic Charities in the Monterey-Fresno Diocese, chaplain of a mission, pastor of Sacred Heart Church in Fresno, chaplain of Soledad prison and founder of the Infant of Prague Adoption Agency in California. See Drury, *History of the*

Chaplain Corps United Stated Navy, vol. II, 161,164; *Pictorial of Father Redmond* (San Diego: United States Marine Raider Association, 1993), passim. Few priests have lived fuller more pastoral lives and few chaplains are more revered by their men than Paul Redmond.

6 Drury, *History of the Chaplain Corps United States Navy,* vol. II, 57,58.

7 Ibid., 58,59; vol. III, 152,237, 242. Neither Knox nor Robinson survived the war. Knox was plagued with ill-health for some time and had to be relieved from a procurement job in the Chiefs' office in September 1942. He died at Bethesda Naval Hospital on March 21, 1943. Robinson left the chaplain school in June 1944 and became the Assistant Director (executive officer of the Chaplains Division) in the Chief's office. He was again reassigned in November 1944 to the staff of the Commanding General, Aircraft Fleet Marine Force, Pacific. On a special assignment he was killed in a plane crash February 23, 1945, near Marion, Virginia. Shortly before his death Robinson was instrumental in securing a number of "portable service kits" for chaplains in the Fleet Marine Air Force, Pacific. These kits were composed of three steel lockers which contained athletic equipment and games, radio and phonograph equipment, and a movie projector with screen and one-reel shorts. Robinson was one of the most well-known and popular chaplains in the service and his death stunned the Chaplain Corps. On his body was found a note written before he died, "Dear Mom and Pop: I have had time to say my prayers. Love, John." Drury, *History of the Chaplains Corps United States Navy,* vol. II, 94, 98, 111, 120, 121, 188, 206; vol. III, 237.

8 Foley diary, April 17, 1942.

9 Ibid.

10 Ibid.

11 In the immediate post-war period and for approximately forty years afterward, many of the American, British and German records concerning the relative efficacy of the U-boat campaign in the final results of the war remained sealed. Popular history followed the claims of the commander

and strategist of the U-boat force, Admiral Karl Doenitz, *Memoirs: Ten Years and Twenty Days* (Cleveland: The World Publishing Co., 1959). This interpretation posited that the U-boats nearly brought the Allies to their knees because of the massive losses inflicted on merchant ships carrying ordnance to England. Its ultimate failure was due to conflicting priorities in the *Kriegsmarine*. For an operational study of a well-blooded boat, see Michael Gannon, *Operation Drumbeat* (New York: Harper & Row, 1990). See also Clay Blair, *Hitler's U-Boat War: The Hunters 1939–1942* (New York: Random House, 1996). Blair, a World War II veteran of the Untied States Navy's "silent service" is vociferous in his condemnation of the standard interpretation, calling it a "mythology" predicated on Nazi propaganda and the Allies' post-war reluctance to open the German records. He claims that the campaign was an abysmal failure, with few merchant ships lost, and that the vaunted U-boats themselves were technologically backward rather than advanced designs. Nevertheless, few sailors on merchantmen or navy vessels who survived torpedoing by the U-Boats would agree that they were an insignificant weapon.

12 Drury, *History of the Chaplain Corps United States Navy*, vol. II, 58, 59.

13 Foley diary, April 18, 1942.

14 Foley diary, April 20, 1942. Definitely more cerebral than physical, Foley did not miss the physical exercises when he left the chaplain school for sea duty, but on board one ship he encountered an eager beaver who hadn't got the word about calisthenics in the tropics. "The only difficulty I had aboard ship was a young officer, and right after breakfast he would be giving us physical exercises under a blistering sun in the South Pacific. Well, I was lagging a bit so he bawls out 'Chaplain! You're not doing it!' He bawls out at me, 'O.K'. I wasn't much better after that. After about fifteen minutes you'd be dripping perspiration, sweating like a gumdrop." Interview with Fr. John P. Foley, S.J., Chestnut Hill, Massachusetts, March 6, 1995.

15 Drury, *History of the Chaplains Corps United States Navy*, vol. II, 62.

16 Another Navy Jesuit chaplain, Fr. Charles Suver, S.J. of the Oregon Province recalled his reaction to the prospect of indoctrination at the Chaplain School, by that time (September 1943) relocated to Williamsburg. "I joined the Navy and went on an overcrowded train from Seattle to Williamsburg, Virginia for Chaplains training. I'd had thirteen years of training before ordination and two years more after ordination. Frankly I wasn't overjoyed at getting four months more training." Charles Suver, speech at 47th anniversary reunion of Iwo Jima veterans held February 20–23, 1992, Biloxi, MI. Suver Papers, Archives of the Oregon Province of the Society of Jesus. Suver opted for service with the 5th Marines and landed on Iwo Jima the first day of the apocalyptic battle. On the troopship heading toward the island he had bragged to the officers in his unit that he would say Mass atop Mount Suribachi, the dormant volcano that dominated the island. On Friday February 23, 1945, Suver scaled Suribachi and celebrated Mass in the shadow of a raised American flag. Charles Suver, "Iwo Jima," unpublished manuscript. Suver Papers. Suver is part of a larger controversy involving the exact timing of the flag raisings. Initially, a small flag was raised and sometime later a larger one, immortalized in the famous Rosenthal photograph, replaced it. Suver maintained throughout his life that he celebrated his Mass under the first, smaller flag. Suver's assistant, Jim Fisk, also confirmed Suver's chronology. "It was on theat day that Father said Mass atop Suribachi—*before* Joe Rosenthal took his famous picture…Upon completion of the Mass the flag which you have seen many times in Joe Rosenthal's famous picture was run up in place of the smaller one. Father and I watched the raising from a little hollow in the ground *between* Mr. Rosenthal and the flag as he snapped his camera's shutter." James E. Fisk, "Mass on a Volcano," *Catholic World* (January 1949): 312-316.

17 Samuel Hill Ray, S.J., *A Chaplain Afloat and Ashore* (Salado, Texas: The Anson Jones Press, 1962), 14,15.

18 Drury, *History of the Chaplain Corps United States Navy*, vol. II, 12.

19 Ibid, 62-64.

20 Ibid, 12, 13.

21 McAvoy, *Father O'Hara*, 213. The Second Vatican Council reversed traditional Church policy on this matter and encouraged "ecumenical dialogue."

22 Drury, *History of the Chaplains Corps United States Navy*, vol. II, 59.

23 Foley diary, April 21, 1942.

24 Ibid.

25 Foley diary, July 4, 1942.

26 Foley diary, July 11, 1942.

27 Foley diary, April 22, 24, 1942.

28 Foley diary, April 30, 1942.

29 Foley diary, May 3, 1942.

30 Foley diary, May 16, 1942.

31 Foley diary, May 7, 1942.

32 Foley diary, May 25, 1942.

33 Foley diary, May 2, 1942.

34 Foley diary, May 31, 1942.

35 Ibid.

36 Foley diary, May 9, 1942.

37 Foley diary, May 14, 1942.

38 Kimmel, who was reduced from four star to two star rank, believed that he had been deliberately framed by the Roosevelt administration, whom he felt had prior knowledge of the planned attack. He spent the rest of his life attempting to resurrect his reputation but failed. His one surviving son continues to push for a new investigation, but the Reagan, Bush and Clinton administrations have refused to reopen the case and restore Kimmel's rank. Though a tremendous bibliography exists implicating Roosevelt, with more works perpetually on the way, there is little chance that the United States government would ever admit to the president's guilt, even if true. See "Pearl Harbor blame hurts admiral's kin," *The Boston Sunday Globe*, 7 December 1997, A-40.

39 When Puller was assigned to command the small Marine complement, which was supposed to function as a machine gun battalion, he
found a few weapons mounted on tripods but no supporting tools, water
cans, hoses, belts or asbestos gloves, without which the guns were entirely
useless. When he demanded that those items be supplied immediately, the
adjutant claimed that he had no idea of the problem. but promised immediate action. The vital pieces of ordnance equipment did not arrive until
months later. Burke Davis, *Marine! The Life of Lt. Gen. Lewis B (Chesty)
Puller, USMC (Ret),* (Boston: Little, Brown and Co., 1962), 53–55.

40 Ronald H. Spector, *Eagle Against the Sun: The American War With
Japan,* (New York: Vintage Books, 1985), 107–109.

41 Spector, *Eagle Against the Sun,* 73. MacArthur's relationship with
Quezon, both personal and pecuniary, can be found in Carol Morris
Petillo, *Douglas MacArthur: The Philippine Years* (Bloomington, Indiana:
Indiana University Press, 1981). The B-17 Flying Fortress rarely operated
effectively against surface ships. A well-designed and extremely tough aircraft, the plane found its proper niche as a strategic bomber primarily in
the European theatre of operations until it was supplanted by the greater
payload of the B-29 Super Fortress. See *The Official Guide to the Army Air
Forces* (New York: Simon and Schuster, 1944).

42 Photographs of the superannuated mortars can be found in Eric
Morris, *Corregidor: The End of the Line* (New York: Military Heritage
Press, 1982).

43 Spector, *Eagle Against the Sun,* 113, 117.

44 Spector, *Eagle Against the Sun,* 117. One of the most outlandish and
unintentionally humorous examples of MacArthur's deification in the
public sphere occurs in the 1945 film *They Were Expendable.* When the
General appears, "The Battle Hymn of the Republic" wells up in the background, common sailors stare in awe and, like Moses and the God of
Israel, his name is never spoken and the audience is not allowed to glimpse
his terrible visage. They see only a trenchcoated form and distinctive corn-
cob silhouette.

45 Giblin, *Jesuits as Chaplains,* 5.

46 John J. Dugan, S.J. "Life Under the Japs: From Bataan's Fall to Miraculous Rescue at Cabanatuan by Yanks," *Boston Sunday Globe* April 1, 1945, 7. Manuscript copy provided by Fr. William J. Leonard, S.J.

47 Karig and Kelley, *Battle Report,* 304, 305; Drury, *History of the Chaplain Corps United States Navy,* vol. II, 35; vol. III, 185, 186.

48 Drury, *History of the Chaplain Corps United States Navy,* vol. II, 35; Dugan, "Life Under the Japs," 28, 40.

49 Dugan, "Life Under the Japs," 42.

50 Drury, *History of the Chaplain Corps United States Navy,* vol. II, 36, 37; vol. III, 186.

51 An analysis of the changing American perceptions of the Japanese is found in John W. Dower, *War Without Mercy: Race and Power in the Pacific War* (New York: Pantheon Books, 1986). Within a very short span of time, western views of the Japanese went from the idea of subhuman, physically inferior brutes who could scarcely operate white man's machines to unstoppable supermen, albeit still bestial ones. The Japanese for their part labored under the fatal delusions that the Americans were hopelessly soft and weak due to "impurities" and Christianity.

52 Samuel Eliot Morison, *The Two-Ocean War: A Short History of the United States Navy in the Second World War* (Boston: Little, Brown and Co., 1963), 138, 139; Spector, *Eagle Against the Sun,* 144.

53 Drury, *History of the Chaplain Corps United States Navy,* vol. II, 38,39; vol. III, 182; Morison, *The Two-Ocean War,* 14, 98.

54 McAvoy, *Father O'Hara,* 233.

55 John Costello, *The Pacific War* (New York: Rawson, Wade Publishers, Inc., 1981), 196, 197; Morison, *The Two-Ocean War,* 139.

56 Costello, *The Pacific War,* 233, 236; Morison, *The Two-Ocean War,* 139, 140; Caroll V. Glines, *The Doolittle Road: America's Daring First Strike Against Japan* (New York: Orion Books, 1988), passim. The *Hornet* was screened by a task force built around the *Enterprise,* commanded by Adm. William F. Halsey. In his 1947 autobiography, Halsey recounted a

trip to Japan during the 1907–08 voyage of Theodore Roosevelt's Great White Fleet. "Despite the entertainments and the tuneless singing of 'The Star Spangled Banner' and the shouts of *Banzai!* (May you live ten thousand years!) I felt that the Japs meant none of their welcome, that they actually disliked us. Nor was I any more convinced of their sincerity when they presented us with medals confirming the 'good will' existing between the two governments. I don't know what became of my medal, but a number of cruisemates sent me theirs after Pearl Harbor, with a request that I return them to Japan at my earliest opportunity. When I took Task Force 16 toward Tokyo in April, 1942, I deputized Jimmy Doolittle to complete delivery for me. He did it with a bang." William F. Halsey and J. Bryan III, *Admiral Halsey's Story* (New York: McGraw Hill Books, Co., 1947), 12.

57 Drury, *History of the Chaplain Corps United States Navy*, vol. II, 59, 321, 322.

58 Spector, *Eagle Against the Sun,* 156–163.

59 Ibid, 166, 167, 174, 175.

60 Foley diary, June 4, 1942.

61 Foley diary, June 6, 7, 1942.

62 Foley diary, June 8, 1942.

63 Giblin, *Jesuits as Chaplains,* 57; Drury, *History of the Chaplain Corps United States Navy*, vol. III, 56, 61, 100, 103, 239; Foley diary, June 12, 1942.

64 Foley, diary, June 13, 1942.

65 Foley diary, June 16, 1942.

CHAPTER 4

▼

"THE LESSON ON NICUS AND NEURILIUS"

The train out of South Station was running an hour late. It pulled into Washington D.C. at 7:30 p.m. and Foley caught the next train heading for North Charleston which arrived at 3:30 a.m. As was his habit in every part of the world, Foley would first seek out the nearest church, hoping to find a gracious pastor who would allow him to say Mass. Fr. Henry Wolfe of Sacred Heart Church on King Street in Charleston was his host on this occasion. After Mass, Foley headed for the Navy Yard and there he saw a ship moored to the dock. He later confided to his diary "…about four when I boarded her, stepped aboard, heart beating fast for 'my' ship was in."1

Foley was destined to steam many thousands of miles on "his" ship, the attack transport *George Clymer* . The *Clymer* was not originally a warship. It was built for the American South African line by the Ingalls Shipbuilding Corporation of Birmingham, Alabama at its Pascagoula, Mississippi Yard. She was christened the *African Planet*, one of triplets, the other vessels being the *African Comet* and the *African Meteor.* The ship's principle dimensions were: Overall Length—489 feet; Beam—70 feet; Displacement—11,058 tons; Speed—19 knots. In civilian life she was meant to carry a crew of 122 and 233 passengers. The *African Planet* and eight other transports were acquired from the Maritime Commission and renamed after signers of the Declaration of Independence. George Clymer was a Pennsylvania politician who replaced a member of the Pennsylvania legislature who had refused to sign the Declaration. Clymer was later a member of the first United States Congress. The *Clymer* was commissioned by the Navy on June 15, 1942 and given the designation AP-57. This was changed in the beginning of 1943 to APA-27, for Auxiliary Personnel Attack ship.2

As the *Clymer*, she carried 33 officers and 314 crewmen. One of those officers was Chaplain Lieutenant junior grade John Foley. APAs, though not comparable in size or complement to capital ships such as carriers, battleships, or cruisers, nevertheless rated a chaplain, whereas other warships such as destroyers and submarines did not. There was a sound reason for this. The chaplain on an APA would have responsibility for his own crew and also the many thousands of army and Marine Corps men who would be brought to their destinations in the ship. Just prior to a landing on a hostile shore is perhaps the most important time of a navy chaplain's ministry. It was certainly his busiest time. The *Clymer* was fitted out with 32 landing boats and could accommodate 2,000 troops. She could also carry enormous quantities of ordnance and ammunition, thereby making her a floating bomb.

Her first day out of Pascagoula heading for Charleston, the *Clymer* was chased by three submarines, but her speed enabled her to outdistance them. The five day journey northward was a nerve-wracking experience because the moon was full—a perfect night light to illuminate the *Clymer* for her submerged pursuers. She made Charleston safely, though passing before other American warships was nearly as dangerous as facing the U-boats. At that point in the war, American vessels on coastal defense were prepared to fire first and ask questions later. Identification signals were changed every three hours and any vessel that did not respond quickly and accurately would be fired upon.3

When Foley went aboard, the news rapidly circulated that a Catholic priest was to be the *Clymer*'s chaplain. One young sailor came up to Foley crying because he had been praying for a priest from the time that he heard a chaplain was joining the ship's company. Another sailor remarked that it was good luck to have a priest on board because the ship was a "suicide scow" meaning a red-hot invasion ship.4

On Sunday, June 28, Foley celebrated his first Mass on the *Clymer* and noted, "Christ came aboard our ship today." This was the beginning of his seaborne ministry. The same day he heard confessions and held general services. He made it a point to introduce himself to all of the crew and found a good deal of piety in some of the men. In the engine room, with the temperature pushing 105 degrees, a sailor told Foley that he said two Rosaries every time he stood his four-hour watch. Foley also checked out who was listed as a Catholic in sick bay so that he would know how many needed the sacraments. Only five officers and sixty enlisted men were Catholic.5

Foley was only on board a few days when he began to fulfill the chaplain's "handyman" functions, those jobs that had nothing to do with religion, but which the other officers disdained. He was told to get down to the local lock-up to bail out a sailor who was in jail for stealing a car and reckless driving. He showed up at the Charleston city jail and asked to see the man. The sailor told Foley that he was drinking in a beer parlor when a stranger offered to rent him his car for the night. Not long afterward, a cop forced him to the side of the road. Foley had his doubts about the story but felt it his duty to appeal to the judge for clemency so he, the cop, and the owner of the "misappropriated" car trudged over to the magistrate's court. There they were jammed in like sardines with white and black flotsam and jetsam while they waited their turn.6

Judge Matthews presided over this motley assemblage with an iron hand. Foley watched him deal with a black man who had been hauled in for breaking into a house and menacing the inhabitants with a knife. The judge told the defendant, "Understand me distinctly if you so much as set foot inside that house again I'll send you under the bridge. You will go under the bridge. Do you hear?" Foley was unclear about what terrors lie "under the bridge" but assumed they were sufficient to make the accused mend his ways.7

When it was the sailor's turn, the principals were brought into the judge's anteroom. The owner was persuaded to drop the charge of misappropriation but the judge wanted to drive home the seriousness of the crime and told him that if it happened again, "the church would be closed and the parson and the sexton have gone home." The group then trooped over to the police station where the charge of careless and reckless driving was filed. The sailor was held in bond of $5 and told to forget about appearing in court on the morrow. A court officer told him he was very lucky. A Marine in there on the same charge a few days earlier was held in bail of $5,000. The sailor was less than appreciative of Foley's efforts. Some time later he was caught trying to steal Foley's sacramental wine aboard ship.8

Over the next two years Foley became expert in talking his miscreant parishioners out of jail. It was all part of the job. He also started to pick up varied types of collateral duties. He was appointed Mess Caterer which meant he was in charge of the ship's officers' mess and rooms and the troop officers' mess and rooms when the ship was carrying assault troops. He was appointed education officer and the ship's insurance agent. In this capacity, he eventually sold about $3 million worth of $10,000 government insurance policies.9

Everyone aboard the *Clymer* wondered when the ship was due to sail and where their destination would be. On July 4, Captain Arthur T. Moen informed the department heads that they would be sailing soon. The next day he called a conference of all officers and charged some of them with breach of confidence. Within two hours after he had told them of the sailing orders the word was all over the ship and brought right back to the captain. He was furious and barked, "I'll be damned if I will stand for that. I tell you that if that happens again I'll have a general court martial on that officer." He wound up giving an "Ours is not to reason why…" speech.10 Though Foley was not involved in the indiscretion it appeared to him that the captain was taking it too far.

Preparations for sailing did continue unabated. When a hull inspection was ordered, Foley described the process to his diary.

> July 14, 1942—Tuesday. USS *George Clymer* undocked this morning about 10:30. Fussy little tugs came chugging in alongside of her about 9:30 making quite a fuss with their whistles, as if saying "We may be small, you may be big, 16,000 tons, but this is a job that requires us to bring you safely without mishap into that drydock over there. Don't forget that good things come done up in small packages." After the lines were pulled aboard, they pulled us out gradually into midstream. When we were apparently going too fast, they would slow us up by putting on full speed snuggling up right under our hull, and pushing with might and main. Coasted gradually into drydock, which when it was drained, revealed hundreds of catfish caught ashore. Collected by negro workmen in baskets.11

The chaplain went about his own business, such as instructing a sailor in the vicissitudes of a mixed marriage and then arranging the said marriage, but he also had time to visit some of the beaches and walk the summertime streets of Charleston. He found a used bookstore in an ancient house in the oldest part of the city. Inside he met the lady who owned the house, Miss Mary Adger, 102 years young, who told him that the house dated back to Revolutionary days. He told her that she looked much younger than a century and she replied, "We don't grow old in Charleston, we just dry out from the heat." Miss Adger took to the flattering Yankee and regaled him with tales of General Sherman's men, who threatened to take her back north with them. She punctuated her story with footstampings but coyly admitted, "All the same they were nice boys."12

After lying at anchor in Charleston for over a month, the *Clymer* got under way on July 27. The first order of business was degaussing practice, to eliminate the threat of magnetic mines. That first night the ship anchored in the harbor at the junction of the Cooper and Ashley rivers. Foley strolled the deck and thought that the Charleston church steeples silhouetted against the evening sky resembled "pencils poised to write but they never did get around to writing before the night closed in and swallowed them up." He hit the sack and was up again at 0300 to celebrate Mass in his room because breakfast was at 0400. Throughout his time in the navy Foley rose an hour early to say Mass when battle operations prevented the men from attending in the Mess Hall. It meant an hour less sleep every night during trying times, but he did it thankfully.13

After some welding equipment was loaded aboard from a tug, the *Clymer* was again underway, slowly maneuvering through the defensive minefield and past the submarine net. Once out of the harbor she headed for the open sea and was picked up by a squadron of navy planes. From the deck of the *Clymer*, Foley and a few of the other officers spied a group of ships heading north and guessed that they would be joining them at Norfolk. Though the morning was bright, General Quarters was sounded and the entire crew sped to their battlestations. 14

For a green crew there was surprisingly little confusion. The chaplain's station was sick bay, along with ten hospital corpsmen and two medical officers, Dr. Daniels and Dr. Harris. Foley had remembered to give a general absolution to the crew when hurrying to the sick bay. general absolution, frowned on in civilian life, was a common practice of chaplains when their men were likely to go into battle. It did not matter that the ship was just off shore. That stretch of Atlantic coastline between South Carolina and Virginia was a "Torpedo Junction." In that last week of July, forty-seven sub contacts were made.15 Death could come at any time from the deep and Foley wanted every man to be ready to face it.

In sick bay, Dr. Harris lectured the group on first aid, describing treatment for burns, hemorrhage, shock, chest wounds and suffocation. The group was attentive, without nervousness, yet cognizant that disaster could strike any moment without warning. Foley hoped that he would have no problems when men were brought in to be operated on. He had seen an operation only once when he was a scholastic at Holy Cross. He had a cousin who worked for a doctor at Worcester City Hospital and she arranged for him to witness a stomach operation. He watched for a time and then thump! The next thing he knew he was lying on the floor wondering where he was. Foley realized that he dropped from the heavy smell of ether, not the blood, but he did not want his crowd back at Holy Cross to hear of the incident. Somehow they did and he was kidded at the dinner table by the other scholastics and priests. 16 The last thing he wanted aboard the *Clymer* was to be known as a guy who couldn't take it. He felt that he had to have the respect of the men at all times, and any display of weakness would go against him in their eyes.

The submarine threat did not materialize this time and the crew were allowed to secure from General Quarters at 0715. The *Clymer* was now about twenty-five miles off the coast, in clear blue water. As standard operating procedure she was zigzagging to foil any U-boats that may still be on her tail. To his delight, Foley found that he was a good sailor. Though he had made an issue with the Military Ordinariate of joining the navy rather than the army, until this day he did not know how well he was going to sail. Again he thought of his early Jesuit days, when he was sent to Heythrop College in England back in 1927 for his philosophate. At that time he sailed for Europe on the German ship *Thuringia* with another scholastic and two priests. The first morning out of Boston he was miserable with seasickness and couldn't look at food. Thereafter he understood the truth of the old saying about seasickness—the first day you are afraid you'll die, the second day you are afraid you won't, the third day you don't care if you do or not.17 As it turned out, Foley was never seasick again, though he sailed through plenty of heavy weather while he was in the navy.

When the first day at sea finally ended he again contemplated the paralyzing effects of fear and as usual found comfort in the Lord. "We have made the first part of our trip successfully. There has been no need to use the Holy Oils that I carry with me all the time, and none for Holy *Viaticum* . 'What need is there for us to fear?' as I asked the men last Sunday. Christ is with us that is the one thing that matters, everything else is secondary."18

The *Clymer* anchored that night with the convoy that had passed it fifteen hours earlier and proceeded the next morning at seventeen knots screened by two patrol craft, two minesweepers, and two planes circling in five mile arcs overhead. Despite all of the protection, lookouts were posted all over the ship, ever watchful for the telltale white feather of an explosive "tin fish." Occasionally the neophyte sailors misidentified the harmless wake of a porpoise's dorsal fin for the fatal variety. Foley spent much of the day working in the library, another onerous job that nobody wanted. He had already spent some time classifying the books according to the Dewey decimal system and now he had it all squared away. He sent a *billet-doux* to all of the officers with a mimeographed list of the collection. That night the ship anchored inside Cape Lookout. Foley wrote, "…the moon, a disk of beaten gold, is coming up to enhance the quiet beauty of the night at sea. Meanwhile, ship has been 'darkened' all lights cut off from outside vision, battleports installed and all hands turn to bunks for we have early rising again tomorrow morning. Thanks be to God for his guidance of us today. He was with us when we zigged and when we zagged. 'Thank you, Lord.'"19

By July 30, the *Clymer* had dropped anchor off Hampton Roads. For the next eleven weeks she would be operating around the Chesapeake making shakedown runs and practicing boat tactics. Foley had time to visit the Norfolk chaplain's school, from whence he had lately graduated. He ran into Fr. Daniel F.X. O'Connor, a fellow Jesuit from Boston College who was then a member of Class H. They had dinner and Foley proudly showed O'Connor around his ship.20

The first week of August, the *Clymer* began to train in earnest. Firstly, the ship itself needed to be thoroughly tested. There was degaussing practice and standardization tests—speed, forwards and backwards, and the instruments—compasses, radios, and other equipment. There were measured runs up and down the Chesapeake Bay. The crew practiced fire drills, abandon ship drills, and gunnery practice under combat conditions. In a letter to his sister back home, Foley described the thrill of exploding ordnance.

> It is quite an experience to be aboard ship when the guns are booming by day but particularly by night. The nights are inky black but starry. The target is idly at anchor two miles away with a big canvas about ten feet square riding on it. Suddenly our powerful searchlight picks it out of the dark as we are making a starboard run. All the guns on that side are manned. The orders come clear from the bridge over the telephone, are repeated by the gunnery officer. "Five minutes to go." The men seem almost indifferent as they stand around with the refills. "Three minutes to go." The trainer, sighter, loader, powderman automatically tense themselves. "One minute to go." They are all poised. "Commence firing." The roar of thunder fills every corner of the quiet night. A tremendous burst of orange flame licks out savagely at the darkness. The hot blast wraps itself around us for a split second even though we are thirty yards away on the boat deck. The ship has shivered from stem to stern but is herself again quickly. Meanwhile the shell is whistling its way to the target—a silver streak of destruction. Somebody shouts in admiration, "On

the nose!" and there is a murmur of approval from the crew—
no histrionics of any kind, just a Navy man's approval of a
good job. Again and again with three second intervals the
operation is repeated for half a dozen times until we steam by
the target, cease firing, turn back for another run with
another gun crew to test its accuracy. Quite an experience, a
test of the caliber of the men.21

Not every man measured up. A young Jewish ensign who was in charge
of a gun crew doing night firing became terrified and deserted the gun
position. He had expected an easy shore assignment and ended up on the
APA by mistake. It was one of the few overt acts of officer cowardice
which Foley witnessed during the war. There was no sympathy for the
transgressor and he was taken off the ship at Norfolk. Foley agreed entirely
with the decision. He felt that an officer, even an ensign, had to be a role
model to the men. An officer panicking and deserting his post could cause
a general panic and endanger the entire ship. Though he disagreed with
many of the attitudes of naval officers, one thing Foley respected was their
lack of tolerance for fellow officers who were incompetent or cowardly. It
was strictly pragmatic, after all, since their own lives could be endangered
by a weakling. Nevertheless, Foley saw no "covering" for fellow officers
simply because they were part of the brotherhood. Foley did sympathize
with an enlisted man who also broke under the naval gunfire. As it turned
out he was a fifteen year old boy who had lied about his age to enlist. The
boy was returned to civilian life.22

At the same time the ship was shaken down, frenetic boat crew training
had commenced apace. The first invasion test was staged off of Cove
Point, at Annapolis, in mid-August, along with three of the *Clymer's* sister
ships. This practice run went amazingly well. All of the invasion boats
were hauled out in only twenty-seven minutes. As each boat went over the
side, it cruised to a predetermined point and circled until all of the boats
were in the water. Then they returned one by one, loaded up their human

cargo, and sped off to a new holding circle. The operation was under the command of Lieutenant Commander Olsen in the Eureka boat, who gave the signal to advance to the "enemy" shore. The roar of the boats shattered the otherwise peaceful afternoon on the Chesapeake. Once ashore, the boats dropped their ramps, unloaded, and headed back to the ship to pick up more troops. 23

Everyone was pleased by this surprisingly smooth performance. The real test would come in actual combat, in which there would be any number of variables and complications that could lead to disaster. For now, training would continue so that every man on board knew his job backwards and forwards. And also for the moment, practice runs in the Chesapeake Bay would have to simulate a hostile, as yet unknown, shore.

Ordinary chaplain duty went on as well. One of the sailors attempted to hang himself from the ramp of an invasion boat though fortunately he was cut down just in time. Foley attempted to succor him but came to the conclusion that the boy was mentally unbalanced. He also made a trip to the Norfolk city jail to make a plea for a pair of sailors who had run afoul of the law. As the case in Charleston, he got them off with only the judge's stern warning.24

Much of Foley's time was spent counseling the sailors who came to him with all of their problems, big and small. He always kept in mind that most of these crewmen were emotionally immature. The average age was between seventeen and twenty-one, and most of them had never really been away from home before. Predictably, the weaker ones quickly found themselves in trouble, either with naval or civilian authorities and looked to the chaplain to bail them out. Other men had legitimate problems but due to their age or background, had difficulty coping with them. A young sailor who was informed that his mother was seriously ill back home came to Foley looking for some consolation. Foley could do nothing about the woman's illness but since the boy was Catholic, he told him to say his Rosary and ask the Lord for the strength to bear his cross. This method could be applied only to Catholics who had been well-catechized. Fallen-away

Catholics or those who had never been instructed in the faith required a different approach. Many of the other men, particularly from the South, were religiously illiterate. Some were overtly anti-Catholic or hostile to God Himself. Foley put an extra effort into these men, though found that bringing them around at all was a "long voyage" most of the time. Still, he found good training in men of all backgrounds. Carver, a Methodist, told him that his one aim in life was to be as much like Christ as he possibly could be.25

Toward the end of September it became apparent that there would be orders soon. Four more doctors and more army troops went aboard the *Clymer*. On September 23, the vessel participated in its second mock landing, accompanied by a number of larger ships. Foley watched the armada in action and wrote,

> All invasion boats, the entire thirty-two of them are manned by their crews, the tank lighters, the Higgins and the Eureka boats. Cargo nets are dropped over the sides of the ship, the order is given to lower away. Down the boats swing out of their nest over the side and "Boats Away." Meanwhile the light cruiser U.S.S. *Wichita,* off our starboard beam sends five seaplanes aloft, her contribution to our umbrella of planes. The aircraft carrier U.S.S. *Charger* steams by at full speed, launching her planes from her flight deck with split second precision. A battlewagon, the U.S.S. *Texas,* on our port side cruises back and forth, forming part of our protecting screen.26

The army troops who came aboard the *Clymer* were enthusiastic about the decent quarters and good chow. These soldiers were generally older than the *Clymer*'s crew. Foley celebrated Mass for them and ministered to them as well as his own boys. These men had more mature concerns. Some were convinced that they would never see their wives and families again. There were some minor casualties during the invasion practices.

One man was knocked unconscious by a gas mask as he descended a landing net. A second had his head smashed by the ramp of a tank lighter.27 The accidents were few, considering the greenness of the troops and the burden of their overloaded packs, some weighing in at 175 pounds. As Foley watched landing operations, he pondered the waste and carnage of war. Suddenly a beautiful orange butterfly with black-tipped wings appeared and hovered around him, a fragile reminder of a better and happier world.28

Foley eavesdropped on a conversation between two of the soldiers, one from Boston College, the other a Notre Dame man. They both spoke of completing college when the war was over and had great plans for the future. Foley hoped that they would come true:

> As they talk I wonder what lies ahead of them. A picture flashes through my imagination of youthful forms lying inert on the hostile shore. Will these two splendid specimens of young American manhood, representative of all that is fine and decent, be among them, their dreams snuffed out by enemy machine guns? May God bless and protect them and bring them safely back to their own.29

On October 22, the *Clymer* returned to Hampton Roads after taking on fuel at Craney Island. The ship also packed on additional stores and ammunition and, somewhat mysteriously, some strange looking rafts with paddles. The chaplain had gone ashore that day and picked up a few instruments for the beginning of a ship's band—two tenor saxes, one trombone, and a set of drums. By 1700 the ship was anchored in her old stomping grounds in the Chesapeake and all of the army personnel that had been training on her for the past month stayed aboard that night. When the day was done, Foley read his office, considered what work needed to be attended to the next day, and then retired.30

At 0700 on Friday, October 23, the *Clymer* weighed anchor and got underway. It was loaded to the gunnels and then some. Gear and crates were lashed all about the deck. Below, the vessel was loaded to capacity with its human cargo. She steamed out of the bay, the leader of seven ships following in Indian file. Soon eight destroyers flanked the column, one for each transport. They passed Cape Henry, Virginia and negotiated the minefields. Taking the van of the column was the battleship *Texas*. The destroyers then fanned out to scout ahead. Directly above the growing assemblage were shining silver dirigibles searching for U-boats. A seagoing tug, the *Cherokee*, also moved into position. As the crew and the army troops aboard the *Clymer* roused, they realized that they were now on their way to battle. Chaplain Foley felt the excitement too. He wrote, "A subtle transformation through crew and soldiers—we are on our way at last! Where??? *Tot sententiae quot homines*—Dakar, Solomons, France, Ireland, Middle East??? One guess is as good as another."31

None of Foley's guesses was correct, though Dakar was the closest. The *Clymer* was one vessel sailing in the largest amphibious operation of the war to date—Operation Torch, the invasion of French North Africa. Foley can be forgiven for not having guessed the destination. The decision to target North Africa as the jumping off point for the "second front" in Europe against the Nazis was a Byzantine one, chock full of political intrigue and Anglo-American jockeying for position. As a result, the target was chosen less for military than political advantage.

Operation Torch had its genesis in the first days of America's involvement in the war. British Prime Minister Winston Churchill was delighted when he heard of the Japanese triumph at Pearl Harbor. He knew that the attack would finally overcome America's reluctance to enter the war and that he and Roosevelt now could plan in earnest to shore up the tottering British empire. Shortly after Pearl, the two met in conference in Washington. The matter of "Germany first" had already been settled, but now a decision on exactly where to strike Germany had to be made.32

For obvious reasons, both Douglas MacArthur and CNO Admiral King still sought in vain to redirect American efforts to a "Japan first" priority. MacArthur had personal business in the Philippines while King and the rest of the navy brass understood the mammoth complexities involved in a naval war that stretched across the vast Pacific. Even commanders who agreed on the "Germany first" strategem were unenthusiastic about the proposed invasion of Africa. Army Chief of Staff Gen. George Marshall, who could usually be counted on to back up Roosevelt in anything, advised the president that French North Africa was a less than optimum choice. Down to earth Gen. Joseph "Vinegar Joe" Stillwell considered the plan sheer idiocy, and resented Roosevelt's fawning to the British while ignoring the advice of all of the top American commanders.

While the American Joint Chiefs of Staff continued to push for a build-up of forces for a cross-channel invasion, Churchill had convinced Roosevelt on Africa by July and the military, with no option, acquiesced. It was now left to Gen. Dwight Eisenhower, who was made Commander in Chief of the operation, to cobble together an immensely complicated land, sea, and air invasion within three months. Speed was of the essence. Roosevelt needed a successful operation by the beginning of November to bolster his party's fortunes in the off-year congressional elections. When he quizzed Marshall about Torch's chances, Marshall told him to expect an easy triumph. Roosevelt mocked a stance of prayer and uttered "Please make it before Election Day."33

In the months prior to Torch, American diplomats and Office of Strategic Services operatives attempted to convince Pro-German Vichy officials in Africa to switch sides to the Allies. The ultimate goal was to secure promises that a naval landing would go unopposed. What transpired was comic opera. Authority among Vichy officials was fluid. It seemed no one could muster enough authority to be considered the voice of Vichy. Some were rabidly pro-German, others were human wind socks, ever ready to switch allegiances as the prevailing breezes blew. The end result was that American forces had to expect an opposed landing by a well armed and fortified enemy. Despite Marshall's assurances to Roosevelt, there was no reason to expect a walkover in North Africa.

Torch was a multi-faceted plan intended to take control of the Atlantic areas around Casablanca in French Morocco and, on the Mediterranean, to seize Oran and Algiers in Algeria. Also, Tunisia was to be captured to facilitate movement eastward to put pressure on Axis forces in Libya.34

The Western Naval Task Force, designated Task Force 34, was assigned to hit the Atlantic coast of French Morocco and capture Casablanca and Port Lyautey. It composed a huge number of ships for that early period of the war. In total, there were 102 ships, including combatants, transports, and service vessels. The three battleships assigned for fire support were the *Texas* , the *New York,* and the newly-commissioned *South Dakota* -class *Massachusetts*. Air cover was to be provided by one full-sized carrier, the venerable *Ranger* and four "Auxiliary Aircraft Carriers" (ACVs) of the *Sangamon* class, later to be designated "Escort Carriers" (CVEs). These vessels were originally tankers converted to small capacity carriers. The Task Force was further broken down into three segments, the Northern, Center, and Southern Attack Groups, whose targets were to be Mehedia, Fedhala, and Safi, respectively.35

Unknown to Father Foley and the rest of the crew of the *George Clymer* , their vessel was assigned to the Northern Attack Group, specifically TG34.8, under the command of Rear Adm. Monroe Kelly. During the shakedown period in Chesapeake Bay, all was not well with the high command. The overall army commander of the Western Landing Force, Gen. George Patton, was characteristically difficult. Until the expedition got underway, he was free to act independently of Admiral Hewitt, which caused predictable conflicts and duplication of effort. Few amphibious warfare specialists were available for the operation. Most of the men skilled in this art were Marines already occupied in the Pacific. A major army-navy difficulty arose over the matter of combat loading the transports. Apart from the *Clymer*, there were seven other transports in the Northern Group alone, the *Henry T. Allen* , *John Penn* , *Susan B. Anthony* ,

Electra (ex-*African Meteor*, sister ship to the *Clymer*), *Algorab*, *Florence Nightingale*, and *Anne Arundel* . In the Center and Southern Attack Groups combined, there were another twenty-one transport vessels.36

The navy intended to land the assault troops as lightly as possible, then bring in the larger equipment and bulky supplies behind them. The army's idea was to pack the assault boats with as much heavy ordnance as could be crammed in with the troops. The vessels themselves had to be loaded on a last-in-first-out principle, so the essential conflict between the services needed to be resolved before the troops and cargo were put aboard. This issue was complicated further by a last minute addition of a large number of troops assigned to the Center Attack Group.37 With time running down, it seemed unlikely that the convoy would be ready for the projected early November invasion date.

In truth, Patton and the other army commanders had legitimate doubts about what they saw. Much depended upon the handling of the attack transports and their assault boats. If even one of the transports was sunk, it would most likely take all of its overloaded invasion troops with it and if the landing craft were incompetently handled, any number of disastrous consequences could result. If troops were off-loaded too slowly, then the whole group circling in the line of departure could be delayed. If troops were landed at the wrong beaches, they would be useless at best and subject to capture or annihilation at worst. This was 1942, not 1945, when much experience had been gained and much specialized equipment had been designed for seaborne landings. The concept, at least on this massive scale, was entirely new.

So too were most of the attack transports, their crews, and junior officers. The performance of these vessels during the Virginia exercises was not exemplary, though probably better than could be expected, considering the extremely short training period. The one ship that looked good right out of the gate was Foley's *Clymer.* Nevertheless, tension had been high and the top one hundred and fifty army and navy officers who met in Norfolk for one last briefing on October 22, the day before departure, had much cause for concern. Admiral Hewitt presided over the meeting and outlined the major facets of the operation. It was the first time most of them were informed of the Task Force's destination.38

Lt. jg. John Foley was not privy to these intimations. All he knew when the *Clymer* headed for the open sea was that they were involved in a massive undertaking. He took inventory of the *Clymer*'s companions and noted twelve vessels of varying types—destroyers, minesweepers, submarines and the battleships as well the aerial cover—dirigibles, P.B.Y.s, scouts and bombers. That evening Foley thought of life back home in New England. Nights would be getting frosty now and the foliage at its peak. Maples, elms, oaks, all would be a riot of color. And in a world at peace, Dean Foley would have been immersed in his administrative work at Boston College. It would be about time for the semester mid-terms and many an undergraduate would be sweating out their Jesuit professor's exams. Instead many of these young men and others like them were on ships or in the jungles of the Pacific and still others were steaming eastward with Task Force 34, their fate as yet unknown. That evening, Foley drank in the scene at sea.

> We stand on the AA gun deck, leaning on the gun shield, silently admiring and drinking in the strange, silent beauty of the scene. From our middle lane we see big ships like ourselves ploughing ahead with not a single light showing, greyhounds straining to cover the distance that separates us from our destination. Off starboard, a lane of hammered silver runs from our ship to the little destroyer directly under the moon in the quarter sky and steadily climbing, a ghostly galleon. Off our starboard, the U.S.S. *Texas*, with reduced speed, leads the parade while we keep on her stern. Even looking at her you sense the massive floating fortress that she is. If we should happen to meet the *Prince Eugene* or any sister ship of the ill-fated *Bismarck*, she and the *New York* could

take care of it. Her steel sides bathed in the soft radiance of the moon, all her war features are subdued.

Suddenly, the ship swings hard to port and the lanyards lace the face of the moon, changing it every minute. They wrinkle her face—now vertically, now horizontally, now on a slant. Now the 20 mm AA gun competes with its own design—its hooded nose ready to be stripped in a split second so that it can start to write its grim message across the night heavens in the tracer ink supplied by its crew that is alert.

We look down to the bow. There the spray is tossed back endlessly, a cascade slivered by a full Harvest Moon in the Atlantic. What a night! All the massed power of modern warfare—soldiers lining the rails and regretting that they didn't join the Navy—unforgettable!39

On the second day out, the crew was informed of their invasion point, Port of Lyautey in French Morocco. An army officer, Major Dilley, showed Foley a relief map of the objective to be taken. The hope was still held out that the natives would offer no resistance. Foley was skeptical. The next day was a Sunday and the Feast of Christ the King. The chaplain scheduled Mass on deck. Without exception, services prior to an invasion were always well attended. Men who cared little about religion and thought little about God in their everyday lives often had a tendency to question their courses when faced with their own mortality. Certainly this did not apply to hard-core atheists or agnostics and many chaplains such as Foley questioned the utility and sincerity of "foxhole" religion in any case. On this particular morning he had hundreds of men crowding the deck in three lanes, acutely attuned to the words of the ancient Latin ritual. Foley thought, "A strange setting for Holy Mass but one that is pleasing to Our Lord and that the men will not forget."40

Foley had hoped to use the homily of this Mass as his first big inspirational talk, but was struck with an unprecedented case of laryngitis so his lesson in fortitude would have to wait for another day but he did give general absolution.41 This precaution was taken because of the ever-present U-boat threat. The *Clymer* and the other transports were as well protected as any ships could be, still, if a wolf pack managed to penetrate the cordon of steel, it was a certainty that the transports would be the targets of their attentions. The entire operation depended upon the APAs delivering the invasion troops to their objective.

The *Clymer* was also carrying a unit of fifteen commandos under Lt. Mark Starkwether of Cleveland. Starkwether became friendly with Foley on the voyage and told him of his unit's mission. The commandos were to negotiate the mouth of the Wadi Sebou, the river that entered the Atlantic at Mehedia Plage, snaked northward around an airport and then veered sharply southward in a hairpin turn, down to Port Lyautey. That city lay directly parallel to another stretch of the river, which then headed northward again, toward Spanish Morocco. A short distance past the mouth of the river, at an area designated Beach Brown was a submarine net which would impede any Allied navigation upriver. Starkwether's commandos were to cut the inch-and-a-half wire of the boom so that the destroyer *Dallas* could move upstream to provide covering fire at the airport and Port Lyautey.42

Starkwether sent one of his men, Ernest J. Gentile, to offer Foley any help he may need. Foley declined the offer but asked why he had volunteered for such a dangerous mission. Gentile wanted to talk and told the priest of his hopes and ambitions for after the war. He talked of how he used to read about such adventures as a boy and now he was actually about to take part in one, in deadly earnest. He said to Foley, "I told my wife that I would give everything I've got; this was a chance to give; will be doing our bit to bring the war to a close in a hurry. I'd hate to think that my two little girls would have to live in a world ruled by Hitler and his gang. That's why I signed up."43

The fourth day out, Foley went to the chart room directly behind the bridge to discern the course they had been following. He learned that the Northern and Southern Attack Groups had left Hampton Roads together and headed due south until they were north of Bermuda, east of Charleston, South Carolina, then sailed east, north, and east again so that by the 26th of October they were about eight hundred miles directly east of Baltimore. On that day, the Center Group, which sortied from Hampton Roads one day after the Northern and Southern Groups, and had headed in a northeasterly direction, linked up with them. A covering group, which included the *Massachusetts,* two cruisers, four destroyers, and a tanker had meanwhile sortied from Casco, Maine, and also joined up with the convoy by twelve hundred on the 26th. The new battleship had to cut its speed down to fifteen knots to stay with the smaller ships. The whole armada was running into high seas. A few hours later, three American subs appeared and rode shotgun on the surface.44

Tension aboard ship was definitely increasing. An army lieutenant asked Foley to mail letters to his wife and daughter just in case he was "ploughed under." Another man wanted to make merry with a harmonica so Foley sought out a Jewish army chaplain aboard, Rabbi Irving Tepper from Chicago, who had one. The rabbi also handed him a pocketknife, an example of the wampum which would be given to the native Moroccans as a goodwill gesture. Brightly colored cloth and blankets were also part of the *Clymer*'s variegated cargo. All aboard continued to wonder about what kind of reception they would get in Africa. Foley learned that the pass-word for Free French sympathizers was "Bordeaux" and that one hour before H-hour, all of the governors of French Morocco would be handed a letter informing them of events in the expectation that they would make the proper decision.45

By the 28th, the Air Group, which had left Bermuda on October 25 with the *Ranger* and four escort carriers had joined up with the main force. This completed the armada that would attack the targets in Africa. The men aboard the ships were informed that November 7 was D-Day.

The convoy, once assembled, charted a course southeastward to give the impression that it was heading toward Dakar.46

Foley's everyday duties went on as usual, even though his schedule was particularly busy, in light of the pre-invasion jitters. One task that he particularly enjoyed was instruction in the faith of Washington, a mess attendant. Throughout the war, Catholic chaplains were often approached by blacks interested in conversion. Foley was obviously sympathetic to the men, who were usually assigned as cooks or stewards in the navy. During battle they may have also been assigned to handle ammunition. He was disturbed by segregation itself, but also by the attitudes of some officers. On one occasion the *Clymer's* wardroom officers were eating dinner and being served by all black waiters. The dinner service on the *Clymer* was refined, if not opulent, as on many other ships. The officers had a silver service and ate off of linen tablecloths. One ensign, a 90–day wonder, asked one of the waiters, a man about twenty-eight, "What were you doing boy, before you went in the Navy?" The reply, "I was a lawyer sir." The young ensign was visibly shaken and Foley felt that he had had that coming.47

With Washington, Foley went over the articles of faith, discussed the truths of the Church, and to make sure he understood them, quizzed him on them. Foley asked him, "Who is God?" Washington answered in correct Baltimore catechism-style, "God is a being who is infinitely perfect." Foley continued, "What do you mean by infinitely perfect?" Washington gleefully replied, "Nothing no better!"48

Humorous interludes were rare on this crossing. After three days of heavy weather, the sea calmed but man-made dangers were still-ever present. Planes from the five carriers made continual scouting sorties and there were several believed sub contacts. Destroyers flanking the *Clymer* and the other transports dropped depth charges to keep any reckless U-boats from attempting a torpedo run. Talk on the *Clymer* was that if she ever shipped a torpedo, she would be thoroughly "disintegrated" due to the vast amount of ordnance aboard.49

Sunday, November 1 was the Feast of All Saints. Mass was at 0650 on deck at the end of General Quarters. There were about three hundred and fifty men in attendance, a terrific showing. Foley preferred Mass on deck though wind and sea always presented some problems with the altar and vestments. He wrote, "Very windy—God is pleased with our primitive surroundings for overhead—the blue canopy of the sky, we have no walls broken by stained glass windows, just sterns and bows;—we boast no marble inlaid floor, just a wooden deck, no fluted columns soaring aloft and carrying on their shoulders tons of masonry and steel, only a strong king post adorned with cables and pulleys and lines that are whistling in the wind."50

The Mass was just the start of Foley's church work that day. At 0900 he conducted a General Service for the Protestants and others. Attendance at this was also good, about two hundred, including Major Dilley. Foley, as was his usual practice with non-Catholics, spoke primarily of Jesus, and in this case, how the men should examine their lives in light of their coming trial. In the afternoon he used his new Benediction kit for the first time, setting up shop on the Boat Deck aft. He had a strong Rosary group which ended with three standard hymns: "Mother Dear, Oh Pray for Me," "Holy God We Praise Thy Name," and "*Tantum Ergo.*"51

The armada continued sailing that week in a rough zigzag pattern. By November 6, Admiral Hewitt was forced to make a decision regarding the landing, scheduled for the early morning hours of November 8. Hewitt was receiving dire weather forecasts of fifteen foot waves, which, if correct, would spell doom for any landing operation. There were contingency plans for a landing on the Mediterranean side of the continent, however, a last minute change of destination would add any number of further complications to this already extremely problematic operation. An emphatic decision had to be made immediately, because the Task Force was due to split into three spearheads on the seventh; one group was to head for Safi, the others to Casablanca and Port Lyautey. Hewitt resolved to stick to the original plan and was rewarded with milder weather the next day. The three groups, accompanied by their Covering and Air Groups, divided on schedule.52

By the evening of November 7, the Northern Attack Group was in position off of Port Lyautey. Nine thousand troops of the 9th Division were to be landed on five beaches, two of them, Beach Red and Beach Red 2, were north of the Wadi Sebou. The other three, Beaches Green, Blue, and Yellow, were south of the Wadi and Mehedia Plage. The objective was to seize Port Lyautey and the nearby airfield, and to take control of the river. The Group was commanded by Rear Adm. Monroe Kelly in the *Texas* , which was to provide naval gunfire support on station north of the transport group. The *Savannah* , a light cruiser, was to provide fire support south of the transports.53 At 2200, the *Texas* , which was also supposed to act as director to the transport group, mistook her own position and in subsequent orders to the transport group, managed to wheel them out of position as well. The *Texas* then left to take up her own station, leaving the commander of the transport group, Capt. Augustine H. Gray aboard the *Allen* , to sort out the mess. More bungling ensued, with misunderstood signals passing between the ships. The only vessel to get in position on time was the *Clymer* at precisely midnight. The *Clymer* was dead center in the line, and her boats were to deliver the 2nd Battalion Landing Team. The *Anthony* and the *Allen* , the two other ships in the front line, were finally in position forty minutes later. Behind them were the other five transports. Instead of the line of departure method, which became standard later in the war, the landing craft were to be guided ashore by three pilot ships.54

Meanwhile, aboard the *Clymer* at midnight, Foley was giving out *Viaticum* to the Catholics in the library after hearing confessions. He had celebrated Mass at dawn that morning and was inundated by men handing him money and last letters home just in case they didn't make it. He then went topside to bless the men preparing to go over the side. Starkwether's net cutting party took off for their objective inside the mouth of the Wadi Sebou. The *Clymer* , still performing better than the others, had three boat waves ready by 0200, but aboard the *Anthony* and *Allen* , confusion reigned. The first wave of boats was supposed to land at 0400, but due to all of the mistakes, the first landings were over an hour behind schedule. The hope that the operation would be a surprise *blitzkrieg* was dashed, and the other hope that the French would see reason and submit without a fight was likewise forlorn.55

The *Clymer*'s luck and skill held. Her first three waves of 24 boats carrying approximately 860 men made Beach Green by 0540, even though the surf was six feet high. Aboard the ship, Foley saw a red cluster flare go up at 0545. He and the others believed this to be a signal from Starkwether that the net had been cut. They were soon to find out differently. At about 0605, the destroyer *Eberle*, which was the *Clymer*'s point vessel lying off Beach Green, began trading fire with the Kasba coast defense battery. At the same time, the net-cutting party was sprayed with machine gun fire from the base of the cliff. The landing boats also came under intense fire from automatic weapons. The *Savannah* and fire-support destroyer the *Roe* poured tons of ordnance onto the shore battery area. The two French fighters that attempted to hit the gunships failed, and Wildcats launched from the *Ranger* and *Sangamon* soon had air superiority and began striking the Port Lyautey and Rabat-Sale airfields.56

By this time dawn had broken on a cloudy day. The *Clymer* got the word that the first three waves had gotten ashore with little difficulty, but the commando net party that straggled back aboard reported that they had not completed their mission. Shortly after 0700, the Kasba battery turned its attention from the gunships to the *Clymer*. For the French, this made perfect sense. There was little chance of sinking a battleship with shore batteries and even if the cruiser *Savannah* or a destroyer were hit, that would not scuttle the invasion. On the other hand, sinking the transports just might do that. When the plan was being discussed back in January, Joe Stilwell had bitterly opposed the operation and wrote to his wife, regarding the landings, "A few lucky hits will jeopardize the whole affair."57

When the batteries zeroed in on the *Clymer* , the landing boats had returned and were clustered around her like a hen and her chicks. Foley and the purser, Mr. Sharp, were topside watching the shelling. At first they enjoyed it immensely, like the Fourth of July. The ship was being bracketed. There were eight near misses, then one so close that it splashed into the water, detonated with a tremendous explosion, and soaked the people on deck. The next shot passed directly over the forecastle, about thirty feet above. Sharp turned to Foley and said, "Father, what the hell are we doing up here?" Foley agreed that they were a couple of fools in navy uniforms. The *Clymer* , all the while, was taking evasive maneuvers and was not hit, but transport commander Gray did decide to pull the vessels back to a point fifteen miles from shore, so the landing schedule was once again delayed.58

While naval gunfire continued from the support ships, Foley went down to his station at sick bay. A large number of wounded had been brought aboard and he waited for the doctors to finish their work before he started his. Two serious casualties were a Lieutenant McCrackin and a Kolfenbach, who was Catholic. The doctors had worked on him for two hours but there was nothing left for Foley to do except administer the last sacraments. He had been drilled by strafing planes as his boat headed for the beach, now his life was slowly ebbing away. Over the loudspeaker, all hands were ordered to General Quarters because an enemy submarine was sighted off the starboard beam, and for several hours the *Clymer* maneuvered in evasive actions as depth charges that were dropped to blast the sub, rocked the ship.59

The chaplain went to each injured man, regardless of faith, and tried to convince them to reject their fear. He was forced to face his own human frailty as well. More than half a century after these events, Foley remembered what happened that day.

> War wounds are not the neat wounds inflicted by a surgeon's scalpel by any means. You wonder where flesh begins

and where the sand begins. Grenades hitting people or something like that. The bullets. The grenades. The human body is just a mess. I was only afraid once in the Navy, when I went down with that purser to sick bay with the doctors. But then the German submarines were bothering us and we were lurching terribly and here all the doors were "dogged down" as they say. So if a torpedo comes in it is only that particular place that would be lost, flooded completely. And here I am, about 100 wounded aboard the ship and they are lying on the tables in the mess hall and boy did I play the hypocrite. I was deathly afraid for the first time. As Shakespeare said, "My seeded heart knocked against my ribs." It was pounding. *Pounding.* And here I am going around as a hypocrite telling the poor wounded boys who were moaning, "we'll be alright." And here I am. I never met a man yet who was in danger, whether from shore batteries or from bombs or submarines who wasn't afraid, no matter who the officer was. That was the only time in all my service days that I was ever afraid. After that, I had had my baptism and I wasn't afraid.60

It became clear that there were severe difficulties ashore. At 1330 a radioman told Foley that the last report indicated Co. F. was completely surrounded by the enemy. Starkwether of the commando net party told him of the disastrous termination of their mission. "We were spotted immediately and caught in the searchlights, withering cross fire of machine guns, both jetties, and then we had to run for it as the fort laid it on us also." Much of this trouble was rooted in a decision of General Truscott to restrain naval gunfire on the shore targets. Originally the landing plan was based upon the assumption that the Kasba could be captured in a rapid assault before the French defenders knew what was happening.61

The Kasba may have been suppressed by field artillery but due to Gray's early decision to pull back the transports, the 2nd Battalion could not get its pieces until the next day. That night, confusion continued to reign on the landing beaches and the situation looked dire. On the morning of the 9th, Foley's Mass was attended by the commando net party and celebrated in gratitude for their safe return. The *Clymer* had moved closer to shore, within one mile, but the situation appeared to have worsened. The surf rose approximately to fifteen feet. The *Clymer* rolled on the swell and the landing boats that tried to get ashore were like cars on a roller coaster. One boat that tried to make shore turned back and four men were dumped out as she was hoisted in. American bombers operated overhead and some naval gunfire was aimed at unseen targets over the hills. On deck in the early afternoon, Foley could see attractive light brown cottages with red-tiled roofs on shore and thought that it must have once been a pleasant summer colony. He was leaning on a nest of life rafts when he was once again visited by a messenger from the natural world. A bright yellow bird appeared from the blue and hovered in front of him. The chaplain reached out his hand and the bird, seemingly exhausted, lighted on it. Foley held the tiny creature while the murder and chaos of war was played out in front of his eyes. 62

Men continued to flow into sick bay. Foley attended them as best he could and noted the different types of injuries. Some had been machine gunned by plane before hitting the beach, others when they landed. There was a concussion and shrapnel cases. One man was blinded when his own rifle blew up in his face. Others were crushed by boats against the side of the ship and still others were crushed by boats on the beach. The word went around that seven men in a tank from the *Penn* drowned when it overturned in the heavy surf. Foley approached another man who was crying. The soldier told him that he had been terrified when he was strafed and the men around him crumbled. Foley tried to console him. He knew what fear was himself, but had learned to control it.63

At 1000, the net party was set to try it again. The Kasba still had not been taken and the *Dallas* , though it had tried to ram the net the day before, had not been able to pierce it to negotiate the Wadi Sebou. The commando unit had to succeed this time, or literally die trying. Foley accompanied them to the side of the ship, gave the six Catholics *Viaticum*, told them to kneel, and began the Latin invocation, "*Benedictio Dei...*" As they scrambled down the landing net in the pitch dark and shoved off from the portside aft, he called, "May the blessing of Almighty God, Father, Son and Holy Ghost descend upon you and remain forever. May He be with you in your mission and bring you back safely." He watched them disappear in the blackness and prayed that he would see them again.64

There was a knocking at Foley's door at 0400. It was three men from the net party. "Well, padre, we made it." They told Foley the whole story from the time he blessed them until they came back aboard. They had run out of fuel early on and had to return to the ship at midnight. They set out again in the tremendous surf. They got by the jetties and were swept onto the net, where they used rocket guns to cut the inch thick cable. The current forced the cable out and they then managed to cut the other side. The party headed for the sea as they were raked by machine gun fire from positions south of the fort. A 75 mm gun opened up as well. Apart from the ordnance, the men had to survive the hellacious surf, which they estimated to be thirty feet high. The boat rode the waves to the crest then dropped off, as if from a cliff. Starkwether was lifted up and hurled down, spraining his ankle and smashing his fingers. He found out later that he had also suffered a broken heel. The commandos' boat made it back to the *Clymer* as if by a miracle even though every man was wounded. Starkwether said to Foley, "would rather face hell of machine gun fire than that surf again." By 0800 the *Dallas* had made it up river and delivered its cargo of eighty Rangers to take the airfield, which was secured by 1030.65

At 1030 four more casualties were brought aboard the *Clymer* though three others were left behind in a tank lighter when General Quarters was sounded and the ship was forced to get underway. A badly wounded Lutheran asked Foley to pray with him. Foley responded with, "Sweet Jesus, mercy. I offer up this suffering for you in union with your suffering on Calvary for my sins, for my buddies wounded and lying ashore without protection or attention."66

Foley also ran into Lieutenant Gilchrist, who had been in the tank lighter that capsized the day before in thirty feet of water. Only four of the crew died, not seven as earlier reported, but that was bad enough. Meanwhile, two Frenchmen had come aboard from a tug. They claimed that the French thought they were fighting Englishmen. Foley gave them food and milk for their children. More casualties were brought aboard also. One man, Huffstutler, died from a stomach wound. The executive officer told Foley that the captain wanted the man buried ashore in the morning.67 It was Foley's first chance to get a glimpse at the now-conquered enemy territory.

The chaplain went ashore in a support boat at 0900 with the body of Huffstutler and a cargo of explosives. The boat dropped him off at Beach Brown near the Kasba. He raised his hand in blessing as he stepped on African soil. The first doctor Foley ran into told him that the cemetery was being set up at Blue Beach, to the south. He hopped in an army jeep and passed rows of American and Moroccan bodies. Foley told the driver to stop when he saw Dr. Cassidy from the *Clymer* working on injured Americans, Frenchmen, and Moroccans in an improvised hospital. Cassidy and a medical detachment of corpsmen had gone ashore on Sunday morning. The corpsmen yelled, "Hello Father!" in unison. While he was there he gave the last rites to two dying Frenchmen. On the way to the cemetery behind the town Foley stopped again to talk to some women with a cluster of children. He identified himself as a Catholic priest and gave them medals of Our Lady and the Little Flower. Their eyes lit up at the mention of St. Terese de Lisieux.68

Foley went next to the Kasba, where a military cemetery was being prepared near a Moslem one. Chaplain Tepper, the rabbi whom Foley had met in the crossing was in charge of collecting the bodies, which still lay scattered around the trenches and concrete block houses beneath the imposing fort. The corpses were frozen like statues as they fell, grotesquely stiff in their death agony. Foley thought, "What a hideous, repulsive countenance war has. It tears the heart to see the tragedy of young faces upturned to the sky, staring with glazed eyes meaningless at the sun."69

At one o'clock Foley began his funeral service for eight men. The graves had been dug by fifty Arab prisoners and there were about fifty American soldiers there for the ceremony. Foley had also brought bugler Conway along to play taps. The scene was one of sadness surrounded by great natural beauty. The sun was shining in a bright blue, cloudless sky. In the harbor the ships rode at anchor, their guns now silent. When Foley finished the service, the bugler sounded taps and the Arabs went back to their grave digging.70

Foley then began to wander around the hill where the Kasba squatted. There were still bodies that had not been collected and Foley wanted to bless them. He saw Lieutenant Sharf, a young officer who had eaten in the Clymer's wardroom with Foley and wondered when he left the ship at midnight on Saturday if he would see his wife by her next birthday in May. He lay about two hundred yards from the east wall of the fort. Foley then entered the concrete pillbox and found two Catholic boys whom he knew well. Their heads were split open. One of them had his brain completely exposed. The sight and the moment were a watershed in Foley's life. He realized at that moment looking at the two dead boys what an old Latin lesson meant. He was brought back to his school days and Virgil's story of Nicus and Neurilius, two young soldiers who were killed, two young flowers cut down in their prime. And he remembered an exam he took on the moral of the story. As a student he just wanted to pass the exam. Now, in a rotten pillbox baking in the African sun, the lesson came home to the priest, a man now in his late 30s. He finally understood Virgil and it was a lesson he could never forget.71

There was more to come. After finding his way out of the pillbox, Foley proceeded to the two trenches along the line of six 5" guns that had almost blown the *Clymer* and its foolhardy chaplain out of the water on Sunday. He found more familiar faces, now frozen in ghastly death masks. He saw a boy from Notre Dame who had served a Mass topside for him on the way over to Africa. The boy had approached him before the Mass and broke down crying. He told Foley that he was afraid to die. Foley replied, "I feel the same way. And our Lord who died for us did not want to die in the Agony in the Garden. And in fact, Mark tells us that He said Lord, if there is any other way to His Father, if there is *any* other way, yes let it be, but not my will but yours be done. Over and over and over again our Lord repeated that. Now he'll give you the courage you need because you're going to receive Holy Communion." The young man who had been afraid to die went ashore and now Foley saw him again, dead, at the base of one of the guns that had been shelling the ships. He and some others had taken the position by storm and paid with their lives.72

At 1600 Foley returned to Beach Brown and saw some prisoners unloading supplies from American landing craft. Chaplain Tepper gave Foley something that he had found in the personal effects of one of the dead boys. It was a copy of Joyce Kilmer's "Prayer of a Soldier in France," written for an earlier war. Foley had distributed mimeographed copies at his last Sunday Mass before the invasion.73 He was deeply touched as he read over the famous convert's words.

> My shoulders ache beneath my pack
> (Lie easier, Cross, upon His back)
> I march with feet that burn and smart
> (Tread, Holy Feet, upon my heart)
> Men shout at me who may not speak
> (They scourged Thy back and smote thy cheek)
> I may not lift a hand to clear
> My eyes of salty drops that sear

(Then shall my fickle soul forget
Thy Agony of Bloody Sweat)
My rifle hand is stiff and numb
(From Thy pierced palm red rivers come)
Lord, Thou didst suffer more for me
Than all the hosts of land and sea
So, let me render back again
This millionth of Thy gift, Amen.74

When he returned to the ship he learned for the first time that a preliminary armistice had been in effect since early that morning. Truly this had been an unforgettable day for Jesuit John Foley. He thanked God that this ordeal, at least, was over, though the killing went on elsewhere.75

For the next two days Foley spent most of his time visiting the sick, both aboard the *Clymer* and ashore at the French hospital in Port Lyautey. He always enjoyed doling out whatever he could steal from the *Clymer*'s supplies, particularly food. In this case he distributed apples, chocolate bars, and cigarettes. He gave these away to the Moroccans as well as the wounded GIs. There was virtually no place on earth where a Catholic chaplain could go that he would not find an outpost of the Church universal, and North Africa was no exception. Foley visited with two Salesian Fathers in a whitewashed Church of Christ the King. There was supposed to be a Catholic population of 17,000 but few attended Mass. This accorded with the notoriously lax observances of the French. Somewhat at a loss for words, Foley asked one of the fathers what he would call the architecture of the church, which featured a large tower. The priest replied, "grotesque."76

At 0630 on Sunday, November 15, the *Clymer* weighed anchor and left Port Lyautey. The anchorage had become just too hot. The Center Attack Group anchored at Fedhala Roads was decimated by U-boats on November 11 and 12. Four transports, the *Joseph Hewes* , the *Edward Rutledge*, the *Hugh L. Scott* , and the *Tasker H. Bliss*, were all torpedoed and lost. Tanker *Winooski* and destroyer *Hambleton* , which was waiting to take on fuel, were both badly damaged by torpedoes as well. Even the *Ranger* and the other flat tops were desperately dodging the white wakes of the infernal devices. Survivors from the sunken transports were brought to the local Catholic church for shelter.77

Admiral Hewitt finally decided to move the remainder of the Center Group and five transports of the Northern Group to Casablanca to finish unloading. The *Clymer* , for one, had only unloaded about one third of its cargo by November 14 at Mehedia Plage. There were anchorage difficulties at Casablanca and there was a back-up convoy due to enter that harbor as well, but a concentration at Casablanca seemed the lesser of two evils, considering the dramatic losses of the last few days. The *Electra* had set out unescorted and earlier than the other Northern Group vessels and paid for it. She was torpedoed about seventeen miles off of Fedhala at 0640 on November 15. The *Clymer* passed the sinking *Electra* at 1210 and continued on to Casablanca. Foley thought the town most modern in design, with large buff-colored apartment buildings. In the water there was evidence of the struggle that had taken place a few days before.78

That afternoon Foley toured the badly damaged *Hambleton*. The destroyer had been towed into Casablanca for repairs after it had been torpedoed. Eighteen men had been killed and another six wounded. There was extensive damage in an engine room, a fire room, and the electrician's room. The *Clymer* , tied up alongside her, was to provide steam and electric power for repairs. Lieutenant Ellery of the *Hambleton* asked Foley to come aboard again on Monday to hear confessions. He did this and went to the machinists' shop to bless the bodies of three of the men who had been killed in the engine room. That night one hundred and fifty English soldiers and merchant marine came aboard the *Clymer*. Their ship, the *Laconia* had been torpedoed in September with the loss of two thousand souls, fourteen hundred of whom were Italian prisoners.79

On Tuesday, November 17 at 1300, the *Clymer* nosed out of Casablanca Harbor, number twenty three on the list of ships shoving off, heading back to Hampton Roads. Before they left Foley was called to pacify a French boy who had gone for DeGaulle and now feared the Darlan faction who were being retained in power under American auspices. DeGaullists were already being shot for desertion. The boy was going to be dropped off at Port Lyautey to join up with some DeGaullists there. For the next few days, Foley tended to his polyglot flock. On Sunday he celebrated his largest service on the ship so far, with over one thousand attending. When he held Benediction and the Rosary, he was sure that Our Lady was pleased by the hodge podge of Irish, Scot, Cockney, and Yankee accents that responded to the first part of the Hail Mary.80

That day the convoy ran into very heavy seas. The pitching was so violent that at dinner in the wardroom, the officers had to hold onto the tables with one hand and eat with the other. The chaplain had just put a piece of turkey in his mouth when Dr. Harris asked him to pass the bread. The ship pitched, the chaplain's two hands were occupied and thus he sailed back and forth like a ping pong ball. "Look at the chaplain!", someone called on his way by.81

That Thursday was Thanksgiving Day. Foley had standing room only for both the Catholic Mass and the General Service. He used the same sermon for both, dealing as it did with the battle experiences of the North African invasion. He enjoined the listeners to be sincere in Thanksgiving, particularly for surviving the battles, but also for all of the gifts of life. He said,

> The personal blessings that God has conferred upon us, we alone know their number. What they are is a sacred secret between us and our Creator, but we do know that deep down in the sanctuary of our hearts where we walk alone with God, where no man treads without intruding, that the protecting arm of God was not foreshortened. 82

He spoke of the poignant burial he performed at the Kasba, with the sun shining down upon the bodies. He assured them that God was not unmindful of their sacrifice and quoted Scripture in regard to fighting the good fight, finishing the course, keeping the faith. All in attendance no doubt had much to be thankful for.

The North African campaign, conceived in haste and executed for political, rather than good military reasons, had been a quick success, achieved with relatively little bloodshed. However, to those who died and those who loved them, Africa was not simply the first step in the "second front" strategy, it was the end of the world. Unknown to Foley, a brother priest had been lost as well. Redemptorist Fr. Clement M. Falter of Rennsalaer, Indiana, who had crossed the Atlantic on the ill-fated *Hewes* landed with the first assault troops at Fedhala on November 8. Shortly after making the beach, around 0800, Falter was killed by a shell from one of the 75 mm guns. This was one more tragedy in the fearful toll the war would take on the American priesthood.83

Fr. John Foley and his ship had survived their baptism of fire. Chaplain Foley had done all he could for the many men who had crossed his path, not the just *Clymer* crew, but also the terrified army troops the *Clymer* had ferried over. And then there were the wounded, and the foreign allies and prisoners, the Arabs and Frenchmen. He had been the spiritual mentor of the commando net party, who accomplished their mission despite 100% casualties. And the middle-aged Jesuit had learned much about himself as he tended to, and buried the dead. The *Clymer* arrived in Norfolk on November 30. Foley's diary entry for that day reads,

> HOME, NORFOLK, VA!!!!! Minus four ships that went East with us——they are now filed in Davy Jones' locker. Thank you, Lord, for bringing us safely back again. We, indeed, have much to thank you for! Thank you, Lord, again, for a safe 7,000 mile round trip.84

Foley was sincere in his gratitude for deliverance but this Jesuit's war was just beginning.

Notes: Chapter 4

1 Foley diary, June 24, 1942.

2 Foley diary, June 14, 1942; "History of the U.S.S. *George Clymer* (APA-27)," Office of Naval Records and History, Ship's History Section, Navy Department. Copy provided by Mr. Saul Knight.

3 Foley diary, June 24, 1942.

4 Foley diary, June 28, 1942

5 Foley diary, June 29, 1942.

6 Foley diary, June 30, 1942.

7 Ibid.

8 Ibid.; Foley interview, March 6, 1995; Leonard Jones, a cook aboard the *Clymer*, caught the culprit attempting to steal the wine, which was stored under lock and key in one of the galley's refrigerators. He ran him off with a meat cleaver. Telephone interview with Mr. Leonard Jones, January 10, 1998.

9 Foley diary, July 2, 1942; Foley interview, March 3, 1995.

10 Foley diary, July 4, 1942.

11 Foley diary, July 14, 1942.

12 Foley diary, July 23, 1942.

13 Foley diary, July 27, 28, 29, 1942.

14 Foley diary, July 28, 1942.

15 Ibid.

16 Foley diary, July 28, 1942; Foley interview, March 6, 1995.

17 Ibid.

18 Foley diary, July 28, 1942.

19 Foley diary, July 29, 1942.

20 Foley diary, August 2, 1942.

21 Foley diary, August 10,11, 1942; September 9, 1942.

22 Foley diary, September 9, 1942; Foley interview, March 10, 1995.

23 Foley diary, August 11, 1942.

24 Foley diary, September 8, 18, 1942.

25 Foley diary, September 9, 30, 1942.

26 Foley diary, September 21, 23, 1942.

27 Foley diary, October 1, 17, 1942.

28 Foley diary, October 18, 1942.

29 Foley diary, October 19, 1942.

30 Foley diary, October 22, 1942.

31 Foley diary, October 23, 1942. "There are as many opinions as there are men."

32 The historical background of Operation Torch and the political/military wrangling behind it is taken primarily from Samuel Eliot Morison, *Operations in North African Waters October 1942—June 1943* (Boston: Little, Brown and Co., 1947) Chapter 1 and Norm Gelb, *Desperate Venture* (New York: William Morrow and Co., 1992). See also Arthur Layton Frank, *The Politics of Torch* (Lawrence: The University Press of Kansas, 1974).

33 Forrest C. Pogue, *George C. Marshall: Ordeal and Hope* (New York: The Viking Press, 1966), 402.

34 Morison, *Operations in North African Waters*, 16, 17.

35 Ibid., 31, 36. The chaplain aboard the *Ranger* was Fr. Joseph T. O'Callahan, S.J.

36 Ibid, 24, 26, 27. In *Operations in North African Waters*, 40, 44, 192, Morison numbers thirty-five transports taking part in the invasion, however the ship roster of Task Force 34 in the same book lists only twenty-nine transports by name. A few cargo ships were also employed for conveying equipment.

37 Ibid., 27.

38 Ibid., 41.

39 Foley diary, October 23, 1942.

40 Foley diary, October 24, 25, 1942.

41 Foley diary, October 25, 1942.

42 Foley diary, October 25, 1942; Morison, *Operations in North African Waters,* 129.

43 Foley diary, October 25, 1942.

44 Foley diary, October 26, 1942; Morison, *Operations in North African Waters,* 43, 44.

45 Foley diary, October 26, 1942. Foley recalled that Tepper was seasick the entire crossing. He told Foley, "Father, I'll never come back aboard another ship if I survive." He was killed in Africa. Foley interview, March 6, 1995.

46 Foley diary, October 27, 1942; Morison, *Operations in North African Waters,* 47.

47 Foley diary, October 30, 1942. Foley interview, March 17, 1995. See also Edward D. Reynolds, S.J., *Jesuits for the Negro* (New York: The America Press, 1949).

48 Foley diary, October 30, 1942.

49 Foley diary, October 31, 1942.

50 Foley diary, November 1, 1942.

51 Ibid.

52 Morison, *Operations in North African Waters,* 49–51.

53 Ibid., 116, 118.

54 Ibid., 119, 120.

55 Foley diary, November 7, 1942; Morison, *Operations in North African Waters,* 121, 122.

56 Foley diary, November 8, 1942; Morison, *Operations in North African Waters,* 122, 123.

57 Foley diary, November 8, 1942; Joseph W. Stilwell, *The Stilwell Papers,* ed. by Theodore H. White (New York: William Sloane Associates, Inc., 1948), 21.

58 Foley diary, November 8, 1942; Foley interview, March 6, 1995; Morison, *Operations in North African Waters,* 123.

59 Foley diary, November 8, 1942.

60 Foley interview, March 6, 1995.

61 Foley diary, November 8, 1942; Morison, *Operations in North African Waters*, 124.

62 Foley diary, November 9, 1942; Morison, *Operations in North African Waters*, 125.

63 Foley diary, November 9, 1942.

64 Ibid.

65 Foley diary, November 10, 1942.

66 Ibid.

67 Ibid

68 Foley diary, November 11, 1942.

69 Ibid.

70 Ibid.

71 Ibid.; Foley interview, March 10, 1995.

72 Ibid.

73 Foley diary, November 11, 1942.

74 Joyce Kilmer, "Prayer of a Soldier in France," in *The World's Great Catholic Poetry*, ed. Thomas Walsh (New York: The Macmillan, Co., 1947), 422.

75 Foley diary, November 11, 1942.

76 Foley diary, November 13, 1942; Foley interview, March 10, 1995.

77 Morison, *Operations in North African Waters*, 169–170.

78 Ibid., 173, 174; Foley diary, November 15, 1942.

79 Foley diary, November 15, 16, 1942; Morison in *Operations in North African Waters*, 169, reports nine men killed outright and eleven missing or fatally wounded. Since Foley was actually aboard the ship and talked to the crew his casualty figures are used. The *Hambleton* lived to fight another day. At Casablanca, Seabees removed a 40 ft. section of her hull amidships, then joined the two remaining sections for the trip to the Boston Navy Yard, where she was permanently repaired. The *Hambleton* later participated in the D-Day invasion and other duties in the Atlantic theatre before being converted into a minesweeper and sent to the Pacific

theatre. See Office of the Chief of Naval Operations, *Dictionary of American Naval Fighting Ships,* vol. III, (Washington, D.C.: Navy History Division, 1968), 220, 221.

80 Foley diary, November 17, 22, 1942.

81 Foley diary, November 22, 1942.

82 Foley diary, November 26, 1942.

83 Grant, *War is My Parish*, 35–38.

84 Foley diary, November 30, 1942.

CHAPTER 5

▼

"THE APPLE FATHER"

The *Clymer* and her crew spent the first two weeks of December 1942 at Norfolk. Preparations were being made for a second cruise, the destination, at least to the chaplain and sailors, as yet unknown. Captain Moen initially issued orders that part, not all, of the ship's complement would have permission for home leave, then rescinded these orders, canceling everyone's leave, including Foley's. Foley asked Moen for permission to go home because he had already told his mother, a widow with three sons in the service, that he would be home to see her, and that he needed to get back to Boston for her sake, not his own.1 Moen allowed Foley to go but did not relent when it came to the crew.

The captain's actions did not endear him to the crew and Foley felt that his decision was unjust. Moen struck him as a man who tried to make up in braggadocio what he lacked in size. Foley loathed the class distinctions between officers and crewmen in the navy. As a Jesuit he respected the discipline of hierarchical systems and understood that senior officers had pressures and responsibilities that enlisted men would never know. Yet he bristled when officers were verbally abusive to the men and he could not abide examples of purposeful humiliation of subordinates or any treatment that detracted from a man's dignity.

There had already been such an incident with this captain. Before the African invasion, when the *Clymer* was sailing from Charleston to Norfolk, she was tailed by a German U-boat. A radio officer came to Foley visibly shaken. He had brought a message to the captain immediately upon receiving it, but the captain told him he had not delivered it fast enough and kicked him, right in front of the enlisted men. Foley considered the radio officer, who was a minister in civil life, to be a fine fellow and a man of integrity, but when the officer asked him what to do, Foley told him to do nothing. The priest saw it this way—the captain was an Annapolis man, the radio officer a reservist. In any court martial proceeding, there was no question which man a naval board would side with. There was a wall there that no reservist could go through. Foley said that the captain must have broken under the strain of the moment.2

The officer accepted that and took his advice, but the abuse angered Foley. This time he let it pass for the officer's sake though there would be other times when he would go at it hammer and tongs with captains and executive officers. He would not challenge authority simply because he disliked particular orders or even the behavior of his superiors but he never failed to respond when he felt the crew's moral welfare was jeopardized. He would pick and choose his places to stand. Once decided, he was implacable. There would come a day with this captain.

After his brief visit home, Foley prepared himself for another cruise. He restocked his own ecclesiastical supplies and recreational materials for the men. On a foray to the City Market in Norfolk to pick up sheet music, he swung into a lunch counter for a steak but was told he would have to buy his own and they would cook it. He found a meat stand and bought a sixteen ounce T-bone for 65 cents, then returned with it to the lunch counter. When the cooked steak was placed before him, it was smothered with onions and tomatoes and accompanied by mashed potatoes, a glass of beer, and a slab of apple pie burdened by two big scoops of ice cream.3 Rail-thin his entire life, John Foley enjoyed a hearty meal and more still enjoyed seeing others eat their fill. On the *Clymer*'s upcoming cruise, he would get the chance (strictly through midnight requisitions) to feed some desperately hungry people, starved by the war.   On December 16, the *Clymer* weighed anchor and headed out to Hampton Roads. The next morning, with the temperature near freezing, the ship departed for its second cruise. Yankees such as Foley were slightly chilled but the southerners aboard headed below decks to escape the cold weather. As the little tenders drew back the submarine nets, the vessel joined an Indian file column directly behind the flagship *Allen*. The ships followed an approved 15 knot zig zag pattern to negotiate the minefield and were soon joined by a screen of destroyers, the light cruiser *Montpelier* , and the carrier *Chenango*, also a veteran of the North Africa campaign. It was only a month to the day that Foley's ship and many others had left Casablanca in triumph. The feeling now was that it would be much longer than a month when they would see home again—if ever.4

The consensus on their destination was somewhere in the South Pacific. One thing was clear; this would not be a beach invasion, as the North African mission had been. This trip the *Clymer* was not carrying assault troops but the 35th Construction Battalion (Seabees) with their tons of equipment, including gigantic cement mixers, cranes, derricks, bulldozers and lumber. The "Can Do" boys of the Navy were loaded for bear and with them was their chaplain, Fr. Francis J. McDonald, S.J., fresh out of the Norfolk Chaplain School only two weeks before. McDonald also happened to be one of Foley's fellow Jesuit professors from Boston College. The two had a joyous reunion though McDonald was ill and one of the ship's doctors diagnosed incipient pneumonia. It was debatable if he could continue and there was discussion that he should be put ashore at the first opportunity.5

McDonald was not the only Seabee on the sick list. Enlisted men and officers alike were conspicuously absent from dinner, illustrating that seasickness has no respect for rank. The *Clymer* continued to chart a course east for sixty miles while her destroyer screen hunted for U-boats in those treacherous Atlantic waters. After veering southward, both the air and water temperature jumped. At two hundred miles out to sea, the flotilla picked up the warming Gulf Stream and the atmosphere became almost balmy. At 0830 the next morning, a thunderous crash was felt. The impact was so great there was an immediate fear that the *Clymer* had been struck by a torpedo. The crash was simply caused by an enormous wave, and the high seas were normal for Cape Hatteras in winter.6 Foley made it a point to visit all of the Seabees afflicted with *mal de mer* , but there was little he could do to succor them apart from reminding them that this too shall pass and that they should cast their bread upon the waters.

By Sunday the weather had moderated. Foley's Mass on deck was celebrated under the azure vaulted canopy of the sky. The priest, always highly cognizant of the natural world, sought to incorporate the men's surroundings with a message of Christ as seafarer in his homily. Foley preached,

> He is one with us for we should remember that sometimes we are inclined to forget that He also went down to the sea in ships. He chose men who wrested a hard living from the depths of the sea to be the first members of His Apostolic company. To St. Peter, a fisherman, He said, "Follow Me and I will make you a fisher of men." He knew what it was to sleep on the fantail of a ship. He knew what it was to feel a ship roll and pitch under Him on the surface of Lake Genesareth in Galilee, a huge inland sea, that was no lily pond but a body of water where storms rushed and whipped down from the mountains, lashing thousands of white horses and made old hands like Peter cry out, "Lord, save us or we perish." Christ also mustered men for His ship's company like St. Paul who knew the privations and hardships of duty ashore and afloat even to the point of being shipwrecked three times. Yes, Christ is no stranger to our way

of life. But the question arises, "Are we strangers to His way of life?"—to Him?...

We can do nothing that counts for eternity, or for time for that matter, which has lasting value in the sight of God unless Jesus Christ is on our side, unless He is with us. And He is only with us when our heart is a good heart when, as it were, it is afloat on the ocean of life and buoyant with His grace, not a torpedoed wreck on the bottom through mortal sin.7

On Christmas Eve day, 1942 the *Clymer* approached the entrance to the Panama Canal. The 2,700 mile journey from Norfolk to the Canal was just the first leg of this cruise. Foley was stunned by his first sight of Panama. At Cristobal, the heat was intense and all of the colors seemed amplified. The hills were covered with the thickest vegetation of the most verdant green. Blue was well represented in different shades—that of the ocean, the sky, the hulls of the *Montpelier* and the *Clymer*. Foley went ashore for supplies for the Crew's Mess and walked through the exotic, palm-lined streets which reminded him of New Orleans' Crescent City. The inhabitants, too were as colorful as those of the French Quarter. Once they roused themselves from the afternoon siesta, Foley observed the locals in all their splendor. Taxis cruised up and down the streets, guitar music and laughter emanated from the crowd, children chased each other and one man menaced another with a leather strap. That night Foley recorded more of the street life in his diary, recalling a

...woman balancing a basket that must have been her own weight disastrously on her head. Huge negro sitting before a pile of coconuts, slashing them open with a murderous looking machete, and eating the small nut about the size of an egg. Then draining the fluid—watery colored—into a bucket.

Madames, overrouged and underdressed, shamelessly sitting outside houses soliciting their customers love—for a price.8

Other Yankees in the flotilla were fascinated by the Canal Zone. James Fahey, a young bluejacket from Waltham, Massachusetts who was a 40 mm gunner on the *Montpelier* confided his impressions to his diary.

> It took eight hours for the ship to go through the locks. It was quite an experience going through the locks and the thick green jungle all around us was beautiful. They say every known animal in the world can be found here. If you go deep into the jungle you will come across savage tribes. If they leave the tribe and return they are killed because the rest of the tribe thinks he will be civilized. We could see some alligators on the beach in this beautiful spot.9

The *Clymer* traversed the fifty-mile-long Canal which runs from Limon Bay on the Caribbean to Balboa on the Bay of Panama on Christmas Day. Foley celebrated Midnight Mass on Christmas Eve in the Officers' Wardroom for a congregation of 250, Catholic and non-Catholic. He was especially proud of the choir, which did a creditable job on the old chestnuts. On Christmas morning he organized the choir to serenade the army families in their homes on the banks of the Canal. In some spots the shore was only twenty feet away. After passing through Culebra Cut, Foley held a General Service on deck. The heat, at a humid 110 degrees, was nearly insufferable garbed in his layered vestments. Foley was not told until afterward that a navy photographer had filmed the service in color. The photographer also filmed his next Mass, which followed immediately and promised Foley a print, but the priest never got the film.10 Later that day he crossed to the *Allen* for Rosary and Benediction so that the Catholics would have some sort of service on Christmas.

The day after Christmas, the *Clymer*, carrying the "Flag," joined the four other transports, *Montpelier* and *Chenango* leaving Balboa for the Pacific. The small convoy hugged the northern shore of the Gulf of Panama before entering the ocean proper. Its surface was as smooth as glass and the ship had not the slightest roll or pitch. The Pacific well rated the name given it by Vasco Nunez de Balboa in 1513. Suddenly the calm was shattered by three dive bombers coming out of the blue and heading straight toward the *Clymer* at full throttle. Foley was on the flying bridge when the first plane made its run from about 2,000 yards away, engines off, heading straight toward the APA at 300 miles per hour. The gunnery officer gave the order to fire and the anti-aircraft crews opened up. The dive bomber banked sharply over the ship and sailed out of range. The other two planes made similar runs, and, along with the leader repeated the attacks, first from starboard , then from port, for a half hour.11 Fortunately, this time, the planes were American, giving the *Clymer*'s AA crews valuable practice in sighting live targets. Before this cruise was over, however, the gunners would have their chance at the real thing.

For some time there had been excitement aboard ship for the traditional "shellback" ceremony, whereby crewmen who had never crossed the equator were called pollywogs and lampooned by those who had made the crossing. The ceremony usually included hosing down the victims, beating them with sticks, shaving their heads, and other ludicrous, if harmless practices. Officers were not exempt from this treatment though of course those who did not care to participate could not be forced to. The chaplain made it clear that he would play along even if it meant enduring "heavy weather" from the shellbacks. A few days before the actual event, Foley led the wretched neophytes in verses of the "Pollywog Song."

I'm a pollywog,
A low pollywog,
How low I am,
No shellback knows.

He thinks he's comical,
When he's anatomical,
He wacks my fanny,
Till I ain't got any.

I grunt and groan,	A shellback's tough,
I sweat and moan,	He boasts he's rough,
How much I moan,	There'll come a day,
No shellback cares.	He'll cry "Enough."

He breaks my back,	I'm a pollywog,
My spine's a crack,	A low pollywog,
Despite this fact,	How low I am,
No shellback cares.	No shellback cares.12

On the big day, pollywog Foley, "a blob plus a tail" was led before Davey Jones and King Nepturne, whacked on the keel by pirates, forced to step onto an electrified griddle, made to kiss the Royal Baby and dumped into a pool fully clothed. The pirates wore long underwear marked with skull and crossbones, slit dungarees, green pajamas and helmets. By noon the ceremony was over and the pollywogs were now full-fledged shellbacks initiated into the "Solemn Mysteries of the Deep." The frivolity was over and the *Clymer* got back to the deadly serious business of war. As if to drive home the point, a destroyer flanking the ships dropped two depth charges a few hours later, in the belief that the column was being stalked by a Japanese submarine.13

The convoy met with tragedy on New Year's Day when one of the *Montpelier's* two scout planes crashed upon takeoff. The planes, ordinarily used for reconnaissance and for towing targets for gunnery practice, also carried two 360 pound depth charges in the event that they sighted a sub close to the surface. Reservist Ensign Thompson and his radioman prepared themselves for a routine launch off the plane catapult, which sent the plane aloft by a powder charge. The blast rocketed the plane skyward but instead of dipping and then gaining altitude, it plummeted into the sea, whereupon the two depth charges exploded, sending a huge geyser of water over the cruiser. Thompson, in the open cockpit, was killed instantly. The radioman, enclosed in pliofilm, was knocked unconscious. When he came to, he found himself hanging upside-down in the wreckage. He managed to smash his fist through the pliofilm and cling to the debris until a boat arrived to rescue him and recover Thompson's body. At sunset, Foley and seaman Mike Rice of the Pontoon Assembly Detachment gazed over at the *Montpelier*'s single plane where two had been that morning. Rice said, "She looks lonesome Father."14

A funeral service for Thompson was held the next afternoon on the fantail of the cruiser. Foley's professional interest led him to borrow a pair of binoculars to follow the proceedings from *Clymer*'s flying bridge. The service was performed by Chaplain Carl Knudsen, a Congregationalist from Plymouth, Massachusetts. The assembled crew were in white and blue. A Marine honor guard stood at attention under the plane catapult. They fired three volleys from their rifles, taps was blown, and the young ensign's body was consigned to the deep. The ocean swallowed him quickly.15

The same day Foley experienced an example of the anti-Catholic bigotry which was prevalent in some of the southerners on board. While he was saying Mass, a group of sailors were heckling him with foul language. His acolyte, Mike Rice, turned to the gang and said, "Quiet please, church services going on." Somebody in the group sneered, "If you were paying attention to the service, you wouldn't hear it." After the Mass was over Rice approached the group and said, "Just came over to say that I was the man who asked for quiet. I heard that remark that was passed. Let the man come topside, put on the gloves, and we'll settle the argument then and there." There was silence and no one answered Rice's challenge. Foley had already been told that some of the crew despised him because he was a priest, "the guy with the nightgown on." These men loathed the Catholic Church and believed the most absurd stories that they had been raised with, even though many had never met a priest in their lives. Catholic sailors understandably reacted angrily to such incidents but Foley felt that ignorance of such a high order should only be pitied.16

Back in Charleston, Foley had already gotten an inkling of these attitudes. One evening a Southern Baptist corpsman returned to the ship after a night of heavy drinking ashore. When he met Foley in a passageway, he stopped him and said, "I just want to tell you something chaplain..." Foley saw that alcohol had lowered the man's inhibitions and readied himself for a harangue. "I've been sizing you up and when I go back home I'm going to tell my minister he was a _ _ liar. The things he fed us."17

In contrast, Foley's dealings with minister chaplains from the South were always amicable. He had no knowledge of what these men told their flocks back home but the atmosphere in the navy was as a rule one of accord. Father Knox's motto for the chaplain school, "Cooperation Without Compromise" seemed to work fairly well in practice. Foley did experience other manifestations of anti-Catholicism while in the navy. The most virulent characters were usually not Protestants or Jews, but ex-Catholics, nursing grudges against the Church. One incident occurred on this leg of the passage to the South Pacific. As a result, Foley for the first and last time threatened a sailor with punishment.

It was Foley's practice to set up his altar on deck at 0400, then from 0400–0500 the ship would stand to General Quarters. Since Father McDonald had recuperated, Foley let him say the first Mass after General Quarters at 0500, and then Foley would follow him with another Mass immediately afterward. The altar itself was a light collapsible affair that had been made for him by one of the ship's carpenters. There was an older bosun aboard who one day deliberately flooded the deck while McDonald was saying Mass. Foley knew he could not let this pass and called him into his office to explain why he had deliberately ruined the Mass. The bosun simply replied that he had his job to do but Foley knew there were other underlying reasons. He said, "You've got a medal of Our Lady and I have never seen you at Mass. What you are doing indirectly is attacking the son of Our Lady. Going to Mass would please Our Lady and her son. What are you wearing that medal for?" The bosun replied, "I don't know. I don't know. My sister gave it to me." Foley retorted, "Well don't you ever do again what you did this morning because it will be serious consequences."18

The "serious consequences" were meant to imply a court-martial, but Foley was bluffing. He knew that preferring charges against a sailor would ruin him with the other men because there would be distorted accounts of what happened. A chaplain had to walk a fine line between being the sailor's crying towel and advocate and yet still retain their respect as an officer and a man. To complicate matters, the chaplain often had to contend with religious animosities such as those that Foley experienced. During his time in the service, he came to reassess his priesthood and more than half a century later, he ruminated on what he discovered about himself in the navy.

> …a priest among Catholics had been on a pedestal , no question about it.
>
> There was a certain amount of deference. In the navy, when you went in as a priest you went in as a man, and you were a complete stranger to the people with whom you were associated and the other way around too. Then they would find out what kind of a man he is, there was no deference and respect for you except as a naval officer. But as a priest you were Joe Zilch and only when they had sized you up, when they said what kind of a person is he, then you were accepted. How you would stand up under very trying situations. In wartime, the word would be passed around, how did so and so stand up. You started on the same level of manhood as the others in the sense that you were just another man as a stranger would be like. That helped me to grow as a man. Being placed in a completely strange situation, no different from the other men. And they finally found out just by the way you behaved. I grew. And I am very happy that I did it. It

was being taken out of the cocoon of religious life and Catholic life. Except you were the representative.19

The small convoy continued on its eastward trek through early January. The route took them north of Tahiti between the Marquesas and Tuamotu Islands. The men enjoyed the weather on that side of the equator, especially being able to tan in the January sunshine. Foley saw something else in the burning orb. While watching Father McDonald consecrate the Eucharist at dawn Mass, Foley was awestruck by the spectacle. In his diary he wrote, "The sunlight caught Our Lord as He was raised on high for the adoration of the men. It seemed that the sun itself wanted to pay tribute to the One who hung it in the sky." It was an image that he never tired of and he recalled the lines in the hymn for Sext in the Office—"*Qui Splendore mane illuminas.*" The meaning had never been so clear to him before.21

The beauty that Foley managed to find aboard his vessel, however, could never subdue the tragedies of war. Another plane crashed, this time one of the *Chenango's* complement. The pilot had apparently made an approach, changed his mind, and spun into the sea. Foley gave absolution from his perch on the *Clymer* and hoped that it was not necessary. This time it was not, as both pilot and crewman were fished out of the water safely. The fatal and near-fatal crashes reminded Foley of the day only two short months before, that he buried the dead at Port Lyautey. That invasion, so meticulously planned and nervously anticipated, seemed a minor tryout now. The men killed by the scrubs of the Axis team -Vichy French and Arabs—were all but forgotten now, except by their families and the pensive chaplain who laid them to rest in the hard African earth.22

Foley had time to remember but not to be maudlin. His immediate concern had to be for the living and he tried to cover all of the bases with the men of the *Clymer* . The group he felt were the unsung heroes of the ship were the Black Gang; the engine crew who worked below deck (in the bowels of the vessel) in 120 degree heat as a matter of course. Foley knew, as the men did themselves, that if the *Clymer* ever shipped a torpedo, they would be hopelessly trapped when the watertight hatches were dogged down. If seawater did not get them, 400,000 pounds of live steam would boil them like lobsters. Foley liked to visit the crew regularly, yet wondered how they could endure the heat. Even the handrails were scalding to the touch.23

Among his other seemingly endless duties, Foley was often asked to hold on to money by the sailors, lest it slip through their fingers. One sailor handed him $200 to hold, a staggering amount for a one month period. The sailor told Foley that a chief in boot camp said to spend one third of his pay on liquor and save the rest. Foley thought this ill-advised, if not diabolical, counsel. Of all the things the young man had been told in boot days, this was the one that stuck. Other aspects of navy wisdom had bothered him for some time. The situation in the Pacific was still not going well, despite the party line of official propaganda, which he despised. While not privy to command decisions, Foley nevertheless felt that the Pacific campaign, particularly the Guadalcanal operation, was a shoestring affair, undermanned and undergunned.24

It would not have been difficult to find others who agreed with him. While the struggle for Guadalcanal *per se* was almost over officially, the battle for ultimate control of the archipelago would continue for another year. Guadalcanal was a somewhat odd choice for America's first big push in the East. Discovered by the Spanish in the 1560s, the island chain itself was christened the Solomons and the ninety by twenty five mile central southern island was called Guadalcanal after a town in Valencia. The Spanish did not colonize their find and except for occasional forays by the French and British, the native Melanesians were little bothered by Europeans until the late nineteenth century, when the island group was partitioned by the Germans and British. After the Germans were displaced as a result of World War I, the islands came firmly under British imperial control.25

Economically, the islands were dominated by Lever Brothers and Burns Philp, an Australian company. The interest was in copra, and the profits were great. The copra plantations were worked by the native Melanesians, a very dark-skinned people, with huge crops of woolly hair. Treatment of these people by their English and Australian masters was oppressive, but the better nature of the white man was exemplified by a small band of Catholic missionaries who wanted to bring the word of God to one of the most primitive people on earth.

When the first Marist missionaries arrived in Oceania in 1837, the natives were still headhunting cannibals who regularly buried alive unwanted children. An order of nuns, the Missionary Sisters of the Society of Mary, soon followed the Marist Fathers and Brothers. Guadalcanal was not the European's dream of a tropical paradise. The island has one of the most toxic environments on earth. Both natives and whites fall victim to the ubiquitous malaria mosquito. Virtually no one who spends any time on Guadalcanal escapes contracting the disease. Other forms of animal and insect life are equally virulent. The jungle itself is a tangible, seemingly evil presence. Because of the daily rainfall, plant life grows continually, creeping over and enveloping anything in its way. The natives were unlikely candidates for conversion as well. The thrall of their pagan god Puraka was strong, and to wean the people off of their customs of internecine warfare, polygamy, infanticide and cannibalism would have daunted St. Peter himself—especially since the British had prejudiced the natives against Catholic doctrine. Not infrequently, the earliest Catholic missionaries just barely kept their skulls from being converted into drinking bowls after crossing swords with jealous witchdoctors. Furthermore, many natives were infectious lepers. Treating them meant that many of the priests and nuns would doom themselves to the same fate as that of Father Damien of Molokai.26

The dangers and challenges only made the Solomons' missions more attractive to both male and female religious, and the orders were never wanting for volunteers, some of whom stayed on station without respite for decades. One Marist nun, Mother Mary Agnes, spent over fifty years in Oceania, most of them tending to the miserable wretches at the Makogai leper colony. All of the missionaries fell victim to malaria and some to elephantiasis. What to most people would be worse than a term on Devil's Island was an eagerly sought assignment by the Marist missionaries.

As a result of these extreme sacrifices, of the approximately 10,000 natives on Guadalcanal at the outbreak of the war, a large number were Catholic. Missionaries had scored similar successes on nearby Malaita, Bougainville, the largest island of the chain, and even on the tiny islands that housed the remotest mission stations. Solely because of the superhuman efforts of the missionaries, many American airmen were rescued by the natives when shot down in the jungle. The colonial capital was on tiny Tulagi, only two miles long by a half mile wide. Apart from the government bureaucracy and commercial center, Tulagi held that other unmistakable hallmark of English rule: a jail.27

The Japanese occupied Tulagi in May 1942 and in June construction began on an airfield near Lunga Point on Guadalcanal. Natives were rounded up to work as slave laborers on the airstrip. The Catholic missionaries were to suffer barbaric treatment by the Japanese, but every mission building was flattened by American airstrikes.

A Boston diocesan priest, James Hennessy, was one of the first victims of the Japanese invaders. Hennessy had volunteered to work for five years in the missions for Bishop Thomas Wade, a native of Providence, Rhode Island in charge of the See of the Northern Solomons. Though Hennessy's commitment was up in 1941, Wade asked him to stay on until a new priest arrived. The Japanese got there first. In March, prior to their occupation of Guadalcanal, they swarmed all over Bougainville. Hennessy was running the mission station at Lemanmanu on Buka at the time. He was advised to head for the safety of the impenetrable Bougainville mountains, where the Catholic natives would protect him. Hennessy said he would rather be killed at his post than to run away in disgrace. A week later, on St. Patrick's day, he was captured, sent to Kavieng on New Ireland and made a slave laborer in a rock quarry. Two months after that he was shipped to Rabaul, New Britain where he scratched on the wall of his cell "*In te domine speravi, non confundar in aeternum*—James Hennessy." On June 22, he was crammed onto the *Montevideo Maru* with a thousand other prisoners bound for Hainan, China. The vessel was torpedoed north of Luzon by an American sub and all aboard died.28

The American response to the seizure of the islands was Adm. Ernest King's brainchild, Operation "Watchtower." Originally the plan was intended to secure the New Britain—New Ireland—New Guinea area, but with the discovery that an airstrip was being constructed on Guadalcanal, the capture of that fetid outpost became an urgent priority. The Japanese had to be denied air superiority in the area or advancement up the archipelago would be near impossible.29

Commander of the Amphibious Force was Rear Adm. Richmond Kelly Turner, with Maj. Gen. Alexander A. Vandergrift commanding the Marine landing force. The invasion went off on the morning of August 7, 1942. Aboard the attack transport *President Hayes* was another Jesuit chaplain, Lt. Comm. Charles A. O'Neill, who published an account of the historic moment.

> We eased in between the islands in the dark, took up our positions while the Japs were asleep and then at 6:20, just at daybreak, everything let go. It was like thunder from the heavens at dawn. The enemy had time to fire only a few rounds before all their guns were silenced. For an hour our planes dived out of the sky, bombs whistled to earth and machine guns rattled away clearing the beaches. Boats in the harbor were set ablaze, subs at the docks went up in flames, oil dumps and tankers exploded, houses and barracks were set afire and fell to ashes. At 8:10 the Raiders went ashore. Our first men were on the beach. Then wave after wave of Marines

followed them in. Not a Jap was in sight except the few lying
dead on the sand.30

Indeed the landing was a stunning success. By August 8, the 11,000
Marines who went ashore seized the Japanese base at Kukum and the
nearly completed airstrip, which was immediately named Henderson
Field by the gyrenes. The ease with which the Marines took this first position was deceptive. On Tulagi the fighting was much tougher and the
actual battle for Guadalcanal—really a series of ferocious sea, land, and air
engagements—would continue for six months.

Foley had closely followed the course of the battle, at least as closely as
the edited press releases had allowed him to. Over the course of those
months, Marine and army troops suffered much and just barely held on to
their precarious position. The several naval engagements were very costly,
and at times disastrous. On August 9, off of Savo Island, heavy cruisers
Vincennes and *Quincy* were sent to the bottom in a furious night battle. In
early September, transports *Colhoun, Little,* and *Gregory* were lost, and
then on the 15th, the *Wasp* went down.31

The sinking of the *Wasp* was particularly bitter for Foley and everyone
else associated with Boston College. The assistant Air Officer on board
was forty-three year old Comm. John J. Shea, formerly a scholar/athlete in
the class of 1918 who had had a successful career in naval aviation prior to
the war. Assiduous religiosity is generally frowned upon in both the navy
and army officer corps, and usually means the end of upward movement.
But Shea stayed close to his roots with membership in the Holy Name
Society and the Knights of Columbus. On the day that the *Wasp* was torpedoed, Shea was directing firefighting efforts when a huge explosion took
his life. Shea would have been forgotten as just another casualty statistic in
this bitter contest except that the *Boston Post* on October 27 published a
letter that he had written to his five year old son Jackie on June 29. The
letter, full of fatherly advice from the doomed man, could not fail to tug

the heartstrings of the most callous reader. The letter was quite long and read in part,

> ...Fighting for the defense of our country, its ideals and homes, is an honor and a duty which your daddy has to do before he can come home to settle down with you and your mother.
>
> When it is done, he is coming home to be with you always and forever. So just wait a little while longer. I'm afraid it won't be as soon as the two weeks you told me over the telephone.
>
> In the meantime, take good care of mother. Be a good boy and grow up to be a good young man. Study hard when you go to school. Be a leader in everything that is good in life.
>
> Be a good Catholic, and you can't help being a good American.
>
> Play fair, always. Strive to win, but if you must lose, lose like a gentleman and a good sportsman...32

The letter was picked up by the Associated Press and run by many papers that used AP. There was an omission, however. The line, "Be a good Catholic and you can't help being a good American" was inexplicably excised from the text. The Jesuit weekly *America* noted that while Shea died fighting for his country, some felt that the mere mention of Catholicism needed to be suppressed in a "democracy."33

As the Solomons campaign continued, losses mounted. The famous carrier *Hornet* had to be sunk after being extensively damaged. Heavy cruiser *Northhampton* , light cruisers *Junea* and *Atlanta* , and six destroyers, *Benham, Cushing, Barton, Laffey, Monssen, Preston,* and *Walker* were all sent to the bottom in a span of three months. In the Battle of Tassaforonga, where *Northhampton* was lost, another heavy cruiser, *Minneapolis* , shipped two torpedoes which ripped open sixty feet of bow. Enormous pistils of water shot into the sky over the wounded vessel and when the water crashed down on deck, sailors were flattened and swept into the ocean. The most badly hurt man on *Minneapolis* was its chaplain, Fr. Arthur Francis McQuaid, who was also a Boston diocesan priest and B.C. alumnus. He was set ablaze and stumbled in agony to the aid station. McQuaid suffered severe burns on his arms, legs, and face and was not expected to live when he was brought to a hospital on Tulagi. He was blind for two weeks and could not walk or use his hands for two months but by March 1943 McQuaid was back on duty.34

It is axiomatic that when great ships are sunk in wartime, large numbers of men go with them to their watery graves. On occasion, the loss of life seems particularly pointless, as was the case with the CL *Juneau* which exploded and sank instantly after being hit by one torpedo. Sister ships not only failed to pick up survivors in the water but did not even send a distress signal. Only ten men out of one hundred who went in the water survived. Apart from them, all 700 crewmen including the five Sullivan brothers from Waterloo, Iowa, perished.35

Into this maelstrom the *Clymer* was sailing along with her small group of accompanying ships. On January 13 *Allen* and *Taylor* left for Samoa while *Algorab* joined the file. The group arrived at Noumea, New Caledonia on January 18. The Seabees aboard the *Clymer* finished packing their gear and prepared to disembark for their new home. Their chaplain, Father McDonald, had started the cruise sick and was ending it the same way, with a bad cold. As the ships pulled into the harbor, the pleasant ocean breezes were suddenly extinguished by the purple, primitive mountains which looked to Foley as if they had been formed at the dawn of creation. The heat and atmosphere impressed themselves on the crewmen from northern climes. They were a long way from home—10,300 miles from Norfolk since December 17.36

When Foley stepped ashore on the 19th, he had two purposes: one, to bless the land as was his custom, and secondly to seek out the missionary sisters who ran the local hospital. He hopped into an invasion boat with a 100 lb. sack of sugar, a box of apples and one of oranges. On shore he spied two Marines in a truck and asked them for a lift because "no Marine ever 'says no' to a priest." When they got to the hospital Foley discovered that the building had been seized by the French government and the nuns had been forced to leave.37

This was not surprising. All over the globe World War II proved to be a disaster for the Catholic Church, which lost an incalculable amount of property, primarily due to aerial bombing and artillery fire. Churches, schools, hospitals, orphanages, convents and monasteries were seized, burned and razed by both Allied and Axis forces in western Europe. The most notorious, though hardly unusual attack was the wanton destruction of the eight hundred year old monastery of St. Benedict at Monte Cassino by Allied forces in February 1944. As of that year as well, more than six hundred Catholic churches had been destroyed or closed in Poland by the Germans. The human and monetary loss was incalculable.38 In the Far East, missionaries in the Pacific were particularly hard hit, maltreated and dispossessed by both sides.

In lieu of delivering his goods to the nuns, Foley found his way to the cathedral and dropped off the food at the rectory. The priests invited him in for a meal but he knew how short of food they were and so declined the invitation. One of the priests told him that the Sisters of St. Joseph of Cluny ran a school nearby, so he and the priest sped to the *Ecole Libre* in the latest model 1920 *Renault* . School was out during New Caledonia's January summer but Foley could see that the sisters, who also provided for the poor, were in desperate straits. After conversing with Sister Joseph and touring the school he made his way back to the ship. Chief Commissary Steward Bonnette was an easy touch. He gave the chaplain three 100 lb bags of sugar, three 100 lb. sacks of rice, and three big boxes of apples and oranges. Once more Foley got a lift and the mule work out of some Marines. When the Leathernecks carried the treasures into the convent, Sister Joseph's eyes nearly popped out of her head. She rang the house bell and all of the other nuns came running for an apple, which they had not seen for two years. Sister Joseph had just bitten into a juicy specimen when she stopped and asked Foley, "Father, did you steal these?" Foley replied, "Yes, of course Sister, every chaplain is an honest thief." From that moment on , the nuns called him *Pere DePomes* , the "Apple Father."39

Pere DePomes was repaid with two glasses of fine French wine and homemade cookies. Mother Superior also insisted he take some of the sisters' handiwork—delicately embroidered table cloths and doilies which he later sent home to his mother. When not playing Santa Claus to the nuns, Foley explored the town of Noumea. As was his wont in every unusual clime, he was fascinated by the people and environment and recorded detailed descriptions of each in his diary.

> Now I see for myself, for the first time in the flesh, the men and women in the pages of the National Geographic for July. There are Chinese, Javanese, and the natives, the Melanesians. The Javanese women, beautiful and petite are dressed in multi-colored blouses and long skirts. Round their waists are swathed sarongs. Now a mother comes along with her sarong slung across her right shoulder for her youngster, riding cheerfully in his chair that the sarong makes on his mother's right hip. The youngsters look too large, a burden for such delicate, slender mothers…
>
> …In the center of the town of Noumea is the place *Des Cocotiers*, a long rectangular shaped park. The lower portion of the park comprises a small botanical garden surrounding the statue of Governor d'Olry, famed for his pacification of the natives after the 1878 revolt. Place *Des Cocotiers* is a misnomer, because the only coconut trees are a few planted around the edges. Most of the trees are the wide spreading flamboyant, which the winter, their flowering season, has transformed the whole place into a one blazing mass of color with their broad crimson flowers. 40

Foley made the convent his second home while the *Clymer* was docked at Noumea. He brought the nuns another box of oranges, still glistening from condensation from the *Clymer's* galley, and they gave him a new handmade alb. In town he ran into Fr. Ozias Bailey Cook, formerly of St. Victor's church in West Hollywood and currently chaplain of the 3,200 men aboard the flattop *Saratoga* . "Sara" had been torpedoed on August 31, 260 miles southeast of Guadalcanal. Though not fatally damaged, she was *hors de combat* for almost three months at Tongatabu. The Japanese reported her sunk several times in propaganda broadcasts but she lived to fight another day in late November.41

On his way back to the ship he met the chaplain of the *Montpelier* , Carl Knudsen. Knudsen asked Foley to come aboard to celebrate Catholic Mass. According to canon law, Catholics were not allowed to participate in non-Catholic services, so men assigned to a ship or a base with no priest chaplain would have to wait until one was in the area to receive the sacraments. Protestant chaplains did in some instances organize Rosary groups and other activities not strictly sacramental, often assigning a Catholic seaman to lead the group. Conversely, Catholic chaplains were empowered to conduct general services, but not when a non-Catholic chaplain was available. When ashore, Foley bent over backwards to bring Protestant chaplains aboard the *Clymer* for services and was very appreciative when he was invited to bring the sacraments to men who had no priest.42

In this case, Foley heard confessions for two hours aboard the *Montpelier* , then crossed the gangplank to the heavy cruiser *Chicago* for another hour's worth of sins. He was up at 0430 the next morning to say Mass aboard the *Montpelier,* which was attended by men from both ships. Foley praised the sailors for the fine turnout and got to speak to some of them from the *Chicago* , which had been torpedoed at the Battle of Savo Island on August 9. She had just returned to Noumea from having extensive repair work at San Francisco. Nine days after Foley said Mass for her crew, *Chicago* would be sent to the bottom in two thousand fathoms of water at the Battle of Rennell Island.43

Pastor Foley was losing his curate when it came time to say good-bye to Father McDonald of the 35th Seabees. The construction engineers had unloaded all of their enormous pieces of equipment at Noumea, which was the nearest advanced base to the Solomons, 1,150 miles distant. He had been a great help to Foley and a big favorite with the *Clymer's* crew and his own men. As they bade one another farewell, they hoped they would meet again at Boston College some time soon.44

On the 23rd, the *Clymer* was at sea again heading for Suva on the Island of Viti Levu in the Fiji group. The ship made additional preparations for sailing into dangerous waters. Already all white uniforms had been dyed khaki. Now the order "Up Rugs" went around. All the rugs on the ship—including Foley's cushy grey office piece were pulled up and stowed away. In case the vessel was hit, there would be less material to burn. Daily General Quarters at 0445 reminded everyone that danger was omnipresent in those waters. The run from Noumea to Suva was approximately 850 miles and took three days. Foley went ashore and was as always fascinated by the exotic populace. He observed the Chinese merchants and the fourteen-year-old Indian child brides hauling babies of their own. He admired the native Fijian women in their colorful dresses and the well-built men. In his diary he wrote "Traffic cop in color is one for the candid camera fiend. He is dressed in a blue jacket with red belt and white skirt, scalloped at the knees. His hair is a thick mop of black that is almost another head."45

Foley also spied a black priest on the other side of the street. He chased him, identified himself, and was glad of the "tie that binds all priests together the wide world over." Fr. Julian Owanga told Foley about his mission in the hills. At the cathedral he met a Marist, Father Foley, and four nuns who gave him some seeds to send back to his mother. As always, the universality of the church bolstered his spirits. The next day he was still pondering his place in the world. January 27 was the Feast of St. Chrysostom. Sixteen years earlier Foley was praising him in a Latin sermon at Shadowbrook. Now he was a navy chaplain aboard a transport loaded with troops bound for Espiritu Santo, New Hebrides, north of New Caledonia. He thought, "*Tempora Mutantur et nos mutamur in illis.*"46

The code name for Espiritu Santo was "Button"; Guadalcanal was "Cactus." *Clymer's* escort was the hard-fighting destroyer *Buchanan*. The two vessels proceeded through Selwyn Straits, a passage about two miles wide between Pentecost and Ambrym Islands. Like the other islands in Oceania, the New Hebrides were covered with steep, heavily wooded mountains and volcanoes. The mined channel was extremely difficult to negotiate. Just recently the *President Coolidge* struck a mine, swung around, hit another and was lost. The *Clymer* gingerly made the field and passed through the anti-submarine net. The anchorage itself looked like the South Pacific version of Pearl Harbor. That day there were thirty-two vessels all told, including cruisers, minesweepers, destroyers tied up to a tender, cargo and combat transports. Seaplanes circled overhead and rode at anchor. Camouflaged bombers nestled in coconut groves. Father McQuaid's *Minneapolis* was there too, its bow still a gaping maw from the November Tassafaronga battle.47

The next day was Sunday, the chaplain's big day. After two Masses with his own crew and the embarked army troops, Foley arranged with the executive officer for a swimming party for the men. About one hundred of the crew headed up the channel to a conveniently constructed diving platform over a swift cool river. Someone had also rigged up a rope swing on an overhanging tree. The sailors, still boys in some ways, stood in line all day to have their turn, swinging out over the water and plunging thirty feet into the river. A second swing was rigged up further down the bank. This one required the athlete to climb the tree and swing out over the river, with a sheer drop of fifty feet. Some of the sailors who tried this one thought better of it, hung on to the rope, and swung back to safety. Foley, too, stuck to the junior model. One sailor said, "This is the life, January 30, swimming in the old river. We didn't do this in New York."48

The *Clymer* got underway at 1630 on Monday, February 1, heading for "Cactus" A.K.A. Guadalcanal. On that day she was also renumbered, from AP-57 to APA-27. *Clymer* was now part of Task Group 62.9, Amphibious Force, South Pacific, along with three other attack transports and four destroyers. The group was not very impressive. Four attack transports and four destroyers to protect them could handle a sub or a couple of counterpart destroyers, but would be sitting ducks for *Dai Nippon's* much heavier cruisers. As the small force thread the needle through the minefield heading away from Espiritu Santo they passed four Yank cruisers heading in. Everyone aboard the *Clymer* wished the cruisers were going with them to Cactus. Soon they spied another group going the wrong way. This group was composed of five destroyers, a cruiser, and Father Cook's *Saratoga* . To add to the tension, the *Clymer* had a sub alarm which kept the men at battlestations for half an hour before being secured. Zigzag plan was #38, the sharpest of angles.49

At dinner, Foley discussed religion with an ex-Catholic army lieutenant named McRaile, who boasted that he lost the faith at Union College in New York and now despised Catholics. The pair went at it for two hours with four others jumping in on occasion. McRaile declared that religious people are one of three types, those in an intellectual coma, ignoramuses, or hypocrites. He put Foley in the comatose category. McRaile shouted, "Schopenhauer was right. The only thing for a man to do is to put a bullet through his head." There was no reasoning with this line of thought. Foley felt only pity for the bitter young man who had no hope and no future. In his cabin Foley went through the books in the Book of the Month Club package. He read a review in the Book of the Month Club news praising a new selection called *Light on the Jesuits From China* . A line in the blurb went: "The Chinese and the Jesuits both have a reputation for mysterious and devious ways; if you would like to know how justified that theory is you may well start your investigation here."50 Foley would skip that one. He had no interest in reading racist drivel about the Chinese and he mused over the thought that a Jesuit could be both devious and in an intellectual coma at the same time.

This time, the *Clymer* would not make it to Guadalcanal. Word came through that a large Japanese task force was heading directly toward the small group. Other ships headed toward Guadalcanal had already been warned but the *Clymer* group didn't get the word until 0100 on February 3. They reversed direction and poured on the steam to put as many miles between them and the Japanese as possible. Two of the destroyers continued on to engage the Japanese. Foley hoped that the reversal had not come too late. Four attack transports flanked by two destroyers would be raw meat for even a token Japanese force. Flying boats and divebombers overflew them also , apparently heading toward the Canal. By evening the *Clymer* group was safely anchored back at Espiritu Santo. The radio informed them that there was a major engagement underway off Guadalcanal, believed to be another Japanese attempt to seize the island. Foley prayed for the American ships and the men on the island who would once more be taking a terrific pounding.51

In reality, the Japanese were not coming in but pulling out. Operation "KE" was the Japanese swan song at Guadalcanal. Japanese destroyers and planes engaged American destroyers and patrol boats on February 1 and 2 and were quite successful, blowing several PTs out of the water at Savo and Cape Esperance. The Japanese destroyers were also successful in the first phase of evacuating their troops, which was the real purpose of their foray. Even after these engagements, the Americans incorrectly believed that the Japanese were bringing in reinforcements, rather than evacuating. On the 4th, another enemy flotilla of twenty-two destroyers accompanied by a cruiser and considerable air power left Faisi off Bougainville, steamed down the "Slot" and met resistance only from a token force of American planes. Again the Japanese successfully evacuated a number of troops.52

The crew of the *Clymer* were anxiously awaiting news of the battle, which would decide if they were to embark for Guadalcanal again or stay pinned down at Espiritu Santo. On February 5, a radio communiqué from Washington came through, a non-committal item simply stating that a Japanese-American sea battle was being waged in the Solomons. The report did not indicate that the Americans had the upper hand; nevertheless the *Clymer* weighed anchor at 0530, once again heading northward. Foley read between the lines and figured that the report was deliberately vague to deceive the Japanese. He looked forward to finally setting foot on Cactus.53

Notes: Chapter 5

1 Foley interview, March 3, 1995.

2 Foley interview, March 17, 1995.

3 Foley diary, December 14, 1942.

4 Foley diary, December 17, 1942.

5 Ibid.; Giblin, *Jesuits as Chaplains,* 72.

6 Foley diary, December 18, 1942.

7 Foley diary, December 20, 1942.

8 Foley diary, December 24, 1942.

9 James T. Fahey, *Pacific War Diary 1942–1945,* (Boston: Houghton, Mifflin Co., 1963), 7, 8. Fahey's diary was one of the first published which gave the enlisted man's point of view of life aboard a warship in World War II. The "Innocents Abroad" naivete of much of the narrative rings true and would have been representative of the vast number of teenagers in the service seeing the remotest parts of the world for the first time. Like Chaplain Foley, who knew diary keeping was strictly against navy regulations, Fahey's account and the countless others published since the war indicates that the order was widely ignored.

10 Foley diary, December 25, 1942. Foley believed that the film was kept from him for security reasons. A check of the National Archives, which is the depository of much of the film footage shot during World War II, has not turned up the Foley footage. Without question, color

footage of a fully vested priest celebrating Mass on the deck of a warship passing through the Panama Canal would be a stunning visual document.

11 Foley diary, December 26, 1942.

12 Foley diary, December 19, 1942.

13 Foley diary, December 30, 1942. On board the *Montpelier* even Capt. Leighton Wood participated in the ceremony by "walking the plank." Fahey, *Pacific War Diary,* 9. In recent years the shellback ceremony has come under attack from various quarters. In June 1997 the Commandant of the Marine Corps, Gen. Charles C. Krulack called the shellback ceremony "hazing" and signed order 1700.20, threatening disciplinary action for anyone involved in the festivities. Some salty Marines are sad to see this time honored tradition go and feel that Krulack's agenda is another example of political correctness ruining the Corps. *Leatherneck* (September 1997): 2,4. Krulack's dictate obviously applies only to Marine Corps personnel. Naval personnel still stage shellback ceremonies when crossing the equator.

14 Foley diary, January 1, 21, 1943; Fahey, *Pacific War Diary*, 9, 10. Fahey also notes that the radioman fell into the ocean a few days later when his plane was being hauled aboard the ship, after another patrol, "We thought he was gone for good because he was out of sight for some time. One of the whaleboats finally rescued him. This fellow must have a charmed life. The Good Lord does not want him yet."

15 Foley diary, January 2, 1943.

16 Ibid.

17 Foley interview, March 3, 1995.

18 Foley interview, March 10, 1995.

19 Foley interview, March 17, 1995.

20 Foley diary, January 4, 6, 1943.

21 Foley diary, January 8, 1943. "Thou who lightest up the morning with splendor, with glory."

22 Foley diary, January 9, 12, 1943.

23 Foley diary, January 11, 1943.

24 Foley diary, January 12, 1943.

25 Background and operational data are from Samuel Eliot Morison, *The Struggle for Guadalcanal August 1942–February 1943*, (Boston: Little, Brown and Co., 1951). Guadalcanal is one of the most studied of World War II battles and the bibliography is extensive. Large and dry is Richard B. Frank, *Guadalcanal* (New York: Random House, 1990) Histories of particular battles within the campaign are common. See for example, Bruce Loxton, *The Shame of Savo* (Annapolis: Naval Institute Press, 1994) which examines the disastrous sea engagement of August 9, 1942.

26 Rev. Charles F. Decker, S.M. ed, *Saving the Solomons: From the Diary Account of Rev. Mother Mary Rose, S.M.* (Bedford, Massachusetts: The Marist Missions, 1948), 1,4, passim. A number of brave priests were, in fact, killed and eaten. See Richard J. Cushing, *The Missions in War and Peace* (Boston: The Society for the Propagation of the Faith), n.d.), n.p.

27 Ibid., 110.

28 "Fr. Jim Hennessy 1905–1942," pamphlet printed for private circulation by the Mission Academia of St. John's Seminary, 1950, 3, 7–12; Decker, *Saving the Solomons*, 88–91. Hennessy's fate was unclear until after the war. To honor his memory, Cushing formed the "Jim Hennessy Club" which helped the missions. See Bishop Richard Cushing, "An Open Letter to Friends of the Mission," *The Boston Pilot*, 6 March 1943.

29 Decker, *Saving the Solomons*, 113; Morison, *The Struggle for Guadalcanal*, 12, 14.

30 Charles A. O'Neill, S.J., "The 1st Invasion," *Jesuit Missions* (November 1945): 249.

31 Loxton, *The Shame of Savo*, passim.: Morison, *The Struggle for Guadalcanal*, 130–138.

32 Paul L. Blakely, S.J., "A Father's Letter That Will Live," *America* (November 21, 1942), 178, 179. James Patrick Sinnot Devereux who shot to fame as the "hero of Wake Island" was another career officer who was conspicuously devout. It was reported that he led a rosary group during his years of captivity and he too wrote a letter to his son "Paddy," which

was released to the press. The text of the letter appears in James P.S. Devereux, *The Story of Wake Island* (Philadelphia: J.B. Lippincott Co., 1947) 227, 228.

33 *America* (November 7, 1942), 115. In its heyday, *America* was a leading organ of muscular Catholic orthodoxy, patriotic yet willing to criticize the government or any other faction when Catholic rights were violated.

34 Foley diary, January 12, 1943; Sexton and Riley, *History of St. John's Seminary*, 295; Drury, *History of the Chaplain Corps United States Navy*, vol. II, 179, vol. III, 187. McQuaid entered the naval reserve prior to hostilities in February 1941 and had two assignments before shipping on to *Minneapolis* in October 1942. Only four weeks later he nearly lost his life in the Tassafaronga engagement. After recuperating, he served at various stations, including a hitch with the 1st Marine Division. He finished the war as a full commander and transferred to regular navy in July 1946.

35 Morison, *The Struggle for Guadalcanal*, 257.

36 Foley diary, January 13, 18, 1943.

37 Foley diary, January 19, 1943

38 Brig. Gen. William R. Arnold, "We are Strong in Spirit," *Faith of Our Fighters*, ed, Ellwood C. Nance, (St. Louis: Bethany Press, 1944), 99; Bernard R. Hubbard, S.J., *Father Hubbard's report on the need for Jesuit relief and reconstruction in Europe* (Chicago: National Jesuit Fund), 1945, passim.

39 Foley diary, January 19, 1943.

40 Ibid.

41 Foley diary, January 20, 1943; Morison, *The Struggle for Guadalcanal*, 110. Morison theorizes that the "Sara" was the only ship known to the Japanese by name, and so every large ship that was hit was presumed to be the *Saratoga*.

42 Foley diary, January 20, 1943; Drury, *History of the Chaplain Corps United States Navy*, vol. II, 214. For more on the subject of faculties regarding the Mass, see "Military Faculties," *The Ecclesiastical Review* 107 (July 1942): 29–45.

43 Foley diary, January 21, 1943; Morison, *The Struggle for Guadalcanal,* 359–362.

44 Foley diary, January 21, 1943.

45 Foley diary, January 23, 24, 26, 1943.

46 Foley diary, January 26, 27, 1943. "Times do change and we change with them."

47 Foley diary, January 27, 30, 1943. The *Buchanan* was later involved in much of the fighting in the Pacific war, earning fifteen battle stars. On January 22, 1944 she sank the Japanese submarine *RO-37* off Espiritu Santo.

48 Foley diary, January 31, 1943.

49 Foley diary, February 1, 1943; "History of U.S.S. *George Clymer* (APA-27)."

50 Foley diary, February 1, 1943

51 Foley diary, February 3, 1943.

52 Morison, *The Struggle for Guadalcanal,* 364–370.

53 Foley diary, February 5, 1943.

With an unidentified *Clymer* Officer.

Refugee children and three nuns of the Missionary Sisters Society of Mary who fled the Japanese on Bougainville and were carried to Noumea by the *Clymer* in early 1943. Left to Right: Sr. Mary Martial (or Martian), Sr. Mary Ignatius, Sr. Mary Adelberta.

Foley with rescued waif.

Sr. Mary Theresa Cartier, another nun who survived the Japanese onslaught on Guadalcanal, photographed in 1997. (Author's collection)

Saying Mass for Marines and sailors on the deck of the *Clymer* just prior to the invasion of Bougainville. Draper's painting immortalized the scene in oil.

Foley preaching the Gospel during the same Mass.

Clymer officers at one of the "scandalous" ships' dances in Aukland, New Zealand. Left to right: Lt. Cdr. McRae, Dr. Walker, Capt Talbot, Lt. Myer.

While Foley was fighting the war shipboard, his friend and fellow Jesuit from Boston College, Fr. William Leonard, was a chaplain with the army in New Guinea.

Leonard saying Mass. His soldiers assembled a collapsible altar out of ordnance material and carved a crucifix from native hardwood.

Foley saying Mass at Bethseda Naval Hospital, Christmas, 1944. Most of the Congregation were WAVES. He considered his time at Bethesda as purgatory and prayed to be returned to a fighting ship.

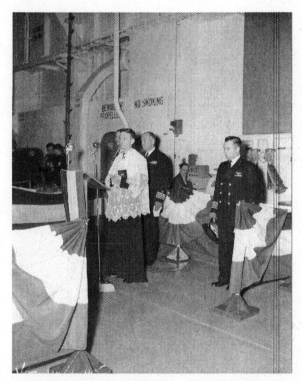

Preparing to speak at the commissioning of the escort carrier U.S.S. *Vella Gulf,* April 1945. Behind him are Capt. McGuigan and Capt. Morse.

Memorial service in the *Vella Gulf* hangar deck for Marine pilot Edward Groves, May 13, 1945. Groves was killed upon takeoff the day before. Note Groves' empty chair, first row left. This service precipitated a blow up between Foley and the executive officer, an ex-Catholic.

Outside Tokyo's "Ginza" in September 1945. Foley's brief escapade in Japan included a joyride in a stolen truck.

Yet another fellow Jesuit from Boston, Fr. Joseph O'Callahan with his kid sister, Rose Marie in Malabon, Philippine Islands, at war's end. Sister Rose Marie had been a prisoner of the Japanese since the beginning of the war. O'Callahan had the signal distinction of being the only chaplain to win the Medal of Honor in World War II.

Lt. Cdr. John Foley aboard the *Vella Gulf* upon its return to San Francisco, Columbus Day, 1945. Like the great mariner himself, Foley loved the sea, but was happy to see America.

Catholic volunteerism in America was so strong in World War II that Catholic schools
such as Boston College and Holy Cross were practically deserted. Jesuit faculty mem-
bers who served as army or navy chaplains assembled at Weston, Massachusetts in
1946.
Front row left to right: Frank Sullivan, William Leonard, Leo MacAulay, Dick Shea,
William Kinneally, Daniel Lynch, Vincent DePaul O'Brien, George King.
Back row left to right: Dan O'Connor, Jim MacGlaughlin, Frank MacDonald, Jim
Geary, Tony Carroll, Carl Morgan, John Bonn, Foley, Joe Shanahan

Rector John Foley welcomed Richard Cardinal Cushing to the dedication of Xavier High School in Concord, Massachusetts on September 10, 1962. Years earlier, Cushing had given Foley a chaplain's "Mass kit" which he used until his death.

First year faculty of Xavier High School. Rector Foley fourth from the left, front row.
Like many other Catholic schools, Xavier soon closed in the chaotic wake of Vatican II.

Fifty years after the war ended, Foley reveals his "forbidden" diary.

The chaplain with the author in 1995.

CHAPTER 6

▼

"GREEN HELL"

Steaming back toward Guadalcanal, lookouts on the *Clymer* spotted a large plane off the starboard beam heading straight for her. Foley plopped on his steel pot, adjusted his lifebelt and took up his station in sick bay. If this was "it", sick bay was where he would be needed. Next to a man's mother, the chaplain was the person he wanted to see when wounded. A few minutes later, the crew stood down from General Quarters. The plane was friendly, a PBY heading for Espiritu Santo. When the excitement abated, Foley went back to his "crying towel" duties. A despondent sailor came to his office worried about his child at home. The sailor's wife had written that the youngster had whooping cough and the sailor could not get it off his mind. Foley succored him, and could not help wondering what the young man's wife was thinking about. Thousands of miles from home the boys wanted to hear about last Sunday's dinner, the latest news from the corner, and what everybody was doing. What they needed was a glimpse of home, in all its day to day ordinariness, because that's what they wanted to come back to. Bad news was like poison, Foley confided to his diary.1

The *Clymer* arrived at Guadalcanal on Sunday, February 7. After 0300 Mass, Foley watched the army troops prepare to disembark in the APA's twenty-seven landing boats. A G.I. who stumbled over a cable was met with gales of laughter and his buddy's barb, "What's the matter,—got a case of the Solomon shakes!" Both crew and passengers were abuzz with anticipation upon landing at Cactus. Only two days later, Lt. Gen. Alexander "Sandy" Patch would inform Admiral Halsey that the island was secure, but everyone knew the high price that had been paid for this particular piece of real estate, and an aura of foreboding still hung in the air like rotting moss.2

Foley went ashore with the troops, carrying a black bag crammed with Chesterfields, Oh Henry candy bars, and apples. His brother Ed Foley had been on the island for two months and Father Foley was eager to see him. Foley stopped a Marine officer for directions but was drowned out by the roar of three P-38 Airacobras that climbed out from behind a grove of coconut trees. Foley admired the sleek deadly look of the ships that the Germans called "fork-tailed devils." As the fighters passed overhead, Foley asked one of the nearby soldiers, "How do you like them?" The G.I. answered, "I like them with that star on them."3

The chaplain bummed a ride to the area of the 101st Medical Regiment, where his brother was supposed to be stationed. To Foley's delight he came upon an open tent with a priest inside vesting for mass. It turned out that the priest was another fellow Bostonian, Fr. Edward B. Flaherty, who had two brothers, Anthony and Walter, also diocesan priests. The Flahertys were known to be tough guys and Anthony even fought professionally under the name of Jack Dillon. When Ed's unit, the 181st Massachusetts National Guard Regiment was mobilized and sent to the Pacific, the group was dominated by a bully who fancied himself a good fighter. A clash was inevitable. A boxing match was arranged on shipboard and Flaherty punched out the loudmouth easily. In the 1940s, two-fisted priests existed in life as well as on film. From that moment on, nobody would take liberties with the chaplain.4

Foley's brother Ed finally showed up, but the three had to postpone their reunion until after Flaherty's Mass. Foley made himself useful hearing confessions to take some of the load off of Flaherty. The men had to shout to be heard as planes were taking off nearby, causing an hellacious din as they did so. The circumstances of confession in the "tropical paradise" of Guadalcanal struck Foley as somewhat different from the dark privacy of the carved oak confessionals back home. Artillery blasted away at Jap positions while parakeets flitted from one coconut tree to another, by this time inured to the noise and chaos of man at war. Foley recorded another unusual wrinkle in his diary. "A pet dog of the soldiers comes along to make friends, but I am cold to him. He doesn't realize I am hearing confessions."5

After Mass, the three comrades caught up on old times. Flaherty and Ed Foley's eyes popped as Foley handed them his bag of goodies. Guadalcanal's bad chow was already legend, and a stockpile of candy and smokes from home was worth its weight in gold. Flaherty left to say another Mass while Foley and his brother went to see some sick Japanese soldiers. Foley talked to the one man who spoke English and found him to be exceedingly friendly. They had all been starving when captured. Ed escorted Foley around the area and told him of the nightly air raids of "Maytag Charlie," "Pistol Pete" and "Millimeter Mike." These characters were instruments of harassment, meant to rouse the Americans from their sleep and keep them constantly on edge and tense.6

When Flaherty joined them again, the trio bounced away in his jeep on the roads carved out of the bush by the Seabees. They toured the coconut plantations owned by Lever Brothers. The coconut oil expressed from the copra was a rich distillate for Lever Brothers and the other international concerns that owned the plantations. The profits were not passed on to the natives who worked the fields for six pence a day and were treated little better than slaves. The environment fascinated Foley, ever the amateur naturalist and botanist. There was much to be fascinated by on Guadalcanal:

> On every side tremendous giant hardwood trees tower well over 100 feet into the sky. They have boles about 6 to 8 feet in diameter flared out at the base by great buttressing roots. Among the trees and beneath them thrives a fantastic tangle of vines, creepers, ferns and brush. Up above some white exotic bird flies away. Insects are all over the ground, ants, "whose bite feels like a live cigarette against the flesh," giant spiders and wasps 3 inches long, scorpions and centipedes. There are strange kinds of rats too, said to be distant relatives of the possum, lizards from 3 inches to 3 feet, and a few snakes.
>
> The air is motionless and stifling. The hot humidity is beyond the imagination of anyone who hasn't been here. Rot lies underfoot everywhere and the ground is springy and mushy with decaying vegetation giving off a sour, unpleasant odor. We are constantly fighting off mosquitoes, bearers of malaria, dengue fever and other fevers. Ed tells me that in the Lunga River are giant crocodiles.
>
> This type of jungle is the type known as "rain forest" from the unbelievably torrential rains that come down. It is not surprising that a thick and heavy dampness is everywhere. What a terrain to have to fight through!7

That night Foley brought his brother Ed back to the *Clymer* and feasted him with ice cream, steaks, and more ice cream. He got permission for Ed to stay aboard for the night but at 4:45 the exec ordered him off the ship. The *Clymer* and some of the other ships in the harbor up anchored and steamed away from Cactus at top speed. The word was that a Japanese task force of a carrier, two cruisers and six destroyers were heading toward them. The *Clymer* had about one hundred Marines aboard, which she had picked up on Guadalcanal. The Marines regaled Foley with war stories and told him that they had particularly dreaded the Japanese naval shelling. The feeling of helplessness was total. All that the men could do was dig in to slit trenches or bomb shelters and pray that a 16 inch shell did not fall on top of them.8

The emergency evacuation from Guadalcanal turned out to be unnecessary and the ship headed back to the island, dropping anchor at 1230 on February 9. More Marine wounded and Japanese prisoners were loaded aboard the *Clymer*. Foley got to visit with his brother and Father Flaherty for another brief spell. He told them that the *Clymer* was now going to be part of the "Guadalcanal Local" making the "Cactus Run." For the next nine months the vessel would indeed be on ferry service to and from Guadalcanal. Foley also told them that like all train schedules, theirs too would be "subject to change without notice.9

The *Clymer* shoved off with over one thousand tired and wounded Marines and army troops. All they wanted now was sleep and hot chow. Many were in poor shape, the majority having had malaria at least once and others succumbing several times. Even the sick ones retained a sense of humor, however. One man told Foley that once he dove into his foxhole during shelling and then felt a tremendous weight on top of him. It turned out to be a horse that stumbled into the trench. The man exclaimed that he had never felt safer while on Guadalcanal.10

Although the 110 Japanese prisoners aboard were generally in very poor condition, a Zero pilot was both healthy and willing to talk to interpreters. He told them that the Japanese called Guadalcanal the "Island of Death" and that Tokyo radio always minimized Japanese losses and inflated American losses incurred by Nippon. The pilot had been forced down in the water and pantomimed to Foley his experience by making a coughing noise indicating his sputtering engine and then using his hands to signal a nose dive and splash down.11

As to the others prisoners, the jungle had taken its toll. Some had beriberi, others distended bellies. Foley tended to these men as solicitously as if they were Americans, though none were Catholic and in other circumstances may have killed a chaplain without compunction. He felt that they should be treated as Americans would hope their own POWs would be treated by the Japanese. Needless to say, Japanese behavior toward American prisoners was generally merciless. Foley never had difficulty separating reality from the attitudes dictated by the government and War Department. A pacifist he was not, and he had no illusions about the transgressions and cruelties of the Japanese; yet his nature and his vocation guided him to see every man as God's image, whatever their sins. He spent some time with a prisoner who spoke a little English. The man had run in the 1932 Olympics, was a physical education teacher in Japan, and had a wife and three children. The man told him that he denied the oath he had taken to die for the emperor under any circumstances for his family's sake. Foley could not hate a man like that and felt that hatred actually diminished a serviceman's efficiency.12

The doctors, too, were more than kind to the Japanese. One doctor attempted to help a young soldier, who adamantly refused to be treated. Through an interpreter Foley asked him why. The youth said that they were told they would be tortured if captured. Foley explained that his stomach was full of water and the doctor could relieve it with a small bunghole. After talking to Foley the boy consented to treatment. Gallons of water flowed out and the boy began to cry.13

One prisoner did succumb to the effects of beriberi and a bullet wound in the chest. Strangely, Captain Moen ordered Foley to conduct a funeral service for the Japanese. At 0400 on February 13, Foley went to the fantail of the ship, where the body was waiting for him. Foley said some prayers over him and asked God to count in his favor the circumstances of his death and burial far from his loved ones. He then gave a signal and the body was consigned to the deep. A man of endless self-examination, Foley pondered the bizarre scene. In the early morning light, a Jesuit far, far from his home in Boston gladly tended to the last earthly needs of a Japanese, with a prayer delivered to a God who the man never knew. Foley was following in a very small way the work of Francis Xavier who attempted to evangelize that inscrutable people in 1549. Jesuit successes with the Japanese had waxed and waned, and in the 1940s Japan was nearly as mysterious to Westerners as it had been four hundred years before. Foley's ceremony was as simple as could be, yet one that he would never forget.14

In fact chaplains were often detailed to bury the enemy. During the battle for Guadalcanal Chaplain James J. Fitzgerald on Florida Island was notified to report to the medical company and given no other information. When he arrived he was told to bury a Japanese flier who had been shot through the wrist and developed gangrene. The flier and two comrades were later captured but he was beyond hope and soon died. Fitzgerald recorded the scene:

> A pitiable site greeted me at the prisoner tent. The one was dead. Another was reading a Bible printed in Japanese. A working party was called out and a guard of three Marines accompanied us to a nearby plot. A few more Marines gathered around. The working party started to dig the regulation grave. The one Japanese continued to read his Bible. I indicated to the other one that he should mark the name of his dead comrade on the cross.
>
> 'Engliss?' he queried.
>
> 'No,' I replied, 'in Japanese.'15

Fitzgerald then allowed the prisoner to recite his ritual in Japanese, which ended with a very distinct "Amen."

Foley's curiosity about the Japanese prisoners extended to reading the naval intelligence reports on each one. The reports revealed the prisoners' military careers, where they fought, period in service, and casualties in their regiment. Most of the prisoners needed to be encouraged to talk by telling them that their names would be forwarded to Japan as POWs. The prisoners knew that information would disgrace their families in the homeland.16

While the prisoners whom Foley dealt with were a sorry lot, the Marines told him about the supposedly gigantic "Imperial Marines" from northern Japan who had been detailed to defend Tulagi. These men were said to be magnificent physical specimens and extraordinarily fanatic and had to be killed to the last man. This story became legend and passed as scuttlebutt through all of the services. As the story traveled, the Japanese Marines became taller and more bestial with each retelling. James Fahey, the young diarist of the *Montpelier,* heard it this way:

> They say the Japs also have some Imperial Marines who are 6 ft. 4" tall. The Japs are expert at jungle fighting and they know all the tricks. You would hardly believe the tricks they use. In the darkness for instance, they like to throw dirt in your eyes and then attack you. Many of our troops get killed learning their tricks. The Japs take all kinds of chances, they love to die. Our troops are advancing slowly, it is a very savage campaign. Very few Japs surrender, they die fighting, even when the situation is hopeless.17

The *Clymer* arrived at Wellington, New Zealand on February 16. The sheer mountains rising up from the shoreline were ruggedly beautiful and when Foley went ashore he found the city to be a true corner of the British Empire. He felt transported back to Heythrop College where he had studied between 1927–1930. Sailors on shore leave usually had predictable desires, namely whiskey and women. Foley went in search of something else, something that he had been dying for since the previous December. He found a tea room, settled himself at a table and gave a waitress his order. He wanted a glass of fresh milk. Upon arrival, he gulped it down and found it to be the creamiest draught he had ever tasted. To wash down the milk he also made a selection of diamond-cut sandwiches, cakes, cream puffs and tarts. To make his fantasy complete, there was also a large slab of butter on the table just waiting to be eaten.18

Not all of Foley's time in Wellington was spent in guilty pleasures. He purchased altar supplies such as incense, vigil lights and charcoal and in the church, St Mary of the Angels, he came upon the most stunning *pieta* he had ever seen. As he gazed on the stricken image of Christ, he thought,

> Our Lord *is* a dead man! There is no doubt of that. "There is no beauty in Him." His eyelids are half open, the eyeballs have the dull glazed look of death, are half hidden under the eyebrows. His mouth is bloody, stained, cracked. He is what he was, a shattered remnant of a man, whose manhood was ploughed and furrowed by the lash of the Roman soldiers until he was no longer Himself. Our Lady is looking off into space with eyes that are most expressive. It seems that she was looking off to Bethlehem.19

Wellington was the last stop for the Japanese prisoners, and, as it turned out, their final resting place. Foley heard sometime later that the Japanese had been mowed down while trying to escape but he had his doubts about this story. Where, he reasoned, would the Japanese go in New Zealand? He knew that the Anzacs were terribly afraid of a Japanese invasion and perhaps eliminated a problem that way.20 Atrocities on both sides would continue until the awful denouement would ring down the curtain on the tragedy in the summer of 1945.

The *Clymer* shoved off from Wellington on February 18. The crew had expected and been promised more than two days in port, but the war would not wait. This time out the vessel was carrying another celebrated group, the 2nd Marine Raiders commanded by Lt. Col. Evans F. Carlson. The detachment had become media stars after a daring raid on Makin in the Gilberts in August 1942. In 1943, a didactic propaganda film, *Gung Ho,* further lionized them. Carlson himself was a bizarre individual, completely out of sync

with Marine Corps thinking and an extreme leftist in politics. He had spent
some time prior to the war with Mao Tse-tung's Eighth Route Army and
had become imbued with a Marxist vision of a New World Order. Carlson
introduced his political theories to his style of command when he returned
to the Marine Corps to organize the Raiders. His principle of *Gung Ho*
(work together), a term that has passed into the language as a synonym for
enthusiasm, was a hodge podge of Communist doctrine and Eastern mysti-
cism. Nor surprisingly, Carlson was an unpopular character with Marine
Corps brass and he only got mixed reviews from his own men.21

The Raiders that boarded the *Clymer* were very unhappy men. They
were promised at least a month of rest at Wellington but were recalled
from liberty after a mere six days. The orders to move came through so
rapidly that more than a few of the Marines were still inebriated. Others
were so hung over they could barely shoulder their equipment as they
struggled up the ship's ladder. A few foolhardy souls attempted to bring
bottles of contraband liquor aboard with them. This was most definitely
not allowed as American warships, unlike the ships of some other nations,
were dry. As each Marine reached the top of the ladder the officer of the
deck ordered them to produce any bootleg they were carrying and smash
the bottles over the scuppers of the ship. Foley stood at the ladder as well,
offering his condolences to every brokenhearted Raider.22

Other passengers along for the ride were members of the New Zealand
Radio Detection Group and two Koreans of the Marines' Intelligence
Department. The ultimate destination was Guadalcanal but there would
be a stop at Espiritu Santo first. Foley heard through official channels of
the losses suffered at the end of January during the Japanese withdrawal of
Cactus. He was glad that he had gotten to hear confessions and give
Communion to the *Chicago*'s crewmen just the week before she went
down.23 He envisioned, too, the likely fate of the *Clymer* had she been in
the area that night. The Japanese had been successful in sinking swift
patrol boats, so a ponderous APA would have been like a slice of rare roast
beef for them. So far, the *Clymer*'s luck had been good, almost too good.

Which is not to say that navy life was free of vicissitudes. The chaplain's Mass was always conducted under somewhat difficult conditions. When held below decks, the congregation was crammed into a space certainly not designed for divine worship. Mass on deck was less confined but presented its own problems. The weather did not always cooperate, even though the environment in the Pacific was more conducive to open-air activities than that of the Atlantic. Even on bright, sunny days the wind could play havoc with the portable Mass equipment. Foley had difficulties along this line while rigging for church on this cruise. As he covered his altar with a linen, the wind whipped it off and it was clear that it was not going to stay put until secured with navy-issue thumbtacks. Candles too were out of the question. Though he attempted to light them behind the stern of one of the boats, when placed on the altar they were immediately extinguished by one puff of wind. Furthermore, Foley had to modify the rubric regarding extending the hands during Mass. He was forced to use both hands to hold down the pages of the missal.24

These were not meaningless inconveniences. The Tridentine Mass in the pre-concilior era orchestrated every hand movement and prescribed every piece of altar furniture. Military and naval chaplains were expected to carry out their faculties in strict accordance with rules laid out by the Military Ordinariate even if (or particularly since) there were no ecclesiastical superior in the area. 25 A concern of some bishops when allowing their men to enlist in the services was that they might "go Asiatic" if they were far away from their diocese for an extended period of time and that they would relax the strict observance of Mass regulation. In fact, a number of ex-chaplains were later involved in the Second Vatican Council and became vocal advocates for major modifications in the Mass, including use of the vernacular and even more extreme changes in the life of the Church.26

Whatever changes were to come in the future, John Foley was determined to observe the letter of the law as far as wind and tides would allow. After the *Clymer* anchored at Espiritu Santo on February 23, the Marine

Raiders were disgorged and Foley boarded the AK *Alchiba* with books and magazines for her crew. The sailors told him *Alchiba*'s hard-luck story. The vessel had done yeoman work delivering ammunition, fuel and supplies during the Guadalcanal campaign but was torpedoed by the Japanese submarine I-16 off of Lunga Point on November 28. The tin fish detonated the gasoline and ammunition packed in the holds and the explosion sent flames 150 feet in the air. The two casualties were soldiers who jumped overboard in a panic and were sucked into the propellers. The ship was saved only by beaching, though fires continued to rage for five days. Repairs had hardly begun when she was struck by two more torpedoes on December 7, resulting in more casualties. In January she was brought to Espiritu Santo for a patch-up to make her seaworthy for the journey to Mare Island for permanent repairs. Foley described the extensive damage: "Decks like tiddle winks from heat of the explosion. Port side same wave motion. Holes in her side like pieces of paper pierced by pencil."27

There was little time for shore leave when a ship was making the "Cactus Run." The *Clymer* headed back toward Guadalcanal on February 26, this time ferrying the 35th Seabees bound for Russell Island, north of the Canal. Foley was kept busy again, since many of the men were Catholics from Boston. The pace was glacial because the *Clymer* and the *John Penn* were slowed down to eleven knots from their usual speed of eighteen knots due to the two Liberty ships accompanying them. Three destroyers screened the column, but APAs had only their relative speed for protection and plodding along at eleven knots in those hot waters was an engraved invitation for any Japanese sub fortunate enough to come upon the sluggish group. Again, the *Clymer*'s luck held.28

Once back on Guadalcanal Foley sought out his brother and Father Flaherty. Foley invited them to spend the night aboard the *Clymer* and neither one of them needed to be coaxed. The trio piled into Flaherty's jeep and headed back toward the harbor. Flaherty was known as a maniac driver and he gave Foley the full treatment on this outing. At some points, the vaunted Guadalcanal mud enveloped the tires to the hubs but Flaherty kept them from getting stuck through speed and nimble maneuvering. The jeep tore through the primeval ooze and headed into what seemed to be black, impassable jungle. Foley felt the menace in his bones. "The tall trees were being strangled by thick vines, some were dead already, mats of heavy vines hung from others. The atmosphere was dank and the ground was alive with creeping crawling things, lizards, bugs, etc. Through here the sun never came. The trees were alive also with talking things, toads and whatnot. The green hell of popular imagination all right."29

Foley's brother had already shown him the Lunga Point area, where a furious battle had raged the previous October. He also heard the inspiring story of a fellow navy chaplain, Fr. Matthew Keough of Philadelphia. Keough was with the 7th Marines 1st Division, but on the night of October 25, when it appeared that Col. Chesty Puller's position was about to be overrun, Keough shepherded the Third Battalion of the Army's 164th to the front. The army troops were green and had mistakenly been brought to regimental headquarters rather than the combat area where they were desperately needed. Keough knew the terrain and even though it was pitch black and heavy rain was falling, he guided them over a mile through the jungle. Puller greeted him when he arrived with the reinforcements and Keough accompanied the bombastic colonel through the night, feeding squads of fresh troops into the depleted line. Puller, an Episcopalian, had great respect for Catholic chaplains and contempt for those of his own faith. He put Keough in for a Silver Star but the navy brass downgraded it to a Bronze Star.30

Stories such as Keough's always elicited a little pride in Foley's breast, even if Keough was not a Jesuit. For the time being, Foley's services would be taken up in the role of gracious host. After the trio boarded the *Clymer* from nets, they feasted on steak, fresh vegetables, real butter, fresh peaches with ice cream, lemonade, Coca-Cola and orange juice. Since Flaherty and Ed Foley had been eating from cans for months, the food was like manna from heaven. When ushered into their staterooms, they feared that the soft mattresses would keep them awake. They were used to good, hard army cots. The next day, after Flaherty and Foley did their Masses, Chief Bonnette whipped up hot donuts for the guests. Before leaving the ship, they were served more steaks and more desserts until they were finally gorged. Foley packed a box of apples, oranges and chocolate bars for them and lowered it down into the tank lighter that took them back to Cactus. 31 It paid to know a navy chaplain stationed aboard a warship. Whatever dangers sea duty afforded, the men ate well.

The *Clymer* shoved off again for New Caledonia. En route she traversed the Coral Sea, graveyard of the *Wasp*. This time the ship was empty of passengers except a dozen Marines and two army stowaways. Foley got the story out of the latter. The two young men had been ordered to kill flies in the Officers' Mess, but were glared at by some officers during their meal. The commanding officer insisted they carry on so they were damned if they did and damned if they didn't. They decided to go over the hill. Foley thought the story a little thin, though he well knew that enlisted men were often squeezed by conflicting orders.32

Once docked, Foley made arrangements to say Mass for the ships tied up with her including the *John Penn*, the *Argonne* and the *San Juan*, one of the cruisers in the task force of the *Saratoga*. Foley also wanted to catch up with old friends such as Fr. Frank McDonald, S.J., who made the Pacific voyage with him. McDonald had a thriving parish with the 37th Seabees and had not been sick a day since disembarking the *Clymer*. Foley also had to check on his new friends, the Sisters of St. Joseph of Cluny. They were overjoyed to see *Pere De Pomes*, the "Apple Father." *Pere De Pomes* blessed the children in the polyglot classroom. There were Japanese, Chinese and Javanese all under the sisters' care. The world may have been at war, but the Church's work for all people went on. A six year old boy, mesmerized by the priest, followed suit and blessed everybody.33

On Ash Wednesday, Foley had Fr. Fred Gehring, C.M., as dinner guest. The two had not seen each other since their days at chaplain school together. In the interim, the flamboyant Vincentian had become a celebrity, if not a full-blown war hero, due to his exploits during the

Guadalcanal campaign. After leaving the chaplain school, Gehring had been assigned briefly to the 12th Naval District and then reassigned to a Seabees unit that was sent to Cub #1 at the end of September 1942. Cub #1 was navy code for Guadalcanal, at that time the most forward and important of advance bases.34

At the same time that Foley and the Torch expedition were training for and then executing the North African campaign, Gehring was making a name for himself, like Father Keough and the other "Padres of Guadalcanal," as a hero to the bedraggled men on Cactus. As was the case with so many other Catholic chaplains, admiration for Gehring reached across religious lines. An oft-told story of the period related the Christmas 1942 celebration that Gehring arranged for the men, many of whom had thought that they would be home for Christmas but were still in the oppressive Solomons. Gehring said a midnight Mass and arranged a concert in miniature, enlisting a Jewish boxer, Barney Ross, to hammer out a few tunes on a tired hand organ while he accompanied on violin.35

As a Vincentian missionary in China prior to the war, Gehring had often worked with orphans and in a strange twist of fate, he would also become the caretaker of an orphaned Chinese child on Guadalcanal. Catholic natives had found the girl in a ditch bleeding to death. Her skull had been fractured, apparently by a rifle butt, and her arms and legs had been painstakingly carved by a saber or bayonet. The natives brought her in to the American lines. A navy doctor dressed her wounds but held out little hope for her survival. The C.O. placed her in the care of Gehring who put a medal around her neck and consigned her to Mary's providence. Her mere existence was a baffling mystery. There was no apparent reason for a young Chinese girl to be found in the Solomons' jungles. Needless to say, she became the Marines' mascot, and was pampered and fawned over by the hardened Leathernecks. Gehring christened her "Patsy Li" which he claimed meant "little white plum blossom" and in January 1943 he brought her to Espiritu Santo to turn her over to *Pere* Jean, a French missionary who ran a hospital for the natives there. A few months later, the girl who never should have been on Guadalcanal and who never should have survived her wounds was recuperating and being schooled by Marist sisters on Efate. Thus the Church's "jungle telegraph" worked one more minor miracle.36

Gehring had also had a memorable run in with Admiral Halsey when that august personage went to Guadalcanal to inspect conditions after he replaced Vice-Adm. Robert Ghormley as COMSOPAC. Halsey's jeep became bogged down in the mud and one of his aides flagged down Gehring, who happened to be passing by in his own jeep. Halsey inspected the chaplain intently and asked him to sum up the situation with no holds barred. Gehring told the admiral honestly that morale was suffering due to the poor supply situation and that there was a general fear that Guadalcanal was going the way of Bataan. Halsey snapped back, "This won't be another Bataan, dammit. It won't be another Singapore either. It'll be more like Thermopylae. Maybe that's the wrong comparison too. The Greeks held at Thermopylae, but they didn't win. We're going to win , and you and I will both see Yamamoto in hell!" When Gehring got Halsey to his destination the admiral hopped out with a final word, "I didn't just come here for a two dollar tour of your jungle!"37

While Gehring was a particular favorite with war correspondents it would be wrong to characterize him as a showboat, as his dedication to the men was thoroughly real. He was decorated with the Legion of Merit both for his work on the front and his hazardous missions behind enemy lines to evacuate groups of missionaries escaping the Japanese. Ultimately Gehring was a man who certainly enjoyed his richly deserved spotlight. One young writer for *Yank* on Guadalcanal, Mack Morriss, whose diary was published posthumously in the 1990s, summed up the feelings of any number of men on Cactus regarding Gehring. Morriss, a non-Catholic, was told to write a piece on a front-line chaplain but had no respect for the ones he had worked with. He decided to seek out the two Catholics in the area for the story. He confided to his journal, "I know for a fact that Father Finnegan of the 35th was in the middle of it because I saw him up there.

He and Father Gehring of the navy have bolstered my faith in the cloth after a couple of pretty unwholesome instances I've run into in others. There are Chaplains and Chaplains, I've found out."38

When Foley and Gehring dined together on March 10, the latter related his many exploits since their June graduation from chaplain school. Little did Foley know that he too would become a caretaker to a group of nuns and others who had escaped the Japanese. Foley was most impressed by Gehring's description of the mass burials he conducted on Guadalcanal, sometimes two hundred men at a time. Though Foley would not swap his shipboard billet for anything, he regretted that so many men died without the comforts of Last Rites. He compared that situation with the problems his boys had. A few days later one of the *Clymer*'s pharmacist mates attempted to commit suicide with sleeping pills. Foley had already counseled this man who had been brooding over past misdeeds and reading Poe, which apparently sent him over the edge.39

Reunions with old comrades were all too brief, and the *Clymer* was one of the busiest ships on the Cactus run. She continued making her rounds, primarily between Espiritu Santo and Guadalcanal throughout the month of March. But the fraternity of Jesuits was everywhere, and the Boston College cadre was ubiquitous. On one trip to Guadalcanal the *Clymer* loaded up the 182nd Infantry, a Massachusetts National Guard Regiment in the 26th Yankee Division along with their chaplain, Fr. Laurence J. Brock, S.J., another B.C. man. Brock too had earned his stripes on the "Island of Death." Like Gehring, he was awarded the Legion of Merit for outstanding service on Guadalcanal and would spend another tough year in the Southwest Pacific Area.40

Brock was also known as a great fund-raiser for the missions. As noted, every mission building in the Solomons was destroyed, either by Axis or Allied action. The Catholic chaplains who served on Guadalcanal and through the rest of the war took up collections especially for the Society of the Propagation of the Faith to rebuild the missions after the war. The director of the Boston office at the time was Bishop Richard Cushing, soon to assume control of the entire diocese, and a fervent supporter of the missions. Brock returned over $3200 to the Society, raised from the ranks of the 182nd. Division Chaplain (Lt. Col.) James E. Dunford, a Boston diocesan priest, sent in $1600. John F. Culliton, a priest from Rhode Island serving in the Russells delivered over $1000. The story was the same with the other "Padres of Guadalcanal," but chaplains in every theater had the same idea. Thomas A. Duross, S.J., from the New York Province took up collections from his men for the support of the local native chapel in North Africa.41 The chaplains never ceased to be amazed by the generosity of the men of all faiths in their fund-raising for the missions.

While funds for the missions flowed from the battlefronts back to the United States, chaplains did often find themselves short of devotional items that needed to be sent from home. Individual parishes often did this but the most effective organizations in this line were the Chaplains' Aid Association in New York, The National Catholic Community Service, and the Confraternity of The Most Precious Blood. Over the course of the war these groups sent approximately three million dollars worth of prayer books, missals, New Testaments, leaflets, holy pictures, and rosaries overseas. The provision of rosaries was somewhat difficult at the beginning of the war because some of the areas that produced the traditional cocoa beads from which they were made fell under the control of the Japanese. Plastic beads were used as a substitute for the duration. The most ornate and expensive items that the aid associations provided were Mass kits and Benediction sets. Many priests had the Mass kits given to them by their home parish but Benediction sets were valued prizes that were much sought after. Often a chaplain's flock would fashion a monstrance, censer, boat, and candelabra from G.I. material at hand and many of these items were beautiful examples of religious "trench art."42

When Foley first saw Brock, he was wrestling with his mattress, trying to pound the lumps out before boarding the *Clymer*. When Brock, Father Flaherty and Ed Foley were treated to Foley's customary largesse, courtesy of the *Clymer's* larder, they gorged themselves on steak and peaches and cream until they were ready to burst. While waiting to depart Cactus for another run to Espiritu Santo, Foley was amused by an example of "nose art." On one recon plane he saw "a queer little fellow. He wore a top hat and tails, was apparently flying, with his four legs dangling down; in his hands was a camera that he was pointing at the earth below. On his face was a big broad smile. We asked the mechanic what he was. 'Shutterbug' was the answer."43

The *Clymer* ferried Father Brock's 182nd regiment to Suva, Fiji, to engage in maneuvers, presumably for a future attack on New Georgia. En route Foley and Brock were angered by a controversy that was raging in the newspapers back home. From January 1942 detective writer Rex Stout had chaired the War Writers Board, one of many government propaganda organs. Stout had an implacable hatred of Germans as a people and from the Board's beginnings, he directed all efforts with the racist thesis that the "German character" was at the root of the war. He also lashed out viru-lently at anyone who offered any criticism of Roosevelt. His increasingly hysterical writings and radio broadcasts reached a crescendo on January 17, 1943, with the publication of an article, "We Shall Hate, or We Shall Fail" in the *New York Times Magazine* . His advocacy of genocide was indistinguishable from the Nazi product, simply with the names changed.44

This latest polemic was so virulent, even given the low standards of tol-erance and reason prevalent in wartime, that it caused a firestorm of protest. Foley and Brock, discussing the issue, were repulsed by Stout. As clergymen who were themselves risking their lives on a daily basis along with their charges, they saw the bald hypocrisy of a Park Avenue writer ordering them to hate the men they were forced to fight. Foley consigned his thoughts to his diary:

> Strange, spreaders of gospel of hate are those sitting behind
> comfortable desks, far from the front lines. I have spoken

with men who fought in the second front in Africa, when soldiers from our own ship were assault troops, I have been with Marines on Guadalcanal, and soldiers, 147th, 164th, and 182nd regiments, and Carlson's Raiders, and not one of them ever said that he was motivated by blind hatred. Yet these are men who have killed their fellow man…

Attitude of Leslie McNair, Gen. of Air Ground Forces, who made a speech in a similar vein, hardly squares with President Roosevelt's expressed wish that this war must result in a re-Christianization of the world. That means not when the war is over, merely, but now also. Our boys are still Christians when they fight, and not pagans.

Their spirit with others—duty to fight, but not duty to nurse vindictive hatred. Spirit with selves—unselfishness, self sacrifice, self-denial, unity, cooperation for the common good.45

Despite the rhetoric of the stateside fireaters it appears that very few men were in the service due to a fanatical hatred of the Germans and Japanese, even taking into account the atrocities committed by the Axis powers. Foley's philosophy, and that of many of his fellow chaplains, was that the men were fighting for what men have always fought for: to get home.46

On the way to Suva from Guadalcanal, the *Clymer* was dogged by a submarine and fired on, but the torpedo went wide, a near-miss being as good as a mile. Foley wondered how the chairborne warhawks would react if they could see the white signature of a murderous torpedo bearing down on *them*. The doughty APA managed to shake the sub and make it back to Suva on March 29. The 182nd was debarked and again, Foley was sad to see an old friend go, but he and Father Brock planned to meet back home when the war was over.47

The pace for the *Clymer* would not slacken. On April 7, she embarked the entire First Battalion of the 132nd Infantry Regiment, a Chicago National Guard outfit from Tulagi. The Second and Third Battalions were boarded on the *John Penn* and the *General Fuller* respectively. Forty miles south of Guadalcanal, the TWEET, TWEET, TWEET of General Quarters was sounded, and the ships in the convoy were descended upon by torpedo bombers. At the same time, back on Cactus, a swarm of enemy bombers pounded the "secured" island in the most intense action there in months. Miraculously, none of the ships in the *Clymer* group were hit and a sub that tailed them that night was likewise unsuccessful, and sent to the bottom by an accompanying destroyer. An official navy communiqué claimed that of ninety-eight Japanese planes that hit Guadalcanal, thirty-seven were brought down. Once again, the *Clymer* was undamaged. "Our Lord has been taking care of us," thought Foley.48

On April 15, the *Clymer* was once more heading for Guadalcanal, this time carrying the 145th Regiment. An army officer, Captain Love, told him that he and few others were doing a reconnaissance problem forty miles into the Fijian hills. The Americans had talked to a French missionary priest and then decided to go swimming. They were surrounded by natives young and old, who stood, mute, watching them as they prepared to enter the water. Love emptied his pockets of change and a knife, then took out his Rosary. The children shrieked with glee and ran to the priest to tell him that the Americans were the same as them. Then they returned to swim with the G.I.s. As always, the universality of the Church reached across racial, cultural, and language differences. Foley enjoyed the story, but little did he realize he was about to become Mother Hen to his own eclectic group of refugees. 49

Notes: Chapter 6

1 Foley diary, February 5, 1943.
2 Foley diary, February 6, 1943.

3 Foley diary, February 7, 1943.

4 Foley diary, February 7, 1943; Sexton and Riley, *History of St. John's Seminary,* 271; Foley interview, March 6, 1995. Information about the Flahertys was also provided by Fr. John A. Saunders, retired Boston diocesan priest who has an encyclopedic knowledge of the diocese from the 1930s to the present.

5 Foley diary, February 7, 1943.

6 Ibid.

7 Ibid.

8 Ibid. The same feelings were expressed in Richard Tregaskis' *Guadalcanal Diary.* In the popular film version of the story, a naval barrage is used as the vehicle for a serious discussion of religion. In an underground shelter, a Marine, "Taxi Potts," played by William Bendix, agonizes over his lack of attention to religion and his fear and helplessness at that moment. He is unsure if he is sorry for all he has done but he "can't tell them bombs to hit somewhere else." The chaplain, "Father Donnelly," played by Preston Foster, listens intently and "Amens," giving his blessing to Taxi's sentiments. While a powerful scene, Taxi's lack of contrition for wrongdoing would have been unacceptable to Catholic doctrine and certainly would not merit approval by an orthodox priest. Starting with Pat O'Brien's portrayal of Father Duffy in Warner Brothers' 1940 film, "The Fighting 69th," the Catholic chaplain became a stock character in many World War II movies. The padre was inevitably a devout but bare-knuckled Irish American, as ready to throw a punch or dance a jig as intone a prayer. While the figures were stereotypical, the images were overwhelmingly positive, unlike almost all modern film depictions of Catholics. Steve O'Brien, "Perhaps We'll Land on Friday': The Catholic Chaplain in World War II Films," paper delivered at "World War II: A Dual Perspective" Conference, Siena College, June 4–5, 1998.

9 Foley diary, February 9, 1943.

10 Foley diary, February 10, 11, 1943.

11 Foley diary, February 12, 1943.

12 Foley interview, March 10, 17, 1995. See also Yuki Tanaka, *Hidden Horrors: Japanese War Crimes in World War II* (Boulder: Westview Press, 1996). This recent account describes various Japanese atrocities such as cannibalism, enforced prostitution, massacres of civilians (including nuns), biological warfare and ghastly "medical" experiments conducted by Unit 731, similar to those carried out by Dr. Joseph Mengele at Auschwitz.

13 Foley interview, March 10, 1995.

14 Foley diary, February 13, 1943. For the early Jesuits in the East see William V. Bangert, S.J., *A History of the Society of Jesus* (St. Louis: The Institute of Jesuit Sources, 1986); George Schurhammer, *Francis Xavier: His Life, His Time*, 4 vols. (Loyola University Press, 1973–1982); Neil S. Fujita, *Japan's Encounter with Christianity* (Mahwah, New Jersey: Paulist Press, 1991).

15 Grant, *War is My Parish*, 117, 118.

16 Foley diary, February 15, 1943.

17 Fahey, *Pacific War Diary*, 46. Also see Burris Jenkins, *Father Meany and the Fighting 69th* (New York: Frederick Fell, Inc., 1944) 22. "The Jap is stripped to athletic shorts and contrary to reports appears big and muscular—confirming later discovery that the island is manned by picked Japanese Imperial Marines." Meany, A Jesuit and formerly the business manager of *America*, was one of the chaplains of the vaunted "Fighting 69th" who followed in Father Duffy's shoes. Meany participated in the invasion of Makin Island in the Gilberts and was badly wounded by machine gun fire in the arm, shoulder and chest on November 20, 1943. As if in a movie, the bullet struck, bent and detached a religious medal from his neck. Meany suffered for an hour before being rescued.

18 Foley diary, February 16, 1943.

19 Ibid.

20 Foley interview, March 10, 1995.

21 An idolatrous biography of Carlson is Michael Blankfort, *The Big Yankee: The Life of Carlson of the Raiders* (Boston: Little, Brown and Co.,

1947). In a recent magazine article, one of Carlson's officers, John Apergis, gave his opinion of Carlson's indoctrination. "The West Coast Marines— we referred to them as the Hollywood Marines—had a more liberal atti- tude toward this philosophy than those of us who had joined up in the East. To us, it seemed that Carlson was launching a subliminal attack on our minds, striving to convert us to Oriental thinking." Though a junior officer, Apergis later had a blow up with Carlson after a blunder of Carlson's nearly got him and his column wiped out in a Japanese ambush. Greek-American Apergis was depicted in the film *Gung Ho* by J. Carroll Naish, though in real life, he was not along on the Makin raid. See inter- view of John Apergis by John Moens, "Marine Raider in the Pacific," *Military History* (August 1998): 42-48.

22 This story was related by one of those said Raiders, the memory still vivid of that "unholy destruction of perfectly good booze" fifty-five years later. Letter to author from Mr. Ben F. Carson, "B" and "E" Companies 2nd Marine Battalion, 2/42 to 2/44 dated December 26, 1998

23 Foley diary, February, 20, 1943.

24 Ibid.

25 Strangely, naval chaplains were allowed at least one special consider- ation that army chaplains were not. They could dispense with the Eucharistic fast "whenever the weather is oppressive, avoiding all danger of scandal and wonderment, those belonging to the naval services stationed in the Philippine Islands, who must rise early in the morning to perform their laborious naval duties, so that they can take some liquids on Sundays and Holy Days of Obligation before the reception of Holy Communion." "Analecta," *Ecclesiastical Review* (July 1942): 32.

26 One such character was Bernard Haring, *Embattled Witness: Memories of a Time of War* (New York: The Seabury Press, 1976). This book is a brief account of his life in the German *Wermacht*. Since the German army had very few chaplains and clergymen were not exempt from military duty, Haring was officially a medic and acted as a priest surreptitiously, to avoid arrest. After the war he became a celebrated modernist theologian.

No causal link can truly be discerned between service as a chaplain and modernist views however, since other former chaplains remained sincerely orthodox and committed to the Latin Mass.

27 Foley diary, February 24, 1943; Naval Historical Center, *Dictionary of American Naval Fighting Ships,* 154. The *Alchiba* remained a troubled ship. Repaired extensively, she soldiered on until the end of the war, but was constantly laid up with engine troubles.

28 Foley diary, February 25, 26, 1943.

29 Foley diary, March 1, 1943. On this date Foley was promoted to Lieutenant senior grade.

30 Keough had been wounded in a bombing raid only three days earlier, on October 22 and would receive the Purple Heart. The reasons for the downgrading of the Silver Star decoration are inexplicable though certainly there was reluctance in some quarters to issue decorations to chaplains in any case. Keough's citation read in part, "Courageously volunteering to act as guide for a reserve battalion ordered forward to reinforce our lines. Keough skillfully directed the battalion's night advance to the front and, despite the hazards presented by difficult terrain and heavy rainfall, promptly brought it to the designated position thereby preventing a possible serious penetration of our territory by attacking enemy forces." Drury, *History of the Chaplain Corps United States Navy,* vol. II, 177; vol. III, 147, 148. Puller was once approached by a Protestant chaplain who wanted him to order Protestant soldiers not to join the Catholic Church. He replied, "Holy smoke, man, we can't do that! If they're deserting you, there must be a reason. If you fellows would get down to work like the Catholic chaplains, you'd have no trouble." He later found the same chaplain away from his unit during a battle and observed that the Catholic chaplains were always in the line and Protestants always seemed to avoid it. Puller told his officers, "In all our fighting I've known only a few Protestant chaplains worth their rations." He later excoriated his own Episcopal bishop over the issue and told him that while Protestants sent poor characters to the chaplaincy, "Catholics pick the very best, young,

virile, active and patriotic. The troops look up to them." Davis, *Marine!*, 158, 159, 188, 189, 201.

31 Foley diary, March 1,2, 1943.

32 Foley diary, March 2, 4, 10, 1943.

33 Foley diary, March 6, 8, 9, 1943.

34 Foley diary, March 10, 1943; Drury, *History of the Chaplain Corps United States Navy*, vol. III, 103.

35 Paul MacNamara, "Father Gehring," *Catholic Digest*, (Jan 1945): 45–48. The story was published originally in *Cosmopolitan*. Others concerning Gehring appeared regularly in newspapers and periodicals.

36 The Patsy Li story also was widely circulated, particularly by *New York Times* war correspondent Foster Hailey. The padre himself wrote it up as a biography of the girl grafted on to his own autobiography in Frederic P. Gehring, C.M., *A Child of Miracles: The Story of Patsy Li* (New York: Funk & Wagnalls Co., Inc., 1962). The tale had a bizarre conclusion. A Chinese woman named Ruth Li lost a daughter named Patsy when the Japanese torpedoed her ship fleeing Singapore in February 1942. After the war she heard the story of Gehring's Patsy Li and was convinced it was her own daughter. Gehring could not believe that the child, whom he named arbitrarily, and who was found four thousand miles from Singapore, could be this woman's daughter. Ruth Li traveled to the Marist orphanage, became convinced that the girl was hers, and returned to the East with her. However, the woman's personal life was troubled and after a few years she told Gehring that she could not keep Patsy. Gehring arranged a Catholic schooling and she eventually married and went into nursing. Patsy Li married a second time and now Mrs. Fasano, attended Gehring's funeral at Philadelphia's St. Vincent's Seminary in April 1998. See Obituaries, *The New York Times*, May 3, 1998, 47.

37 Gehring, *A Child of Miracles*, 130, 131. A sanitized version of this incident was portrayed in the 1959 film *The Gallant Hours*, produced by actor/director Robert Montgomery. The movie was a semi-documentary that centered on Halsey's retrieval of the Guadalcanal situation.

Montgomery, who knew Gehring and Halsey well, had the admiral picking up the chaplain on a trail, rather than vice-versa, and then conversing in polite tones. The character of Halsey, played by Jimmy Cagney in one of his last roles, soft pedaled the demeanor of the oft-profane admiral. Likewise the characterization of the chaplain as an exceedingly gentle, almost angelic entity hardly mirrored the reality of the Brooklyn-born Gehring, who had seen the world and all of the evils in it. Whether or not Halsey and Gehring are with Yamamoto in hell is another story.

38 Mack Morriss, *South Pacific Diary 1942–1943* (Lexington, Kentucky: The University Press of Kentucky, 1996), 79. A portion of Gehring's citation for the Legion of Merit is found in Drury, *The History of the Chaplain Corps United States Navy,* vol. III, 177. Sister Mary Theresa Cartier, SMSM originally from Holyoke, Massachusetts, was one of the missionary sisters who had a series of harrowing adventures escaping through the jungle one step ahead of the Japanese. The butchery of Fathers Engebrink and Duhamel and Sisters Mary Sylvia and Mary Odilia convinced the remaining missionaries to make a break for it before they too were slaughtered. The firebombing of the cathedral by the Americans helped decide the matter as well. Mary Theresa and the others were tended to by Fathers Reardon and Gehring upon their arrival in the American lines. Mary Theresa spent the rest of the war nursing lepers on Fiji before returning to Guadalcanal and continuing missionary work until being sent home in 1983. The feisty nun, now in her 90s lives in her order's retirement home in Waltham, Massachusetts and regularly tells her story at Guadalcanal veteran reunions. See Sister Mary Theresa, "Horrors Start As Yellow Men Strike," Pictorial Review, *Boston Sunday Advertiser,* June 27, 1943.

39 Foley diary, March 16, 1943. After leaving the navy Gehring continued a close relationship with veterans of the Guadalcanal campaign until his death at the tender age of ninety-five. Toward the end his memory failed him. In 1995 the author contacted him for reminiscences of John Foley, but Gehring did not remember knowing him.

40 Foley diary, March 23, 1943. Brock eventually was promoted to lieutenant colonel. Part of Brock's citation for the Legion of Merit reads, "In his unceasing efforts to carry the word of God to troops fighting in perilous forward areas Captain Brock disdained all hazards and expended his every effort. The altruistic, courageous quality of his superlative work was best illustrated at Christmas time, 1942, when he traversed from fox-hole to foxhole under hostile sniper fire to receive confessions and thus administer religious solace to men." Giblin, *Jesuits as Chaplains*, 38, 118.

41 Cushing, *The Missions in War and Peace*, n.p.; Grant, *War is My Parish*, 91.

42 Society for the Propagation of the Faith, *Priest Goes to War*, n.p.; *America* (January 24, 1942): 424; Photographs of holy items made from a Jeep piston, ordnance tools, and New Guinea mahogany can be found in Leonard, *Where Thousands Fell*. Amateur military artists produced innumerable pieces of religious art during the war including hand-carved crucifixes, paintings of Mary and Jesus, vestments, and even entire altars and chapels made out of exotic woods.

43 Foley diary, March 24, 1943. World War II nose art ran the gamut from cartoon characters to pornographic images, which were painted over before the craft returned to the United States. There is no evidence Foley ever saw yet another category, one that surely would have delighted him, and that was a group named after Mary and the saints, including "Queen of Heaven," "St. Sebastian," "Our Lady of Loretto," "Notre Dames des Victoires," "St. Christopher," "Our Lady of the Skies," and others. Society for the Propagation of the Faith, *The Priest goes to War*, n.p.

44 Stout believed that the Germans must be forced to "cooperated with democracy." If not, they must be convinced "by killing twenty million of them." Another time he broadcast, "I am willing to grant to any grown German one right and one right only—the right to a decent burial." Stout quoted in John McAleer, *Rex Stout A Biography* (Boston: Little, Brown and Co., 1977), 306, 307. There is a large collection of Stout material in the

Boston College archives. This is an irony, since fellow traveler Stout was not enamored of Romanism much more than he was Germans.

45 Foley diary, March 26, 1943. McNair's speech was criticized in *America* as well. A portion of McNair's harangue, originally published in *Time*, 7 December 1942, was reprinted in the Jesuit periodical. "We must hate with every fiber...We must lust for battle; our object in life must be to kill; we must scheme and plan night and day to kill. There need be no pangs of conscience, for our enemies have lighted the way to faster, surer, crueler killing." *America* (January 9, 1943): 390.

46 Many years after the war, the last surviving World War II Jesuit chaplain from the New England Province assessed the motivations of the servicemen he knew a half-century before. "I don't think anyone felt enormous hatred for the Germans and Japanese...let's finish the filthy business and get home. That was what I heard most. Maybe the Marines talked it up a little bit, but I don't feel that the G.I.s across the board had any great hostility or enmity in them at all. They'd fight but of course that was self-preservation. Kill them before they kill you." Interview with Fr. William J. Leonard, October 4, 1995, Chestnut Hill, MA.

47 Foley diary, March 30, 1943.

48 Foley diary, April 7, 10, 1943; Robert C. Muehrcke, *Orchids in the Mud: Personal Accounts by Veterans of the 132nd Infantry Regiment* (Chicago: J.S. Printing, 1985), 190. This anecdotal regimental history numbers the Japanese attack at 273 planes but there is no documentation for the figure.

49 Foley diary, April 16, 1943.

CHAPTER 7

▼

"TRAGEDIES GREAT AND SMALL"

The *Clymer* was back at Guadalcanal on April 19, still moving when Foley scrambled down a net on the side of the ship and dropped into a boat which sped him to shore. As usual he had a care package of candy and cigars for his brother Ed and Father Flaherty. However, this time the chaplain was to pick up and take charge of some special cargo: three Marist nuns and thirty-four refugees. The captain told him "it's your family." The nuns may have been his family but the others were Chinese, Fijian and half-caste. Foley went to meet them and assure them that they were now safe. They were glad to be leaving Guadalcanal, as the island had been bombed the night before. The nuns had been through a great deal of suffering, but the whole story would have to wait until they were underway. 1 He then went to the Port Director's office to arrange their transportation out to the ship. After a brief visit with Ed and Flaherty, inspecting the handmade monuments erected over the many graves at the Henderson Field cemetery, Foley took a boat back to the ship. A coxswain showed him a skull he picked up floating ashore. "Bloody waters, these." he thought.2

The *Clymer* was already underway but the refugees had not yet appeared by 5:30 so the vessel steered toward Kukum where they had been staying. On the way, a tank lighter finally delivered the group. Foley described the unusual picture to his diary:

> I introduce the Sisters as they come aboard. The little Chinese kids are howling with full lung power as they are carried up the ladder by our strong sailors. They want their mamas. Set down on the quarter-deck, they instantly quiet down when mother climbs the starboard gangway and slings them in the saddle, multi-colored, black, green and red on her back. One little tacker about two years old is screeching at the top of his lungs until his little sister, all of four years old, swings him on her back. Off we go, Sisters, Chinese and Fijians, myself leading the procession to their staterooms, where they marvel at their quarters. A bath, a cold drink and a hot meal make them forget their ordeal. Before long they are sound asleep in bed.3

The next day, as the *Clymer* steamed toward Noumea, Foley got the entire story from the relieved nuns. The leader, Mother Mary Ignatius, had been on Bougainville since the turn of the century. Her order at that time was known as the Third Order Regular of Mary but had not yet been approved by Rome. When the Vatican did recognize the order in 1931, they became the Missionary Sisters Society of Mary, which tended to the Solomons and other pagan areas of the South Pacific. She had been the first nun to set foot on Bougainville from a station in Samoa and had rarely left the island for any purpose in nearly half a century. When the Japanese arrived in Holy Week of 1942, they robbed and abused the missionary fathers but did not initially imprison them. By late summer the

Japanese began round-ups of priests and nuns and started cramming them into concentration camps.4

A few religious did manage to avoid capture, with the help of friendly natives. The two other nuns in Foley's party, also women of advanced age, were Sister Mary Adelberta from Germany and Sister Mary Martian, originally from France. They fled their station at Sieve on December 28, 1942. They stayed nights in native huts, wandering from district to district, unsure of where to go, since there appeared to be no safe refuge on the island. Their trek was a genuine ordeal. They forded rivers, slid down trails and climbed mountains, always just one step ahead of their relentless pursuers. Finally they met an Australian group who told them of a rendezvous point at Timbuts where an American submarine would evacuate them. Upon their arrival at the designated spot, however, they found a Japanese foraging party stealing food from the locals. To their relief the Japanese left with their booty and the nuns were brought out to the *Nautilus* in native canoes along with the variegated group of women and children.5

The senior nun, Mother Mary Ignatius, had left her station at Turi Boiru in the Buin District on October 14. The Japanese had smashed their way into the convent and dragged off the other seven sisters. They left her there, unwilling to waste rice on an old woman, probably expecting her to die due to her advanced age. Some natives brought her to the rendezvous point where she joined her two sisters and the others on the *Nautilus*. They were transferred to a sub chaser which brought them to Guadalcanal where they had been for two weeks. The youngest sister noted that the trip on the *Clymer* was only her second "aboard a steamer" in twenty-five years.6

The Fijian and Chinese women and children had likewise taken to the bush when it appeared that their days were numbered under their Japanese masters. One of the Chinese women was raped by over fifty soldiers before she managed to escape. Aboard the *Clymer* their nightmare ended at last. Foley tended to not only his "family," the nuns, but also coordinated activities for the children who ran wild throughout the ship. The children were awed by the two destroyers flanking the *Clymer* as the sleek greyhounds zigzagged back and forth, sending tendrils of foamy spray over their bows. Foley was less entertained than the children because he knew what the destroyers' maneuvers meant. The day before, there had been two General Alarms. They were being dogged again by a Japanese submarine. The destroyers were running interference for the APA and searching for the sub, which could very well have still been on their tail. As Foley watched the children screaming in glee, he thought, "God grant that if we are to ship a torpedo, it happens on some other trip rather than this one. On the starboard side, they can see a big aircraft carrier sending its birds aloft to make sure that the skies overhead are safe from the hawks that would wreck us."7

April 22, 1943, was Holy Thursday, the anniversary of the institution of the Holy Eucharist. Ordinarily, Masses would not be celebrated, but Pope Pius XII had anticipated the difficulties military chaplains would face in the war and had allowed special faculties for priests in service dating from 1939. One of these special considerations was permission to celebrate Mass on Holy Thursday for the duration of the war.8 Foley took the opportunity to compare the plight of the *Clymer's* guests with the countless others then suffering, just as Christ had suffered. As he said to his little congregation:

> …this Mass is an extraordinary one. Among our congregation are three Missionary Sisters of Mary and other passengers. Perhaps you may have heard of their harrowing experiences of the last few months.
>
> They have been walking in the footsteps of our Lord, yes, literally stumbling as He stumbled on the road to Calvary. Their road has been a bloody one. You would never guess it from speaking with them, but the truth shines through their humility.

Our ship is blessed in having them aboard. It is an honor
to serve them, and a privilege to carry them as passengers.
They won't be with us much longer, but they go their way
attended by our prayers. We hope they will never be the inno-
cent victims of a war as men wage it. And we ask God to bless
and keep them always. 9

The star of the group was a three year old cherubic waif named Aloysius
Chin Yung. At one meal the boy stood on a chair to better attack his
chicken. He would stop periodically to wipe his hands on his only gar-
ment, a "Perry Flour" sack. He scrambled all over the ship making friends
with the sailors, twenty of whom watched as he tried his first taste of ice
cream. Foley no sooner fed him a spoonful when Aloysius spit it out,
shocked by the cold. He gathered the courage to try it again and was converted. After the treat, Bosun Grymen approached Foley with a bomb helmet full of money for the children. The sailors thought the flour sack was
funny but rough too, and wanted the nuns to buy the children some
clothes and shoes. Foley did not solicit the money, but he was not surprised at the gesture. He swore by the generosity of the American sailor
and expected nothing less.10

The refugees' time aboard the *Clymer* drew to a close when the vessel
pulled into Noumea on Holy Saturday. It had been a strange interlude for
the crew, and a welcome one. The APA had been a hard-working ship
since her commissioning eleven months earlier. First, she made the
African invasion, then the tedious and often hair-raising Cactus Run. The
ship needed maintenance and the men needed liberty. For some of the
crew, the refugee children reminded them of home and the normal things.
When they were gone it would be back to the war as usual. Foley too was
unhappy to see them go. The captain showed him the order he had
received from shore regarding the disposition of the refugees.

COMSERON SOPACFOR
USS GEORGE CLYMER
    REFERENCE MYDIS 230521 X REQUEST YOU DISEMBARK 38 EVACUEES VIA SHIPS BOAT WITH COMMISSIONED OFFICER IN CHARGE AT SUCH TIME AS WILL PERMIT BOAT WITH EVAC-UEES TO ARRIVE AT NAVY LANDING AT 1300 TODAY X REQUEST BOAT BE INSTRUCTED TO TAKE COMMISSIONER OF POLICE AND HIS FINGER PRINTING EQUIPMENT ABOARD AT NAVY LANDING AND THEN PROCEED TO NOUVILLE ON ILE NOU AND LAND COMMISSIONER AND EVACUEES X REQUEST YOU SEND WITH GROUP A LIST OF NAMES OF EVACUEES AND ANY OTHER AVAILABLE INFORMATION FOR DELIVERY TO COMMISSIONER OF POLICE REF: (230521) UNFORESEEN DIFFI-CULTIES HAVE DELAYED THIS EMBARKATION OF 38 EVAC-UEES DUE TO THE LACK OF PREPARATION OF THE LOCAL AUTHORITIES X EXPECTED THAT THIS EMBARKATION WILL TAKE PLACE APRIL 24.

                                  CHAPLAIN FOLEY _____
                                  INT. OFF. _____ 11

    The Police Commissioner of Noumea came aboard at ten o'clock and it was immediately apparent that he and Foley would have trouble. He was a typical example of a colonial police official: haughty, imperious, venal and thoroughly corrupt. He told Foley that Sisters Martian and Ignatius would be allowed to go to the local convent. Sister Adelberta however, because of her German birth, was considered an "enemy alien" and he was there to arrest her. Foley calmly explained that she was not to be arrested; that the nun, who had served in the Solomons for decades, was no more an enemy than he was. The Frenchman was adamant; she was to be arrested and interned for the duration of the war. Foley gave up on gentle persuasion. He told the Police Chief that he was *not* taking her to jail. If he attempted it, he would have to arrest Foley too. 12

The Frenchman stepped aside to confer with his aide. He had not reckoned with this meddlesome American priest. Perhaps he had expected a bribe to forget about the "enemy alien." If so, this shakedown attempt failed. After a few minutes he returned to Foley and told him that all three could go to the convent provided he would "guarantee their good behavior." Foley was appalled by this uniformed crook. He snapped, "I'll guarantee their behavior" then, sweeping his arm toward the many American ships in the harbor, "and the U.S. Navy stands behind the guarantee."13

The incident upset the normally easygoing Foley. When he went ashore to deliver his charges he told a shore-based chaplain about the functionary. The chaplain was not surprised. He told Foley that the Police Chief ran the biggest brothel in Noumea, the infamous "Pink House," which catered exclusively to American service personnel.14 The Pink House was an open secret to every serviceman who stopped at Noumea and everyone knew that it operated with the forbearance of the American military officials. For homefront consumption, military policy was to discourage prostitution. In reality, the military's only real concern was that servicemen would be unavailable for duty if infected with venereal disease so prostitution was perfectly acceptable as long as men did not lose time in sick bay.

The Pink House situation went far beyond brass hats looking the other way at the world's oldest profession. In this case the bordello was owned by several French entrepreneurs, including the Intendant-General and the Police Chief whom Foley encountered. A building had been purchased, painted pink, named "Chateau Moreau" and had many toilets installed. Then the policeman approached the commanding general, Lt. Gen. Alexander "Sandy" Patch regarding protection, since a bordello that serviced Americans would have to have his blessing to stay open. Patch brought in his Provost-Marshal and Medical Inspector to help the business run smoothly. He told them in no uncertain terms that "I am never to know that the house exists or that its activities are connected in any way with the United States forces."15

The Pink House operated for some time with obvious but unofficial army supervision. M.P.s acted as bouncers while corpsmen examined the "Johns." The enterprise folded when a new Inspector-General found that the brothel was operating with stolen government property. The Medical Inspector, now Service Command Surgeon, told him that it was "entirely a French installation" and begged him to forget the matter so as to avoid publicity. The racket finally ended when Patch was transferred and a new commanding general removed the M.P.s and corpsmen.16

Foley was not privy to the whole sordid story but the mere fact that the Police Chief demanded a guarantee of "good conduct" from refugee nuns while at the same time running organized vice on the island disgusted him. American political and military policies regarding cooperation with French and British colonial regimes in North Africa, the Pacific and elsewhere were not admirable. The tendency was to keep these regimes in place no matter how rotten and abusive. Foley understood the nature of the characters who ran colonial outposts. The French policeman would be running his fleshpot in collaboration with the Japanese if the shoe were on the other foot, since the profits from crime know no patriotism. Foley also understood the hypocrisy of the military commanders. They were more than willing to aid procurers and pimps but were deathly afraid of publicity. Wives and mothers back home were likely to rethink their support of the war if the government's involvement in the prostitution business became known.

The refugee nuns were finally delivered safely to a clinic on Noumea run by their own Missionary Sisters of Mary. Their erstwhile host Chaplain Foley bade them good-bye and went back to his usual duties. On Easter Sunday he celebrated Mass aboard the battlewagon *Indiana* directly under the aft turret, the middle 16" gun. Because of the gargantuan weapon, he could not raise the host to its normal height during the consecration. It was a Mass unlike any he had ever celebrated, with his congregation of five hundred kneeling and praying under the long rifles;

he thought that this was why he became a priest, a Jesuit, a chaplain in the first place.17

Back at sea, there was a general uneasiness. The *Clymer* was being dragged back by two eleven-knot Liberty ships, which the sailors called "submarine bait." Foley scanned the waters for undersea predators, the same as everybody when on deck. He had more unpleasant duty after reading an old copy of the *New York Times* from March, which published a list of New York boys killed in the invasion of North Africa the previous November. On that list was the boy who had come to him crying in fear before the landings and who died fighting the next day. At that time he was forbidden from writing personal letters to casualties' families but the military situation had changed and he now took the opportunity to write to the boy's mother, who perhaps found some solace from his carefully worded letter:

> Please accept my sincere condolences on the occasion of your sad bereavement. If military reasons had not prevented me, I would have written to you sooner to extend my sympathy.
>
> It so happened that as a naval chaplain I was in a position to know the circumstances of Michael's death. Thinking that knowledge of them may help to lighten the burden of your sorrow, I am writing to acquaint you with them.
>
> On the morning of November 11, 1942, it was my priestly privilege to bless, and later bury the bodies of the first boys who died in the battle that raged for three days and three nights. I came upon Michael lying at the base of one of the coastal guns that had been shelling our ship heavily. He had died taking it by storm. He gave his life that we might live. Because of his bravery, our ship and her men were not at the bottom two miles off shore.
>
> About one o'clock in the afternoon of the same day, Michael was buried a short distance from the spot where he

fell. It was a beautiful day, clear blue sky overhead and warm with sunshine. As I started the burial service, fifty of our soldiers flanked me on the left and fifty native Moroccans, prisoners of war, on the right, all of us facing Michael and his brave comrades. When the order was given, the entire group snapped to attention. I read the prayers for the dead, taps were sounded and the last blessing given. Michael is buried on the crest of the high hill next to Fort Mehdia that looks out over the broad reaches of the Atlantic toward country, home, and those near and dear to him for whom he gave the last measure of devotion. God, I am sure, has been mindful of his sacrifice.

May these details of the death and burial of your boy help to console you in your loss. You have my heartfelt sympathy and assurances that Michael will have a constant remembrance in my daily Mass.

Sincerely yours

John P. Foley, S.J.
Chaplain, USNR 18

The sluggish Liberty ships were left at Efate, New Hebrides and the *Clymer* headed out immediately for Guadalcanal at her usual speed of seventeen knots with a destroyer escort. On that morning, Saturday May 8, Foley was talking to two chaplains along for the ride in his cabin, Father Tennyson and Chaplain Bartholomew. He had to run topside on an errand and when he got on deck he saw a mob of passengers portside. Half a mile astern the water was ablaze with acrid smoke billowing from below. Only moments earlier, a P40 had been showing off, "buzzing" *Clymer's* destroyer escort. A wing clipped the water, the plane flipped and sank immediately. Then her fuel tanks ruptured, exploded and burned underwater. The tanks were still feeding the fire on the surface as Foley gave the pilot absolution, "*Ego te absolvo ab omnis censuris et peccatis in nomine Patris et Filii et Spritius Sancti, Amen.*"19 He prayed that night for the pilot's mother who would soon be receiving a cold impersonal telegram curtly stating the fate of her son.

Upon arriving at Cactus, the *Clymer* began unloading its human cargo, sick soldiers who were to be treated at Guadalcanal's medical facilities. Foley hit the beach again with a hoard of edible treasures including a big baked ham for his brother Ed and Father Flaherty. This trip he brought along Dr. Kirkpatrick from the ship, who was awed by the evidence of the past struggle, including the sight of coconut trees sheared in half. Flaherty took them to the Naval Operating Base to meet Bishop Jean Marie Aubin, S.M., Vicar Apostolic of the Solomons. At Visale, Bishop Aubin had developed a thriving missionary diocese of two hundred buildings prior to the war including a cathedral, school, hospital and other structures. The Japanese landing in July meant the end of everything he and the priests and nuns of the mission accomplished in decades of work. At first, the Japanese under Ishimoto merely stole food and other property. When Ishimoto demanded that Aubin "cooperate" and work with him to subdue and pacify the natives, who were put to work as slave laborers at Lunga, Aubin adamantly refused. Ishimoto made it clear that the missionaries were prisoners in their compound and Aubin would not be allowed to visit the sick or otherwise leave his residence unless he began collaborating.20

Aubin also clashed with Ishimoto over his Provicar, Father Brugmans, whom Ishimoto dragged off to confinement but who was released in three days. Japanese looters continued to return on a regular basis to steal everything not nailed down. They also established an anti-aircraft position in the bush near the cathedral over Aubin's protests. When American planes overflew the mission on August 7, the missionaries were momentarily joyous over the thought of being rescued. Then the Japanese fired from the cover and the planes turned back to strafe the mission. It was a First Friday and the compound was crowded with churchgoers. Everyone scattered screaming into the jungle; natives with their children, priests and nuns ran for their lives. A bomb smashed the church, a second flattened the boys dormitory, windows in the other buildings shattered from the concussions, and nearby trees were set aflame.

During the attack, Aubin continued to say Mass in his private chapel. When there was a lull he tried to cross the compound but a plane swooped down and riddled the presbytery. The ship banked to make another run so the bishop, well into his sixties, bolted for the bush. As the plane bore down on him, he threw himself to the ground. He just barely missed being stitched with armor-piercing .50 caliber bullets. He crawled to the comparative safety of the jungle in time to see more American bombs falling on his life's work. Surely the Japanese were enjoying the show.

Aubin and his bedraggled flock of religious spent the next weeks living like animals in the bush, unable to start cooking fires for fear the Americans would spot them and take them for Japanese. The bishop did furtively return to his ruined mission during the day to conduct business. But he came to the sad conclusion that the mission was a total loss and the group had little chance of survival if found now by the Japanese. On August 30 they seized a local boy and demanded he show them the missionaries' hideout. He ran them ragged through the jungle before they realized that they were being led a merry chase, and shot him in the head.

With nowhere else to go, Aubin decided to try to make it to his Tangarare station, thirty-five miles northwest of Cape Esperance. The band left before midnight with no supplies and almost no personal effects. Only hours later the Japanese arrived, furious that they had again missed their prey. Aubin was so sick with dysentery that he had to be carried by natives slung in a blanket tied to bamboo poles. For most people, a thirty-five mile trek into the Guadalcanal jungle with no food or water pursued by a merciless foe was not an encouraging prospect. But the missionaries' works had preceded them and their faithful native companions guided them through the unforgiving bush. The Islanders would step into the sandaled footprints of the missionaries so the Japanese would be tricked by the tracks of bare feet. Nevertheless, other natives arrived, warning them not to slow down as the Japanese were closing. After climbing a mountain, they found rest in a village for a few hours. Almost miraculously, the group made it to the Tangarare Station by September 5. The Japanese had given up the chase for the moment but the missionaries were not yet safe. After several failed attempts, the group was finally evacuated to an American position on October 4th.21

Most of the nuns spent the rest of the war in New Caledonia or Fiji. General Vandergrift did give permission for Bishop Aubin to remain in the islands, an act for which he was grateful, since some of his charges were still in Japanese hands and he felt he could not leave the Solomons even if there was nothing he could do to help them.22

When Foley met Aubin, the bishop was wearing a khaki army uniform and sun helmet. The only indication that he was not American military personnel was the large bishop's pectoral cross hanging from a chain around his neck. He was about sixty-five, thin and frail, with white hair and gentle eyes. He had been through a lot physically though the emotional toll was worse. His life's work was in ashes, some of his clergy had been grotesquely murdered and the others made refugees. He asked Foley about himself and his ship before moving on to the other guests. When Foley left, the bishop gave him his episcopal blessing. Foley thought as they parted, "It is not often that one has the opportunity to be blessed by a saint in the flesh."23

Flaherty was being transferred to New Caledonia so this was the last time Foley would see him on Guadalcanal. The *Clymer* departed the next day with two hundred Marines and the 147th regiment 2nd battalion. Foley was in the wardroom about 1230 when General Quarters sounded. A four engine Mitsubishi heavy bomber made a run at the ship using the sun to blind her gunners. A bomb hit off the portside and Foley could feel the vessel shudder at his station in sick bay. Another explosion failed to hit the mark. The vessel hove to port then starboard and back again to evade the deadly missiles. An escorting destroyer blazed her guns into the sky trying to knock the raider down. One more bomb run and the Mitsubishi was away. That afternoon at Rosary and Benediction, Foley used the day's fireworks to drive home the lesson of God's providence.24

The *Clymer's* next few cruises were uneventful in comparison. On May 19 she landed at Pago Pago, another island that seemed unchanged from the prehistoric age. Foley was met by Glyn Jones, the Baptist minister who attended chaplain school with him. Jones was with a Marine unit that had been there for months practicing jungle warfare. The atmosphere at Pago Pago was not identical with Guadalcanal, yet it had its own terrible aspects. Average rainfall was three hundred inches per year. A rainstorm would appear and dump torrents of water on the surface, soaking every-thing in its path. Foley, Jones, and another chaplain stationed there, Father Burns, enjoyed a beer and had a few laughs after being drenched in one of the passing cloudbursts. The topic of conversation was, however, deadly serious. Jones told Foley that there were three divisions of Marines in the area and it was assured that another major campaign was near. The game turned to handicapping the date of the next assault. Jones guessed about six weeks. Foley thought it would be closer to four months. Both were off though Foley was closer. The invasion of Bougainville would have to wait until the beginning of November.25

While on Pago Pago, Foley attended to his usual duties of picking up films and this time he even wangled a 35mm projector. He found a school run by the Marist Sisters and told them about their three refugee sisters who had been carried by the *Clymer*. One of them, Sister Mary Florentine from Lynn, Massachusetts, shed a few tears when she learned that Foley was from back home. He entertained the native children with tales of the war including the *Clymer's* recent close shave with the bomber.26

At the beginning of June the *Clymer* was once again in Wellington where she would remain for over a week, a long stopover for this APA. Her work had shifted away from Guadalcanal, and though New Zealand was safely south of the Solomons, it was apparent that the war was moving north. Wellington was a beehive of activity. The Third Marines were loaded aboard the *Clymer* with all of their cargo for debarking practice. A few nights before shoving off, Foley was invited to an interfaith gathering of chaplains and civilian clergymen at the house of the Anglican bishop, Mr. Barb-Holland. There were two priest chaplains, Fathers Kelly and O'Neil, who were serving with Marine units and a mixture of Protestant chaplains, all of whom wore their uniforms. Foley was stunned by the nine civilian ministers, all but two of whom were dressed in black and wore Roman collars. Even the one rabbi was wearing a collar, which floored him.27

Back at sea, Foley was more in his element among the Marines who had come aboard. He was not much of an ecclesiastical politician and saw little point in functions such as the bishop's. He joined the navy to minister to his boys on the ship and the many others that the ship ferried. He wanted the war to end so that the men could go back to their own homes and he could return to his own home at Chestnut Hill. He would return to the tragic vicissitudes of freshmen who were cut out of a course and he would love it. He received a copy of the *Heights*, the Boston College newspaper, and learned of the deaths of some of the young men he had taught in class. The war was sparing no one.

Watching the Marines preparing for boat drill Foley heard this exchange between two gyrenes, "What wave are you in?". "Sixth. What's yours?" "First wave, first boat." "Boy, oh boy, I'll put a blanket on you as I go by." There were fresh faces in the Third mixed with hardened countenances, veterans of the Guadalcanal campaign. This time boat drill would be different. It was decided that the landing boats would be lowered completely loaded with men and gear, rather than lowered and then have the men climb down the nets into the boats. It was a risky new maneuver. Lowering them loaded would save valuable time during the actual operation, that was true, but the tactic was risky. There was some doubt if the boats could take the strain and if the bottoms collapsed the whole batch of Marines, weighed down with equipment, would sink like rocks. Furthermore, there was a greater chance of tipping when being lowered.

The drill went well the first day. Whether or not disaster would strike on invasion day when the stakes were much higher was still problematic.28

On June 12, the vessel steamed for Paikakari for maneuvers, thirty miles to the north. She passed through Cook's Straits, the channel between North Island and South Island, which make up New Zealand. Foley enjoyed the natural beauty of the land from the steel deck of the APA, "Off on our portside, Mt. Cook, 3800 ft. high, raises her majestic snow-crowned peaks into God's azure blue. The color contrasts are breathtaking. The blue sky, the white of the snow, the slaty grey of the mountain below the snowline, then the blue of the Tasman Sea washing the feet of the mountains; and over all, the clear, bright sunshine, flooding the crisp day."29

That afternoon the Marines did another drill, this time condition 1–A, a troop landing to practice taking a shore position eight miles away. The practice went smoothly and there was the usual Marine mix of jest and braggadocio during the whole affair. Despite the facade of confidence there was not a man among them who did not know that the real thing against an enemy-held objective was murderous business. As Foley was watching the spectacle, his eye caught a chance for evangelizing. Not for nothing had he been a Jesuit for twenty years and here was an opportunity to use the fine hand. A very young Marine was shivering in his shirt, ostensibly from the cold. Foley asked him if he needed a sweater and brought him down to his cabin. "Father Foley is my name." The boy told him his and added, "sorry I'm not a good Catholic, Father." "How long since last confession?" The boy admitted it was too long. "All right, but you'll be squared away before tonight, right?" "Right, Father." Ha! bagged another one. Foley thought that God works in wondrous ways if an old sweater can be a means of grace for the boy. Perhaps the lesson would stick during his trials ahead. Foley believed that no matter how long a person had been away from the sacraments, God never abandoned him.30

So far the exercises had just been boat drills. On June 14, 15, and 16, there were going to be full scale simulated attacks on the "enemy-held" shore. The other attack transports *Hunter Liggett, American Legion* and *Crescent City* were involved in this training operation, which reminded him of the North African invasion the previous November. These "war games" were startlingly realistic, the idea being that the rehearsals would iron out some wrinkles though the fog of war could never really be replicated by rehearsals. Foley described the ersatz air raid staged for the event:

> 0815—Simulated dive bombing attack. Eight fighters and dive bombers come in from all angles repeatedly, strafing and bombing and torpedoing our ships. They wiggle as they come in to splatter their machine guns over a wide area, i.e. their bullets to knock out as many men as they can, then the work of the dive bombers and the torpedo planes will be so much easier. Were these the real thing, we should have been at the bottom in two minutes after the first wave came in on us. This squadron is a unit from the New Zealand Air Force that has been doing such splendid work in the Middle East and Tunisia.31

There were dreadful forebodings during these exercises which seemed to indicate the course of the true invasion. On the 16th, the surf was wild. The APAs moved forward within two miles of shore but the landing boats could still barely make it through the raging waves. Eight boats were wrecked, their human cargo thrown into the water to die or to make it to shore as best they could. The defenders had them at their mercy, and had this been the real thing, the waterlogged Marines would have been mowed down like wheat stalks before a scythe. Two boys were killed in the confusion, one of them chopped to pieces by a propeller. The decision was made to sail to Wellington to make repairs on the boats that could be repaired and to assess the results of the rehearsals, which so far had been disastrous.32

The group returned to Paikakariki on Sunday June 20, to try it again. Foley could not celebrate his usual Mass for the crew as most of them were on duty hoisting the landing boats. The weather was again treacherous, with high winds and whitecaps tossing and rolling the boats like so many toys. Foley went on deck and wanted to know if there were more casualties this day. A Marine returning to the ship informed him that the operation was again a gigantic SNAFU, with boats smashing on the shore and being disabled. The plan called for all the troops and cargo to be unloaded and the APAs to leave the area within eight hours lest they be sunk. After a few hours it was apparent that the schedule would never be met. That night salvage parties worked furiously on the beach to refloat the damaged landing craft. To cap off the day, it was learned that eight enlisted men and one officer were killed when their boat turned over. Two of the bodies washed ashore with large gashes on their heads, indicating that they had been killed by the boat's propeller. Monday was spent searching for survivors and then steaming back to Wellington.33

Foley was livid over the events of the past week. While it was inevitable that people would be killed in wartime, the losses experienced in those rehearsals seemed particularly pointless. How many men had to die and boats wrecked before the brass understood that there was nothing to be gained by continuing in those turbulent seas? He was further incensed when he picked up an Auckland paper and learned of the high casualties experienced by American flyers during a one hundred plane Japanese raid on Guadalcanal recently. He knew for a fact that the figures had been omitted from American accounts. It was bad enough that American boys were being killed senselessly and it was even worse to deceive the folks back home, particularly the ones with sons, fathers and husbands in service. He believed that the Office of War Information (O.W.I.) and fiction writers such as Rex Stout were salesmen for war and that the American people deserved the truth, for good or ill.34

And as bad as the situation was, the chaplain continued with his handyman and crying towel duties. He had come aboard exactly a year earlier, unsure of all that a naval chaplain was expected to do, and he had learned on the job. He had seen stupidity on the part of higher officers and among the men he observed behavior that was not admirable. Yet he continued to be exhilarated by his floating parish and his young congregation. He always made himself available for the most mundane and sometimes off-beat duties. For example, a radar man came to him with a Dear John letter, telling him that his steady girlfriend of two years jilted him. There was nothing Foley could do to patch up the relationship but, like Cyrano de Bergerac in reverse, he wrote a letter to the girl and had the radar man sign it. He hoped the sailor's erstwhile lover would read it and think, "And I gave up that kind of man. What a mistake I made."35

The questions on everyone's mind were where and when the big strike would be. "When" was obviously soon. As far as "where," it was well known that overall strategy called for the reduction of Truk, the "Japanese Pearl Harbor." Truk was defended by a powerful base at Rabaul on New Britain, which had been in Japanese hands since January 1942. Though Guadalcanal was more or less securely held by the Americans, it was still subject to harassment bombing raids from the Japanese positions. It was certain that there could be no more advancement toward the Philippines until Rabaul, which lay northwest of Bougainville, was smashed. Further, New Guinea would never be secure while the Japanese held Rabaul and Truk. Flank attacks on Trobriand and Woodlark Islands were successfully conducted in June. Operations were also conducted against Rendova and New Georgia itself. Where the major strike would occur was still a mystery, at least to small fry like Foley and the others who would be called upon to do or die.36

On June 28th, the *Clymer* loaded up the 9th of the Third Marine Division, while the *American Legion, Hunter Liggett* and cargo vessel *Fomalhaut* ferried other elements of the Third. On the way to Guadalcanal the group was dogged by a sub and survived a pass by enemy planes. These diversions had not become boring, just part of the job on the "Cactus Ferry." Foley laid out some essential items every night before turning in: long underwear, Vaseline, white cap, sweatshirt, sunglasses. If the ship were hit and did not sink instantaneously he would don the clothes and grab the Vaseline before going overboard. The items were supposed to help one survive freezing at night and roasting during the day. In any case, it would be better than hitting the water in skivvies.37

The Marines were disembarked at Guadalcanal on July 6 for more intensive jungle training. If anyone still had doubts about the invasion, this more or less settled the issue. The *Clymer* was scheduled to head for Noumea the next day, so Foley had only a fifteen minute visit with his brother Ed. He had much to do, and when the destroyer *Renshaw* came along the *Clymer*, he ambled down a ladder and asked the exec for permission to hear confessions. Then it was back to his own ship to start tending to a group of ninety-eight casualties from the northern operations. These men were seriously hurt, blinded, deafened, shot and with mangled limbs. Foley made the rounds once they were settled in. Some of the men asked him, "Do you recognize me Father?" They were men that the *Clymer* brought to the area months ago. Now their faces were gone and Foley could not have recognized them if they were his own brother. One of them cried, "I never thought I would be coming back this way, Father."38 He spent the two day trip to Noumea trying to keep the men from losing hope and providing them with clothes, underwear and socks. Some of them had been loaded aboard stark naked except for the sheet on the stretcher. His diary entry for July 8, 1943 read:

0615—Mass

Busy taking care of the material needs of the 98 wounded we have aboard. They are a pitiable lot, this sample of the human debris of war, most of them bombing victims. One squadron of 15 bombers did this work. What must it be over Europe where hundreds of them concentrate on one area in a thickly congested modern city?

McMullen, from Bangor, Maine, is stone blind, will always be. Was a clerk in a Division Headquarters; bomb fragment scooped across center of face, wrecking both eyes and leaving only tip of his nose.

Pathetic, as he asks me to describe the Purple Heart to him, award for Military Merit. Purple and white ribbon, medal is heart-shaped, with medallion of Washington in center, is bronze colored.

Some of the concussion cases are still stunned psychologically, others deafened, others with both eyes black and blue, blood shot. Concussion breaks blood vessels.

Hand out cigarettes to the men. They have only what they brought on their backs.

Two army officers, Captain and Lieutenant are psychoneurotic cases. One imagines he has a bad leg; other insists that he wants to see no more blood for the duration.39

Apart from the casualties, an ensign who had only been aboard for six weeks was to be removed. He had begged for a transfer, claiming that he would do better work in another branch of the service. The officers had no doubt that he was a coward and wanted to be rid of him. It was only the second apparent incidence of cowardice since the ship began her naval career. Everyone remembered the case of the ensign who deserted his gun crew back during the Chesapeake maneuvers and this looked like a similar situation. There was no sympathy for this individual either. Lieutenant Morey brought up the subject with Foley and said, "Hope he gets reassigned, Father, and he is with us when we are making the next beachhead."40

Foley had to smile when he saw an account of Marine Corps' ace Joe Foss' crash and rescue in November during the struggle for Guadalcanal. The *Chicago Tribune* reported that he had crashed near Malaita, inhabited by the "worst natives on the Solomons." The true story did not make the papers. When Foss' battered Grumman hit the water he thought the island about five miles distant was Guadalcanal. He was nearly taken to the bottom as the Grumman sank instantly and though his Mae West brought him to the surface and kept him afloat for five hours, he believed he would either succumb to the sea or be feasted on by sharks. The sharks in the area had been treated to a smorgasbord of bleeding human flesh because of the many naval and air battles over the past few months. Out of strength and helpless, Foss heard canoe paddles and muffled human voices approaching. Then he identified English words and called for help. He was shocked when he saw a canoe full of natives armed with war clubs, but was pulled into the outrigger by Fr. Dan Stuyvenberg, the pastor of the Malaita mission. Malaita was the long narrow island to the northeast of Guadalcanal. Not only was Foss disoriented as to which island he was near, he was also swimming for a jut of land swarming with man-eating crocodiles. Foss later thought, "If somehow I'd made it to land, I'd proba-bly have been somebody's supper."41

Foss was warmed at the missionaries' campfire and quizzed about the outside world by fathers, brothers and nuns, including one sister from Boston. He was well fed and allowed to sleep, then awoke to the sound of hymns. Later Foss wrote:

> Following the sound, I came upon an open-sided thatched hut which was obviously a church; the altar was made of carved bamboo and coconut shells, and before it stood one of the priests leading a congregation of seminaked natives. Some of the older natives were a fearful sight, clad in red loincloths and savage-looking jewelry made from shells and animal teeth, their mouths stained red from chewing betel nuts, and their hair standing out like it was charged with electricity. The missionaries had told me the night before that this par-ticular tribe had a reputation for being hostile, but here they were, singing hymns.42

After Mass, Father Stuyvenberg arranged a reception and the natives showered him with gifts of food, though they were very short themselves. A Grumman F4F spotted Foss' parachute and he was picked up by a PBY later that day. As a parting gesture, he gave his chute to the nuns to make altar vestments. The story reminded Foley yet again of the universality of the Church. Just a few years earlier, those "worst natives" of the Solomons would have roasted Foss for the main course. Now they rescued him and other American flyers from the Japanese at great risk to themselves, all because a handful of priests and nuns brought them the good word. Even Foss realized the significance of this, and from then on felt that he had been saved for another day for some good purpose.43

The *Clymer* sat at Auckland from July 15 until the 23rd. During that time Foley had a major blow up with Captain Moen. He had considered the man to be a petty tyrant from the start. The incident wherein he kicked the junior officer was only the beginning. Now a year later he was widely despised by many of the officers and crewmen. Foley had a wise policy of managing trouble aboard ship. Whenever there was a problem such as a theft, Foley would try to handle it himself so that the captain would not become involved. There was a two-fold purpose in this. First, the captain would not be bothered by every minor annoyance that occurred on board. Second, as Foley would tell the men, incidents reported to the captain would doubtless be handled in a severe fashion and self-rectification was the more prudent course.44

The crew's morale continued to deteriorate while the *Clymer* rode at anchor in Auckland. Elements of the 9th Marines and the 21st were loaded aboard along with Fr. Joe Conway, formerly of Brooklyn, now with the 3rd Marine Division. After several days of no liberty the crew and the loaded troopers were hot and restless. Foley noted the tension in his diary entry for July 21. "No liberty for the Crew!!! What a skipper! Men wouldn't go through tissue paper for him !"45

The situation aboard was such that Foley continued along the same line the next day.

July 22, 1943—Thursday

0630—Mass

Men of the ship's company boiling last night and today. No liberty granted by the Captain. WHY? No doubt has a reason, but whatever it is it works a hardship on the crew. To be in port without any ostensible reason for canceling liberty when the other ships in our division have liberty and the OFFICERS ABOARD OUR SHIP HAVE IT and the MEN don't does not make for good morale.

Unfortunately the men will be happy when he is transferred. He is not liked by his men. He has the reputation of being inconsiderate of his crew in the little things that are the big things, e.g. liberty, water for the showers; when he does grant liberty, holding them back for hours needlessly and then bringing them back earlier than the other ships. I share their opinion.46

The chaplain and the captain had already had it out. The previous Saturday, Foley had made all of the arrangements for a dance on Sunday night. He even called on the Lord Mayor of Auckland to grease the skids. That day Captain Moen called him in and asked him if he approved of having a dance on Sunday night. The captain's opinion was that such an event on Sunday would cause a scandal with the New Zealanders. Foley saw nothing wrong with a Sunday night dance if the crew started the day with Mass or general services. The captain told him the dance was canceled. There was also the matter of one hundred cases of beer brought aboard for the crew. Foley discovered that the captain was instead planning on selling it to the Marines aboard. Foley considered the captain's actions questionable, but he was furious when he found out that the captain was indeed holding the dance, for officers only. So much for the scandal of dancing on Sunday.47

The night of the dance Foley did some work in his cabin. One of the Catholic officers stopped by and asked him if he were going. Foley told him if the enlisted men were forbidden from attending, he would not go either. Ordinarily he put in an appearance. Not this time. Foley did not announce his protest but the word went around the ship like wildfire and it did not hurt his reputation with the crew. The *Clymer* continued with her business ferrying fresh troops and wounded between Noumea and Guadalcanal for the next few weeks and the acrimony continued between Foley and the captain as well. On a stop at Cactus, the captain refused to give him permission to go ashore with the sick and then to see his brother as usual. Instead, Foley had a boat go to pick up his brother, who stayed aboard that night.48

It was decided that the *Clymer* was to be the flagship of Rear Adm. Theodore S. Wilkinson's 3rd Amphibious Force for the impending invasion. The appearance of the gold braid meant that old timers such as Foley would be dispossessed from their rooms. It was also decided that the *Clymer*'s bottom would be scraped and the vessel overhauled at New Zealand rather than go home to the states as expected. The work began on August 11 at Devonport across the Waiamata harbor. Foley got homesick when he saw the new radar equipment being installed on his vessel . It was manufactured by the Massachusetts firm of Raytheon and he could not help thinking that the equipment had just come from where he wanted to be. 49

On August 18, Foley went to Mobile Hospital #4 to have dinner with one of the most extraordinary men ever to wear a chaplain's uniform, Fr. Charles Carroll Riedel, C.S.V. Riedel was a thirty-year-old priest of the Clerics of St. Viator out of Illinois. He had experienced some difficulty getting an appointment, as his navy paperwork was lost more than once. After chaplain school he was assigned to the hospital in Auckland. When he got there in February 1943, the place was still swamped with casualties from the Solomons fighting and he was the sole chaplain available. Riedel built up the chaplain facilities from scratch and after a few months the operation was running smoothly. The morning after he had dinner with Foley, Riedel wrote a long letter to Bishop O'Hara explaining that he had been offered the post for the duration but it was too soft for him and he was desperate to get a flattop, cruiser or billet with the Marine Raiders. He wrote, "Not so young or foolish that I want to be a bloody hero but, *ceteris partibus,* an older priest can do the work here just as effectively or better and I can take duty an older man cannot.50

By the middle of September 1943 Riedel had been transferred and was serving with the 10th Marines, an artillery regiment of the 2d Marine Division. At the invasion of Tarawa in November he landed on Betio on D-Day-plus-two under heavy machine gun fire. His actions during this fierce battle were beyond the call of anyone's duty. He cared for casualties on the beach and accompanied corpsmen to evacuate the wounded under sniper fire. He even buried the dead and said Mass under fire. His personal courage and devotion to the men was without peer, yet his relationship with the Marine Corps brass began to sour from this point. Riedel was never shy in expressing his views that the Catholic men were not being cared for adequately. In official reports he pointed out the dearth of Catholic chaplains in particular areas even when there were several Protestants and Jewish chaplains on duty. Because of his devotion to the men in the 10th regiment, he turned down transfers which were effectively promotions.51

Riedel was again a human dynamo at the invasion of Saipan in June 1944. He landed under artillery fire and for the next few weeks scrambled furiously to cover as many units as possible since there was no Catholic chaplain assigned to Division. His heroic actions came abruptly to an end when the senior Marine aerial flight observer asked him if he would like to take a flight over the island. After a short, uneventful flight he returned to work at the 2d Division hospital. There he mentioned the flight to a wounded comrade who had been with him on Tarawa. Unfortunately, Col. David Shoup, the Chief of Staff of the 2d Marine Division was eavesdropping behind him. Shoup informed on him to Col. Raphael Griffin,

Riedel's C.O., who already knew about the incident. Though there were no orders prohibiting such actions prior to Riedel's flight, Shoup insisted that he be arrested. Riedel was confined to quarters on July 4,5, and 6 and was distraught that the troops had no Catholic chaplain available during the battle. He attempted several times in writing to communicate the importance of this principle to his C.O. and even appealled to Lt. Gen. Holland Smith, who told him that he was bound to support the chain of command, and that the flight itself was immaterial, but that Riedel's language was objectionable.52

It was clear that Riedel was being punished because of his volatile personality and his insistence that Catholics be attended to rather than his violation of a non-existent order. Though surgeons at the Division hospital, all of them non-Catholics, wrote letters protesting his relief, a non-Catholic chaplain on the discipline board who claimed to know "all about the Catholic Church" concurred in Riedel's punishment. He was encouraged to take up the matter with Senator David Walsh but did not want to make a public stir. Riedel languished in purgatory for five months until he was reassigned to the Naval Training Center, Bainbridge, Maryland where he served until the end of the war.53

All of Riedel's trials were before him when he and Foley enjoyed their evening of dinner and boxing matches at Auckland. Foley's defense of his men would not result in his removal, yet he was just as adamant that they not be degraded by the captain or other officers. For the rest of the Clymer's time in Davenport Foley had dinner with several chaplains and visited the local churches and orphanage. Being in port so long, he managed to secure several movies for the crew, who continued to come to him with tragedies great and small. Harding of the 1st Division stumbled into his office near tears. It turned out he was only sixteen and falsified his age to get in the navy. A bosun seemed to be picking on him so he wanted a transfer. After a little talk and a piece of cake, he settled down.54

The Clymer returned to Wellington on September 1. A few days later another chaplain problem arose, this one somewhat more substantial. A woman met Foley and asserted that a *Clymer* crewman had impregnated her younger sister. The girl did not know the sailor's name, just his nickname, "Fritz" and described his "MOTHER" tattoo. Foley accompanied the two women to a doctor, whose pregnancy test was inconclusive. He would test again the next month. The doctor glared at Foley and snarled, "Are you the man behind all this?" Because of the seriousness of the situation, Foley suppressed his laughter.55

There was a buoyancy in the crew when the new captain, Frank R. Talbot, came aboard to relieve Moen. The men did not know if they were getting a top skipper this time, they only knew they would not miss Moen. Communications Officer Lieutenant Commander McRae handed Foley his last fitness report submitted by Moen. It was a good one. The ship next made a stop in Fiji. Foley learned that two old friends, Fathers Flaherty and Brock were now stationed at Suva. At Viti Levu, the largest of the Fijis, the *Clymer* embarked a mixed crowd including Merrill's Marauders, the special unit for jungle fighting in Burma. The *Clymer* also got the word that Italy had surrendered unconditionally. The crew broke out into wild cheering and whistling at the good news. On deck Foley uttered a prayer of thanksgiving. A sailor chipping paint off the deck saw him and said, "Well Father, that's strike no. 1. Now we've got to get the other two."56

Joining up with a task force built around the *Enterprise,* the *Clymer* docked at Espiritu Santo on September 16. The harbor was choked with shipping including two more carriers along with cruisers, destroyers, APAs and other support vessels. Foley attended a conference of chaplains aboard the *Saratoga.* "Sara" had two chaplains for her 3200 crewmen. The Catholic chaplain aboard at this time was Fr. Maurice Sheehy, formerly the head of the department of religious education at Catholic University. Prior to America's involvement in the war, Sheehy was a loud advocate for Roosevelt's interventionist policies. He published a long article to that effect in the *Washington Post* in 1939 and in February 1941 delivered a "Fence-Sitters" speech over the Columbia radio network attacking non-interventionists and equating England's policies as those "of Christianity." The speech was widely published in the press as was another delivered in August to support Roosevelt's gambit to extend compulsory military service. Many felt that his speeches helped sway the vote in favor of Roosevelt's maneuver. As a naval chaplain, Sheehy received captain's rank and a Bronze Star.57

Foley was not the admirer of Roosevelt that Sheehy was and he knew England too well to confuse her agenda with Christian principles, yet he enjoyed his tour of the flattop, noting her awesome aerial firepower. As fulfilling as his work on the APA was, he desired service on a floating airfield. He would get his chance before the shooting match was over.

The next two weeks were business as usual, with a hop to Guadalcanal and then Dumbea Bay, Noumea. Foley was kept busy with his own boys as well as other crews who had no Catholic chaplain. He got to baptize Metzger at St. Joseph's Cathedral in Noumea and was pleased at how happy the boy was. In these exotic locales, Foley never got over the constant evidence of the Church's universality. American servicemen attended Mass celebrated by black Fijian priests and could see what work had been done by the missionaries who sacrificed so many years of their lives and labors for the natives. 58

And the natives learned their lessons well. Fr. Francis J. Gorman, the chaplain of the hard-fighting 132nd Infantry Regiment from Chicago thought that the faith of the natives put most American Catholics to shame. Like Brock, Foley and others, he sent contributions home to the Society for the Propagation of the Faith for support of the missions. In a letter to the Society he could not praise the Solomonese natives enough:

> You should hear them chant the Mass; you should hear them pray in Latin. I never realized the value of universal Latin until I had occasion to offer Mass for natives whose tongue I could not speak. Because of Latin, I could pray with them. The prayers after Mass which we are accustomed to

recite in the vernacular they always say in Latin. In each village they recite every evening the Rosary in perfect Latin.59

On Columbus day the *Clymer* was prowling the waters around Guadalcanal. She had made Tassafaronga south of Cape Esperance the day before but a Japanese sub had knocked out two Liberty ships earlier, one of which was loaded with gasoline. Standard operating procedure in such cases is to leave anchorage and cruise at night to avoid being a stationary target. When the vessel returned to Cactus elements of the 2nd Raiders were loaded aboard. Foley tended to them and also made trips to the *Buchanan* and the *Tracy*, all between incessant General Alarms. Something big was in the air and Foley wanted all of his boys to be ready spiritually for their trial. He could not stop thinking about the Liberty ship, burning still a day after she was hit. As he stared into the blazing pyre he thought, "We speak of twenty four hours as a long time, yet Hell burns forever!"60

Notes: Chapter 7

1 Foley diary, April 19, 1943; Foley interview, March 6, 1995.

2 Foley diary, April 19, 1943.

3 Ibid.

4 Interview with Sister Mary Theresa Cartier, SMSM, July 9, 1997, Waltham, MA.: Becker, *Saving the Solomons*, 76–78.

5 Foley diary, April 20, 1943. Sister Mary Thesesa believes the French nun's name was Martial, not Martian, as Foley understood.

6 Ibid.

7 Foley diary, April 20, 21, 1943.

8 "Analecta," *Ecclesiastical Review* 107(July 1942): 39.

9 Foley diary, April 22, 1943.

10 Ibid.

11 Foley diary, April 24, 1943. The correct total, according to Foley, was thirty-seven, including the three nuns and thirty-four Chinese and Fijian women and their children.

12 Foley diary, April 24, 1943.

13 Ibid. Foley interview, March 6, 1995.

14 Ibid.

15 Arthur G. King, *Vignettes of the South Pacific: The Lighter Side of World War II* (Cincinnati, Ohio: ARthur G. King, M.D., 1991), 57–61. King was the Island Medical Inspector whose primary job was to cover up American involvement in the business and deal with the madam who actually ran the place. He would also supply American property when necessary such as a case of lubricant he authorized on the grounds of "humanitarian aid for use when business was 'brisk.'" It is revealing that a doctor, who specialized in gynecology, should brag about his involvement in the prostitution racket, his theft of taxpayers' property and his lying to cover up the army's role. Revealing too is his perception that this was the "lighter" side of the war.

16 Ibid. Patch's biographer does not mention the Pink House incident. William K. Wyant, *Sandy Patch: A Biography of Lt. Gen. Alexander M. Patch,* (New York: Praeger, 1991).

17 Foley diary, April 24, 25, 1943.

18 Foley diary, May 5, 1943.

19 Foley diary, May 7, 8, 1943.

20 Foley diary, May 12, 1943. First hand information regarding Bishop Aubin comes from interviews with Sister Mary Theresa Cartier, SMSM, one of the nuns under Aubin's authority, July 2, 8, 1997 and her article "Horrors Start as Yellow Men Strike," Pictorial Review, *Boston Sunday Advertiser,* June 27, 1943; Also Decker, *Saving the Solomons.*

21 Sister Mary Theresa regularly makes the rounds of Marine Corps reunions, giving her vivid description of the harrowing escape.

22 Though Vandergrift was polite to Aubin and even wrote an article on religion for a Methodist journal, he was reportedly incensed that he

kept getting requests for missionary evacuations. When asked to supply a reserve boat for Aubin's group he said, "Is this what this war is all about, rescuing missionaries and nuns?" Sister Mary Theresa interview July 2, 1997; Lt. Gen. A.A. Vandergrift, "Religion on Guadalcanal,"; Ellwood C. Nance, ed., *Faith of Our Fighters* (St. Louis: Bethany Press, 1944), 239–244.

23 Foley diary, May 12, 1943. A photograph of Aubin dressed as Foley saw him can be found in Decker, *Saving the Solomons*.

24 Foley diary, May 13, 1943.

25 Foley diary, May 19, 1943.

26 Foley diary, May 20, 1943.

27 Foley diary, June 7, 1943.

28 Foley diary, June 10, 11, 1943.

29 Foley diary, June 12, 1943.

30 Ibid.

31 Foley diary, June 15, 1943.

32 Foley diary, June 18, 1943.

33 Foley diary, June 20, 21, 1943.

34 Foley diary, June 21, 1943.

35 Foley diary, June 22, 1943.

36 John N. Rentz, *Bougainville and the Northern Solomons* , (n.c.: Historical Section Division of Public Information Headquarters U.S. Marine Corps, 1948), 1–3.

37 Foley diary, June 29, 1943; Robert A. Authur and Kenneth Cohlmia, ed. Robert T. Vance, *The Third Marine Division*, (Washington, D.C.: Infantry Journal Press, 1948), 53, 54.

38 Foley diary, July 7, 1943.

39 Foley diary, July 8, 1943.

40 Foley diary, July 10, 1943.

41 Foley diary, July 14, 1943; Joe Foss and Diane Foss, *A Proud American: The Autobiography of Joe Foss* (New York: Pocket, 1992), 122-125.

42 Foss, *A Proud American*, 126.

43 Foley diary, July 14, 1943; Foss, *A Proud American*, 126–128.

44 As an administrator in both an ecclesiastical and academic bureaucracy, Foley well knew the arbitrary nature of rules, and his shipboard policy was eminently sensible. What the captain didn't know would not hurt the men. An example of this was the time a black steward came to Foley and told him that somebody stole his wallet. Foley figured that it must have been taken by one of the other stewards so he gathered them all together and said that he was sure that the man who took it was sorry now. He turned his chair around and said that the guilty man should throw the wallet on the floor and there would be no questions asked. No wallet. Later Foley was telling some of the officers about his method and they hooted at him. "You'll never make out with the thief that way Father!" Foley gathered the stewards together again and did the same thing. This time the wallet was thrown on the floor by his feet. Foley returned it to its owner and told him to forget about the whole thing since if the captain knew, there would be trouble for all involved, even the victim. The incident ended there. Foley interview, March 10, 1995.

45 Foley diary, July 21, 1943.

46 Foley diary, July 22, 1943.

47 Foley diary, July 23, 1943.

48 Foley diary, July 30, 1943; Foley interview, March 10, 1995.

49 Foley diary, August 6, 7, 11, 14, 1943; *Dictionary of American Naval Fighting Ships,* vol. III, 73. For a company history of Raytheon see Otto J. Scott, *The Creative Ordeal: The Story of Raytheon,* (New York: Athenaeum, 1974).

50 Foley diary, August 18, 1943; Letter from Fr. Charles Riedel, C.S.V. to Bishop O'Hara, August 19, 1943, from the Archives of Clerics of St. Viator, Arlington Heights, IL.

51 "Statement of Father C.C. Riedel, C.S.V.," Archives of Clerics of St. Viator.

52 Ibid.

53 Ibid. Riedel returned to his religious community and was assigned to the Mission Band, giving retreats to clergy in dioceses across the nation. He was renowned as a captivating preacher and his retreats were well attended. He died unexpectedly during a retreat in November 1958 at the age of forty-six. Riedel's belief that his relief and punishment at Saipan were the result of anti-Catholic animus on the parts of a few officers appears to have been correct. His outspoken defense of Catholic Marines' right to have their own chaplain surely provoked individuals such as Shoup and meant that he had to be dispatched on any pretext. By objective standards, Riedel should have been decorated for his courageous service on both Tarawa and Saipan. Instead he was removed from his charges at a crucial time and then summarily punished. Riedel knew the score. In a letter written to a friend at the Viatorian Seminary soon after all of the fireworks, he wrote, "the Corps is like the Community; you usually get a pat on the back for something that deserves no credit, whether its brains or personality, and a kick in the pants for doing something that needs to be done." Letter from Fr. Charles Riedel, C.S.V. to Father French, 12 September 1944, Archives of Clerics of St. Viator. In the end, it can be judged that Father Riedel was just too tough for the Marine Corps.

54 Foley diary, August 27, 1943.

55 Foley diary, September 6, 1943.

56 Foley diary, September 7, 9, 12, 15, 1943.

57 Foley diary, September 18, 1943; Drury, *The History of the Chaplain Corps United States Navy,* vol. II, 15, 16. Sheehy was an example of a priest who over-identified with the Democrat party and Roosevelt's agenda. Other clerics who opposed Roosevelt's interventionism, such as the popular Fr. James Gillis, were silenced by government pressure. See James F. Finley, C.S.P., *James Gillis, Paulist* (Garden City, New York: Hanover House, 1958).

58 Foley diary, October1, 4, 1943.

59 Grant, *Was is my Parish,* 88. Gorman fought and prayed with the 132nd throughout the Guadalcanal and Bougainville campaigns and was

the recipient of the Bronze Star. He went regular army after the war and served in Japan, Germany and Korea. He retired as a lieutenant general in 1960 and returned to a Chicago parish. It is unknown how he felt about the discarding of universal Latin for the vernacular in the wake of Vatican II. He died in early 1998 at the age of ninety-four. See Muehrcke, *Orchids in the Mud*, 450; *Guadalcanal Echoes* May/June 1998, 24.

60 Foley diary, October 12, 13, 1943.

CHAPTER 8

▼

"FURIOUS BATTLES ON TWO FRONTS"

By mid-October the *Clymer* was steaming toward Vila Bay at Efate in the New Hebrides for maneuvers. Along the way the crew was given the long anticipated word about the expected invasion. Foley wrote in his diary:

> "Today I learn that our next operation is against Bougainville. These Marines we have aboard are to go secure the beachhead, hold it for two weeks until the army takes over. Presently it seems that *Der Tag* is November 3rd."1

Bougainville was the largest of the Solomons group, half again as large as Guadalcanal and with the same forbidding terrain of impenetrable jungles, oppressive rainfall and humidity, crocodiles, insects and the most dangerous game of all—an estimated forty thousand Japanese. To seize Rabaul, Bougainville would have to be taken. Theoretically, if not in fact, the target should have been an even tougher nut to crack than

Guadalcanal. It was closer to air and naval support from both Rabaul and Truk, and the Japanese had worked furiously for over a year and a half to prepare defenses, including four airfields and a seaplane base. Furthermore, the Japanese knew the invasion was coming. There would be no surprise advantage working in the Americans' favor and even the landing point, Cape Tokorina at Empress Augusta Bay on the southwestern coast, was fairly obvious. As always the risks were high. The amount of available intelligence information about Japanese fortifications was not great and the old problem of inadequate transport shipping remained. There would be only four AKA attack cargo vessels involved and eight APA attack transports including the *Crescent City, American Legion, Hunter Liggett, President Hayes, President Jackson, President Adams, Fuller,* and the indomitable *George Clymer* .2

Because of the dearth of cargo shipping, the plan was to land the first wave of assault troops loaded as lightly as possible since speed was of the essence. Heavier equipment, service personnel and backup gear would follow with the succeeding waves. The ships were restricted to five hundred tons of supplies apiece and needed to be completely unloaded within six hours.3

There would be a week of final training and rehearsal at Vila, Efate, New Hebrides. The Marines aboard the *Clymer* had lost some of their cavalier bravado and were scattered over her deck cleaning their weapons as they never had before. Foley made his rounds with them and also went forward portside to greet some other passengers, twenty-four dogs slated to do scout, messenger, and sentry work in the Bougainville bush. The First Marine War Dog Platoon was attached to the 2d Marine Raider regiment which the *Clymer* was carrying and was slated to land one hour after the first wave went ashore. Foley noted that only four of the group were German Shepherds, the rest being Doberman Pinschers. The War Dog program was still in an experimental stage and the Bougainville campaign would either prove or disprove the efficacy of the concept.4

On the 16th, the Marines began landing exercises at Efate harbor, which was the picture of a South Seas paradise. The water was almost powder blue with white coral covering the ocean bottom. The beach was beautiful ivory sand with coconut trees swaying in the breeze and dark natives in colorful array hawking their wares to the strangers. The enticing tropical fantasy was just a brief interlude before the assault on the fetid Bougainville jungle and Foley got more than his share of young men suffering pre-invasion jitters. One boy came to talk for awhile and said, "Father, did I feel good when I heard that there was a priest aboard." Foley told him not to worry. The big day was set for the first of November, not the third as earlier announced. The first was the Feast of All Saints, a good day to go home to heaven.5

Of course Foley did not let on to the men, but in officers' meetings, the picture painted was bleak. Captain Talbot informed them through the Communications Officer that high casualties were expected, perhaps over 30% and as usual, the combat transports were expected to draw the enemy's most concentrated fire. It was recommended that the *Clymer* officers write a final letter home just in case. Foley looked at the others, all with the same expression on their faces. He wondered if some or all of them would be dead in two weeks. He thought about his shipmates' loved ones as most of them had families, and the anguish they would face if the worst happened. And he thought about his own position as a priest of God and gave thanks for the celibate priesthood. When he had embarked upon his vocation he had decided to devote himself solely to the Lord and the task of serving God's people. A family would be wonderful, but a man could not give all of his heart and soul to God if he were concerned with the welfare of a wife and children. His only worry was his mother, who would be devastated if he was lost, but would always be provided for by his brothers and sisters.6

Foley dutifully wrote his contingency letter:

Dear Ma:

I am writing this letter to you just in case anything should happen to me. I mailed it to Sister Flavius to give to you if you had received a telegram from Washington about me. If you read this letter, you will already have learned that Our Lord called me home to Himself.

Although the news will be hard to bear for all of you, I know that with your wonderful faith you will take it as the very best thing that could have happened to me. That is the way I would want you to take it. It was the way Our Lord wanted. Nothing could be better than His will and since it was fulfilled in me, what more could we ask for?

It may surprise you to learn Ma, that we never prayed to be spared in the struggle. We only asked in the words of the prayer that we said at the end of Mass, "Lord, give us the strength and devotion that we need to serve You and our country with courage. If it should happen according to your holy will, that the supreme sacrifice should be asked of us, as it has already been asked of so many others like us, may Our Lady, Your Mother and Saint Joseph, Your foster-father, be with us in our last hour."

You will not be surprised however to learn that like all the other men out here I often thought of you all and looked forward to the day when we would be together again. Never a day when you weren't in my thoughts and prayers. As you know now, Our Lord decided that we should meet only in heaven. Pa and Thomas apparently needed company so He called me to join them.

Looking back over my life, I see nothing but reasons that placed me more and more in His debt as the years spun out. First, there was the gift of such good parents as you and Pa. Your care of us and your years of self-sacrifice were a lesson in love. Then there was the gift of such wonderful brothers and sisters, Mary and Kay, James and Joe, Ed and Francis. There couldn't be any better in the world.

Then Our Lord gave me my vocation to the Society of Jesus. When I first told you shyly about my desire on Memorial Day 1923, you wondered if you would live to see the day of my Ordination and First Mass. He took care of that also after the years of preparation near home and far away in England. In the Society my work has been with those whom I loved most, young men for whom the world was just opening out. It was a labor of love to teach them at Holy Cross and Boston College and to advise them in the Freshman Dean's Office at Chestnut Hill. When the change came to a naval career, I was still with young men, bringing them the word of God and the Sacraments that they would not have had, if I had not volunteered. This year and a half in the Navy aboard ship has been very consoling. Only a mother could appreciate the light in a boy's eyes and the smile on his face as he said, "Father, did I feel better when I learned there was a priest aboard." To many of the boys who said that I gave Holy Viaticum which was just that. To know that through my ministrations they had Our Lord with them on their journey into eternity made me very happy and at the same time humble at the awful powers that I exercised as a priest.

Finally Ma, there was the gift of friends like Sister Flavius, Julia Sheehan, Frs. Barney Boylan, Tony Carroll, John Long, Al Duncan, Tom Herlihy and others whose friendship and prayers meant so much to me.

Yes, my life has been a rich and happy one. Even if I could live it over again, I wouldn't have it any differently. God was so good to me that it would be ungrateful to think of reordering it, not even its ending. He had charge of that also.

Meanwhile, I shall keep pestering Our Lord and Our Lady to take care of you all. Imagine the joy of conversation with Our Lady and her Son. You will understand then why Pa, Thomas and I are anxious for that day of reunion when we shall all be together forever. Until then, Ma, Good-bye, God bless and keep you and Mary and Kay, Joe and James, Francis and Ed.

As usual with love to All. John7

The idea was that the officers would make a couple of copies of their final letters and hand them out to various friends so that at least one might be sent later. Foley was deluged with letters from Catholics, non-Catholics and atheists alike. There was an inexplicable feeling that the priest would survive any disaster. Foley told them it was presumptuous to assume that he would be the letter carrier to come through. Nevertheless, he carefully stored away the letters, hoping that he could return them all to their authors after the invasion was effected. Meanwhile he went about his business as usual trying to keep everyone's morale up. He showed "Men of Boy's Town" with Spencer Tracy and was disappointed that it had no hint of spiritual life. Father Flanagan could not be proud of that!8

On the afternoon of the 20th there was a conference of gold braid aboard the *Clymer* . Admiral Halsey's wrinkled, stony visage was perhaps more furrowed than usual. Marine Maj. Gen. Charles D. Barrett, the overall commander of the operation, fell from the window of his quarters that same day and was killed. Halsey was anxious to get General Vandergrift as replacement even though he had just been made Commandant of the Marine Corps in Washington. The green 3d Marine Division commanded by Maj. Gen. Allen Turnage was scheduled to make the beach assault with the 39th Army Division.9

The Marines aboard the *Clymer* were allowed beach recreation parties after the vessel moved to Pakkelulo Bay, twenty miles north of the usual anchorage at Espiritu Santo. The ship was commended by the COMTRANS GR for speed in unloading, supposedly the first time he complimented a transport in the SOPAC area. Based on the timing of the rehearsals, the transport vessels were expected to completely unload in the span of four and a half hours, predicated upon a 2,500 yard run from the beach. This was optimistic thinking. The surf in that area could be wild, the charted coastline was ten miles off what the aerial survey revealed, and the approach was guarded by uncharted shoals. Much of what information did exist regarding the area had been provided by the displaced missionaries.10

The dog platoon was likewise brought ashore for exercises. Foley dealt with a couple of young handlers who were having spiritual problems. Though a dog lover, the chaplain had a bad experience one night when he had to pass their pens topside. One K-9 started to bark viciously at him, setting off the rest of the pack. "I should hate to meet these dogs unleashed," he thought.11

This was the final period of preparation. The Marines were allowed to frolic on the beach while the *Clymer* was besieged with a mock air attack. Foley recorded the scene.

> At 0910 General Quarters alarm is piped down, "All hands to General Quarters." Peep-Peep-Peep all battle stations are manned. Since this is only a dry run, I go to the flying bridge deck to watch the show. Suddenly as from nowhere, torpedo planes are skimming over the surface of the water, as they get within 100 yards of us, they open their torpedo bays, then swing up and over us. The roar is deafening and frightening. Everywhere, from every side they come in on us. The gunners are training the guns on one plane when another is on top of them. Then suddenly there is a whine straight over ahead, no it is a few hundred yards away, six dive bombers are plummeting straight down on us, with a zing-zing noise that makes us happy that they are our own. As they drop their eggs, dry run, they zoom up and over us, vapor streaking from their wing tips. There is a lull for about ten minutes, then the fighters, strafing the gun crews come in over the low hill straight for the ships. We are all being sunk, the four of us. The other three are the President ships. We automatically duck as we think they are going to crash into us, then they gun her up and away they have gone. For one hour intermittently these attacks go on. When they are over we know what to expect when D day arrives, next Monday. We learn also

from scuttlebutt that we are to have 18 destroyers and 6 bat-tlewagons, plus four aircraft carriers with us, meaning 8 attack transports and four cargo ships.12

On the way from Espiritu Santo to Guadalcanal to pick up the brass hats for the operation, the Marine junior officers gave their men their last instructions including the warning to separate any captured Japanese enlisted men from the officers immediately as they were known to volunteer information in such cases. The gyrenes for their part sharpened their trench knives on whetstones and hummed while loading .30 caliber cartridges into Garand clips and preparing machine gun ammunition belts with a linker. Colonel Shapely gave them the lowdown on the time and location of the invasion over the P.A. system. Foley winced when Shapely's only invocation of God's name came in an expletive.13

Off Lunga Point on October 30, Admiral Wilkinson and Air General Harris came aboard with their staffs. General Vandergrift and his entourage appeared also. Among Vandergrift's group was a young navy combat artist, William F. Draper from Hopedale, Massachusetts. Draper had volunteered at the same navy recruiting office on Causeway Street in the North End of Boston that Foley had. Amazingly, the navy utilized him where he was most useful and he was initially assigned to draw wakes of submarines so that pilots would be able to identify them from the air. He did work in the Aleutians campaign before being reassigned again. Though primarily a landscape artist he was chosen to do portraits of Admirals Nimitz and Halsey. His current assignment was to execute paintings of the Bougainville operation.14

The next morning was the Feast of Christ the King, and the *Clymer's* chaplain celebrated two Masses for the men about to embark on their great adventure. The Masses were standing room only on the hot steel deck of the attack transport. Draper was there, concentrating more on his work than the Gospel. A professional photographer was there too, taking pictures of the scene and the celebrant, and some of the photos showed up in books and magazines in the coming months. Foley was oblivious to these men capturing his image. He was focused solely on the Mass he was saying for these young men, many of whom could be dead the next day. Draper's finished work depicted Foley bowing before his homemade altar with an acolyte next to him and a congregation of kneeling Marines in jungle camouflage behind him. In the background other ships of the convoy steam under an azure sky.15

Operation CHERRYBLOSSOM was only hours away. Most of the attack transport and cargo ships had preceded the *Clymer* to the rendezvous point. A Japanese reconnaissance plane spotted the convoy, but was immediately swatted down by a P-38. The Transport Group Task Force 31 was under the overall command of Commodore Lawrence F. Reifsnider. The group was divided in two, between the Northern Attack Force and the Southern. The Northern Attack Force was further subdivided into three transport divisions, Able, Baker and Charlie and there was also an escort unit with minesweepers. The *Clymer* was in division Able with the three *Presidents Jackson, Adams* and *Hayes. Clymer'*s code name for this operation was DESTINY. The convoy bore on a northwesterly course, with some maneuver for deception, toward Empress Augusta Bay. The sky above on the night of October 31 was very dark, the ocean below glowed phosphorescent.16

The chaplain worked far into the night. The vessel was crammed to the gunnels. An extra two hundred Marines slept on deck apart from all those stowed below. Foley had rosary, Benediction, and Consecration to the Sacred Heart in the afternoon and heard confessions until midnight. He wanted to make himself available to any man who might need him at that point. One of the Marine majors who sat in on the high level planning sessions came to him and told him, "Father, you should know this, that one of the admirals said there is too much _ _ religion aboard this ship." Foley replied, "Is that so? I wish he would say that to me." Foley only occasionally felt that anti-Catholicism in the navy was institutional though certainly there were plenty of individual examples. In any case, the admiral did not pursue his grievance and Foley continued with his business unimpeded.17

Reveille blared at 0315 November 1, 1943. Foley was back at it, distributing Holy Communion and then Mass. By 0550 all of the *Clymer's* boats were hoisted to the rail and made ready. Minesweepers preceded the APAs into the horseshoe-shaped bay and reported sufficient draft for the transports. Shortly after six, the destroyer screen opened fire just as the sun blazed fiery red in the sky. Foley thought, "It is a morning made in heaven and man is making it a hell. We see the angry flames leap from the mouth of the guns of the destroyers and then fourteen seconds later, timed by one of the sailors, we get the noise of the explosion from the guns. What happens on the shore we don't hear, but we see earth thrown up and then lazy smoke drifting skyward."18 The shore itself looked forbidding. The jungle extended almost to the shoreline and in the background a menacing mountain loomed with white clouds surrounding its apex.

A young Marine lieutenant, only about twenty-two, who had served Mass for Foley aboard ship asked him to come down and say hello to his fifteen-man platoon. Foley looked at their faces, "Just children" he thought. The guns pounded overhead. He told them, "Listen to all the noise we are making there, it won't be as difficult as it seems to you now." One trembling boy near tears said, "Father, they mean to kill us." Foley saw that it suddenly dawned on the boy what war is.19 He hoped that the Marine would not soon be a mangled corpse on the beachhead.

The destroyers continued to pour fire onto the target, some salvos landing along the shoreline, others directed inland. By 0721 the *Clymer* had swung into her place in line parallel to the beach, sandwiched between the *Presidents Jackson* and *Adams*. She opened up with all of her firepower as did the other APAs. The landing boats had already shoved off with a benediction and a prayer, and were circling in the rendezvous area. Then, given the go ahead, the LCVPs and LCMs lurched toward the enemy shore. At 0730 the first assault troops landed on schedule and overran the beach. Some crumpled immediately as Japanese machine guns opened up. The

Raiders embarked from the *Clymer* heading toward their sector of Beach Blue 2 were sprayed with fire from dug-in defenders on two small islands, Puruata and Torokina. A boat of Raiders from the *Fuller* headed toward Puruata to silence the harassing elements there.20

The Japanese defenders at Cape Torokina were not impressive in numbers. There were only approximately 270 to 300 soldiers in the immediate area and the jungle was so heavy and overgrown that defense would naturally be localized and reinforcement from inland extremely difficult. However, the small force was entrenched in eighteen tough coconut log pillboxes and they also had a 75 mm gun dug in on Beach Green 2 directly behind the protecting cover of Puruata and Tokorina islands and near the Buretoni Mission. The gun blasted away and destroyed several of the approaching boats. Meanwhile mortar, machine gun, and rifle fire continued to pour from the shore. Further up the line to the left of the *Clymer's* position, there was no Japanese opposition but the surf was wild and men and equipment were dumped into the water by the raging waves. 21 The section was later abandoned due to the insurmountable conditions.

Japanese planes managed to penetrate the screen of American P-38s to make passes at the transport group. At 1005 a group swept over the *Clymer*, which executed evasive maneuvers wildly. Fire from the ships caught one of the interlopers who nevertheless managed to drop his bomb prior to bursting into flames and disintegrating. By 1100 the first wounded were brought back to the ship. Commanding Officer of the 2d Raider Battalion Lt. Col. Joe McCaffery had moved from unit to unit on the beach under heavy fire, trying to reorganize the disjointed groups. He was shot twice while leading an attack on a Japanese position. When brought aboard the *Clymer* McCaffery was dying from a bullet in the shoulder and another that had severed his spine. Foley gave him the last sacraments in his final moments.22

The *American Legion* ran aground on a shoal. Tugs quickly moved in to haul her off but a squadron of forty enemy bombers sighted her and attempted to dispatch the stranded APA. Anti-aircraft fire drove them off.

Two pilots bailed out of their burning planes; one tangled his chute and fell like a rock to his death, the other floated gracefully into the water. A machine gun crew on the *Clymer* cut him in half and he sank out of sight. Foley said to them, "You shouldn't have done that. If we had picked him up he would have given us lots of information." The gunner replied, "Father, he was trying to kill us. We got him."23

Because of all the air harassment the transports had to withdraw temporarily, upsetting the unloading schedule. The *Clymer* and other APAs did move in again and sent shore parties to the beach to facilitate the dispatch of supplies and equipment which went on through the next day. The transport group, less the *Hunter Liggett* and *Crescent City* , headed back to Port Purvis, Florida Island on November 3rd. These ships were joined at Point Purvis by another group that had fought a furious battle only hours before. Fr. Steve Hannon, chaplain of the light cruiser *Columbia* came aboard the *Clymer* that evening and gave Foley a blow by blow description of the fracas.24

Four light cruisers the *Montpelier, Cleveland, Denver* and Father Hannon's *Columbia* along with eight destroyers the *Charles Ausburne, Dyson, Claxton, Spence, Thatcher, Converse, Foote* and *Stanly* pounded the Buka-Bonis airfields on the northern end of Bougainville on October 31, prior to the landing at Empress Augusta Bay on November 1. They had plastered the two airfields with three hundred rounds of six inch and 2,400 rounds of five inch shells before heading south to bombard the Shortlands and Ballale. The task force commanded by Admiral "Tip" Merrill then moved to protect the transport group on the first. The next day the hard fighting group turned north again to engage a Japanese surface force of comparable size, albeit with three heavy cruisers armed with eight inch guns and one light cruiser. The Japanese force was intent on smashing Foley's transport group. The combatants engaged at 0245 on November 2 and the fire exchanged was terrific. The destroyer *Foote* was severely damaged by a torpedo, and CL *Denver* and destroyer *Spence* sustained minor damages. The battle raged until 0536 with the Japanese losing a light cruiser and a destroyer. Even after all of this, Merrill's group had to resist an air attack by sixty-seven bombers from Rabaul as they headed back to Point Purvis.25

Another participant in the Battle of Empress Augusta Bay was the 40mm gunner/diarist Jim Fahey of the *Montpelier*.

> As the sea battle was coming to an end we passed a Jap ship under attack at close range. We did not fire on the Jap ship because we were very low on ammunition and our help was not needed. This action took place on our starboard side not too far away. It seemed like it was getting a little brighter as I watched the action. The Jap ship was dead in the water. I did not notice any other ships around but the three of us. The Jap ship was a mass of flames and red hot steel as the big guns covered it with exploding shells. It gave off a red glow that lit up the area around it. It must have been a nightmare in hell for the Japs as they were roasted and blown to bits. I don't see how anyone could escape. It was a horrible way to die, it was a slaughter. This type of warfare tops them all for horror. There is no safe place to hide and if you land in the water the huge sharks that are longer than a good sized room are always close by.26

The group refueled, rearmed, and removed their wounded at Purvis Bay. Foley's transport group did the same. Foley himself went back to his usual duties when the ship was in port, picking up movies, arranging rec parties and visiting vessels which did not have a Catholic chaplain. On Veteran's Day, the *Clymer* was back at Tassafaronga to load up the 129th combat team for delivery to Bougainville. The objective had been penetrated by the Marines after furious fighting but the island was not secure by a long shot. Army General Roy Geiger relieved Vandergrift of overall command on the 9th. Vandergrift became the eighteenth Commandant of the Marine Corps on January 1, 1944.27

The *Clymer* and her sister ships plodded northward, "into the jaws of the Japs again," with a strong escort. The Japanese were contesting the Bougainville operation with vigor and were desperate to prevent the rein-forcing troops from arriving. The convoy was besieged incessantly by Japanese fighters overhead, and General Quarters were rung so often that there was little point in standing down. Foley described this trip to his diary:

> Looks as though it might be a bad night for us. There is a bomber's moon overhead, bursting with fullness. Easy to read a paper on deck, I pull my note book out of my pocket and read with the greatest of ease. Passengers loll on decks, drink-ing in the silent beauty of the tropical night. Sea is hammered silver. Other ships are no longer dark silhouettes on the ocean, they are as brightly lit up as we are. A short distance away three cruisers and five destroyers come up on our port quarter going the wrong way, then they turn around and steam ahead to intercept any Jap task force that may be trying to annihilate us.28

At Bougainville, the *Clymer's* human cargo was off-loaded with some-what less urgency than on D-Day. On the beach could still be seen a million dollars worth of landing boats splintered like so much kindling on that first day. A wounded Japanese pilot with an eye shot out was brought aboard even as Marine artillery continued to hammer Japanese positions. Unloading was completed expeditiously and the ship steamed off toward Cactus again, under the constant threat of Japanese birds of prey. The area was still plenty hot. The *Clymer* passed the cruiser *Denver* being towed by a tug at five knots. A torpedo bomber had scored with a hit on her starboard side aft and she was dead in the water until being aided by the tug.29

Anchored in Tulagi harbor early on the 15th, Foley was heading for the hospital when he passed the famous sign which read:

Admiral Halsey Says
Kill Japs, Kill Japs
Kill More Japs
You will kill more yellow Bastards
if you do your work well.

Foley thought to himself, "The Chinese are yellow also. The spirit evidenced by that sign is what brought on the war and will hinder the peace. Are we Americans still color conscious?"30

A few days later Foley put up a graveyard marker for the Raider Col. J.P. McCaffery and PFC J.S. Studer, both of whom died aboard the *Clymer*. Apart from the tough Japanese resistance, troops on Bougainville were plagued by continual downpours and the ever present dangers of the jungle. The *Hunter Liggett* and *American Legion*, two of the *Clymer*'s comrades in their transport division steamed off, heading toward home. The *Clymer* crew waved as the vessels departed for God's country. They wished they were going with them. Their motto was "the Golden Gate in '48."31

The crew had no time to feel sorry for themselves. The *Clymer* loaded up the 8th Field Artillery, veterans of the fighting on Guadalcanal and Munda, New Georgia and ferried them to Noumea. On November 25, Chaplain Foley gave his second annual Thanksgiving address over the loudspeaker. He told the men that they had much to be thankful for, that in a year of operations in hostile waters the vessel had come under frequent air and surface attacks and only two crewmen had been slightly wounded. Then he asked the Lord for his continued protection in whatever dangers lie ahead.32

The ship did get an extended rest in Auckland for the first two weeks of December. Foley arranged a dance at the Metropole for the ship's complement. There was some trouble when one of the *Clymer*'s bosuns got drunk and was hauled back to the ship by the Shore Patrol. This was not unusual, as Foley told the men that drunks would be dealt with that way for their own safety. The bosun insisted on going back to the dance and disappeared. The next morning the Division Officer came to Foley and told him that the bosun was missing. What should he do? Foley said to look for him and if he was not found by the afternoon to report him missing. Several days went by and there was no sign of him. Foley remembered a conversation he had had with the boy some time ago. As one of his handyman jobs, Foley was in charge of selling $10,000 government insurance policies. Most of the men took out these policies through they were not required to. The bosun was one of the few who would not buy one. He said to Foley, "Oh no chaplain, its a racket. I won't have that." Foley tried to convince him. The bosun asked him if he had one. Foley told him yes, he had to take out one since he sold the policies. He had sold about $3,000,000 worth, but the sailor was not buying.33

On December 12 Foley was ashore with another chaplain, Fr. Bob Minton from Mobile Hospital #6 visiting the Auckland zoo. A messenger arrived and told him to report to Morrison's funeral parlor on Parneel Street with the ship's dentist to identify the body of the missing bosun. Foley went into the chamber which resembled a pillbox where the corpse was held and viewed the body, now completely unrecognizable after decomposing in the water for a week. Foley staggered out of the chamber, his eyes streaming tears from the stinging formaldehyde. The dentist laughed and said, "You can't take it, huh, Father?" Foley replied, "You try it." The dentist emerged crying as well. The bosun's body was positively identified by dental records and Foley arranged his funeral the next day. The assumption was that after being brought to the ship the night of the dance the bosun took an "anchor chain liberty" to try to get back to the dance and fell in the water. He was so drunk he could not save himself.34

When Foley wrote to the man's mother he was extremely cautious and did not go into the circumstances of his death. Foley later received a heart-breaking letter from the woman who felt that her son must have been the victim of foul play. She also wondered why there was no insurance payment. Foley bit his lip and had to tell her the truth, that he had tried to sell her son the insurance and he refused to take out a policy. It was not a pleasant duty for him and he cursed the evils of drink, which led to the bosun's pointless death.35

For his own part, he had tried to be the men's advocate and crying towel, but much more importantly, their spiritual guide regardless of differences in faith. He felt that they had to respect him as a man first and then they could accept his moral teachings. Foley was guided by the words of Diego Laynez, one of the original members of the Company of Jesus and the second Jesuit chaplain, after Nicholas Bobodilla. In a letter to an Italian duke about to embark upon a military expedition, Laynez spelled out the timeless reasons to have chaplains along.

> ...I believe that our Lord will be very well served and Your Excellency much consoled if you send some good religious along on this expedition, men who will be true servants of God and who will seek the salvation of souls. By prayer and good example, by preaching and hearing confessions, by nursing the sick and helping the dying, these men will do a tremendous amount of good. They will teach the soldiers proper motives for fighting, keep them from quarreling among themselves, and will call them to task for blasphemies and gambling. Finally, I know that the soldiers of our nation will really profit from this, for by their peace of mind and confidence in God they will better fulfill their duties in the war.36

Ironically, Foley would discover what the *Clymer*'s men thought of him the same day he went to view the bosun's body. That morning he said his usual morning Mass and was then told by Bosun Grymen to stick around afterward. Foley had no inkling of what was up and Grymen was not talking. Over the P.A. system the announcement blared, "All hands not on watch report to the Boat Deck forward." When the crew was assembled Grymen delivered a speech and then the chaplain was presented with five gifts: a large statue of St. Patrick, a lovely lace alb, a pen and pencil desk set, a clock made out of kawhri wood with three kiwis perched on top and an order for twenty-five dollars worth of photographs. Foley was overwhelmed by the gesture and could only say that he hoped he would prove worthy of the spirit behind the gifts. He was further edified when he found out that many of the non-Catholics chipped in too. There was some difficulty living in his cramped quarters with St. Patrick so he later gave the plaster apostle of Ireland to his friends the sisters at their convent in Noumea. The clock he carefully packed in a load of towels from sick bay and placed it in a wooden box the ship's carpenter hand made for him. He prayed that it would get back to his mother in Boston without being broken a world away. When she opened the package, a giant New Zealand cockroach jumped out but the clock worked fine.37

The *Clymer* headed out for Suva and there loaded aboard the 164th Infantry Regiment, made a stop at Guadalcanal and then steamed north again toward Bougainville. On the way one of the soldiers, Bucky Connors, sang a few tunes with the 164th's excellent band. There were tears in a few eyes when he crooned "*When the lights go on again all over the world.*" The date of embarkation for the regiment was Christmas Day. Foley said his first Mass at 0350 so that the soldiers would have the sacrament before going over the side at 0700. It was still dark when the vessel approached the familiar anchorage. The airstrip at Torokina that did not exist six weeks earlier was crammed with planes landing and taking off. After the army men were disembarked, a group of Marines that had been put ashore on November 1 came aboard. They looked haggard and talked of the fierce Japanese resistance. This batch was being removed to Guadalcanal. They would have preferred New Zealand. Nevertheless, Christmas aboard the *Clymer* was vastly preferable to the merciless Bougainville jungle.38

The Marines were off-loaded at Guadalcanal and another unit, the 132nd Infantry Regiment, was loaded aboard off Latuoka. The *Fomalhaut* and *Crescent City* carried other elements of the regiment on this foray. There was another new captain aboard as well. Capt. Murvale T. Farrar officially succeeded Captain Talbot on January 1, 1944. Talbot was promoted to commodore of the transport group and consequently there was a distinct feeling of loss to the *Clymer's* crew. Unlike Moen, the first captain, Talbot was well respected and morale was high under his leadership. Foley recalled one meeting with him over beer for the sailor's shore parties. Talbot asked him if he thought it was a good idea and Foley, who had no objection to alcohol in moderation, said yes. Naturally Talbot put Foley in charge of picking up the beer and he watched as it was loaded from the boat to the below decks of the *Clymer*. When Foley went down to the refrigerator one case was missing. Foley asked the bosun who had accompanied him who swiped it. The bosun feigned innocence but Foley knew that he knew exactly what happened to the case. The word got back to the captain who asked Foley if he was surprised. Foley said no and told him that he had an idea. He wrote a letter and posted it up so that the whole crew would read it He told them that Captain Talbot was violating a navy regulation in bringing beer aboard for them and that they had abused the confidence he placed in them. No other captain would give them the privilege and they would lose it by such actions. After this Talbot again allowed beer aboard and not a bottle was unaccounted for.40

It remained to be seen if the new man Farrar would be another Talbot or more like Moen. He came on as a by-the-book character and immediately read the officers the riot act. Foley recorded his initial reactions to the man, "New Captain believes in far more drills than the other. He seems to be regulation also, for orders have been issued about uniforms, jackets, etc. All will be well—PROVIDED he is generous to the men with liberty when we hit a New Zealand port. He stands or falls there with the men. They will slave for him if he is considerate of their desires in a liberty port."

The 132nd was off-loaded at Bougainville on January 9. As Foley watched the troops head toward shore a stranger approached him and introduced himself as Father McNeil from Syracuse. He asked him if he would like to say a Mass ashore. He did not have to be asked twice. On Bougainville he was brought to a makeshift altar on roads that did not exist two months ago. The "Can-Do" Seabees apparently *could* do anything. Fresh graves were dug on the Epistle and Gospel side of the homely altar and planes from the nearby airfield blasted off throughout the service, making it difficult to communicate. Foley was distracted by the face of one of his former B.C. students in the congregation. After Mass he was joined by Father McNeill, several soldiers and who was that coming up the rear? It was Fr. Laurence Brock again, chaplain of the 182nd regiment of the 26th Yankee Division and magic man of the foreign mission collections. Foley brought the assemblage out to the *Clymer,* fed them ice cream and loaded them up with food, cigars, and Oh Henrys. Then he told them to skedaddle unless they wanted to take an unscheduled boat trip for which they had not made provisions with their commanding officers.41

As usual the *Clymer* was transporting spent troops out after bringing in fresh men. The vessel headed back to Guadalcanal again loaded with veterans of the tough Bougainville fighting. One man, Marine Capt. Jack Delahanty told Foley an amusing story. Delahanty went ashore in a rubber boat from a submarine five days before D-Day to scout Japanese positions. He was discovered by 150 natives who may have been planning to place him in a stew pot before they saw a crucifix and Mary medal around his neck. They knelt before him, exclaimed, "Catholique, Catholique" and kissed his hands, thinking he was a priest. He did not want to let them down so he gave them all an Irish blessing.42

Anchored off of Teteri, Guadalcanal, Foley and Delahanty topside on the *Clymer* watched a group of Liberators take off. As each bomber lumbered into the sky, Foley gave them his blessing. The air crews never knew the prayers that were being said for them. Foley thought, "There is something melancholy about the whole setting and the atmosphere as we stand out on the deck and watch them disappear into the night. Young men, in love with life, to whom killing is alien, bound for a mission whose sole purpose is to wreak death and destruction on an implacable foe. They are gone and the silence of the tropical night wraps everything again. We are alone with our thoughts." 43

By January 11 the *Clymer* was swinging around the buoy at Purvis Bay. She spent the rest of the month doing boat drills, division, flotilla and group maneuvers. Otherwise there was little happening. Now scuttlebutt was saying that the *Clymer* would be involved in an invasion of New Ireland, projected for March. The vessel moved on to New Caledonia on February 2. Mail call that day brought important news from the Bureau of Naval Personnel. A letter dated December 15 informed Foley that his orders for transfer were on the way. It did not tell him where he was being sent. He only hoped it would be another combat vessel. The next day he made it in to Noumea to meet his brother Ed who had been transferred there. Foley always felt that his brother had been underutilized in this war. He was a college-educated man who had spent over a year doing menial tasks. As they said good-bye after a brief meeting, Ed appeared the spitting image of their father. Since Foley did not know where he was being reassigned, there was some uncertainly when they parted. It was a mystery when or if they would meet again.44

On the morning of February 5, Foley was called into Captain Farrar's office. The captain said, "Well we were just about to get to know each other when you leave," referring to Foley's transfer. Then he handed the chaplain three type-written sheets with liberty regulations for the men in Wellington. One section with the heading "Venereal Disease" read:

> Overlooking the after effects of Venereal Disease on your life and health, a man on the sick list due to not taking the necessary precautions during and after sexual intercourse is a damned slacker. He becomes a burden to his country in time of war instead of pulling his own weight in the war effort.

A green box with a red cross painted on it will be handy to
the gangway and will contain sanitubes. If you feel that there is
any possibility of exposure, take a couple with you. This is not
to encourage intercourse but to provide you with some protection. In addition you must report to the sick bay on return to
the ship, sign the book, and take supervised treatment.45

The captain wanted Foley to okay the regulation. He handed the
papers back to Farrar and said that he could not give approval to that section. The captain wanted to know why. Foley said, "What you intend is an
insult to every decent, clean-minded man aboard this ship besides being
an encouragement to vice." The conversation then became more heated.
The exchange went, "Be practical chaplain." "Not by flying in the face of
God's law." "Fornication is not forbidden by the Bible!" "I'm shocked at
your ignorance." "State laws don't arrest a man at home for it." "The State
doesn't make morality, God does. You don't encourage stealing by saying if
you're going to steal, here's a way to avoid being caught."46

Foley continued, "I have friends in Wellington captain. What you are
doing will get around to these people. They will ask me 'Is it true what I
hear about your ship and that box on the Quarter Deck?' I will hang my
head in shame and say 'Yes' and they will say, 'Well you have some captain.'" Farrar could not have known what a hornet's nest he had stirred up
in this feisty chaplain. Foley warned him that he would speak on this subject at the services the next day. The captain insisted that the crewmen's

parents would approve. Foley disagreed and told him he would have to
answer to Almighty God for his action. The captain retorted, "Have a lot
to answer for. Further I did this on other ships." Foley then told him that
had the regulations been posted without consulting him, he would have
been in the captain's office like a shot. Once this went around the ship the
men would ask, "I wonder what the chaplain thinks of this?" Foley then
registered his most emphatic disapproval. The captain snorted,
"Registered. Interview ended chaplain, over."47

Foley had not taken to the new captain from the start, and this incident confirmed all of the impressions that he had already made. He considered the man's moral ignorance to be appalling. The chaplain later asked the senior medical officer if there were a high rate of venereal disease aboard. The doctor told him that there were four cases out of 529 men from the last liberty at Auckland. If the rate had been high Foley could understand but still not approve of the captain's action. With the rate so low, it did not even make any sense.48

If the captain thought Foley would buckle he had surely misjudged his man. In the 1940s there was little of the moral relativism and uncertainty that would later plague the Church. Most Catholic chaplains would have lodged a protest over the encouragement and supply of prophylactics by the military. The issue was by no means a trivial one. The Jesuit journal *America* , then a voice of orthodoxy, questioned government policy various times throughout the war. In one editorial, *America* noted that while rubber was a high priority in the production of war material, it was also being diverted for stocking prophylactics at army bases. There was no equivocation in the Jesuits' stand. The piece declared, "That cynical disregard of morals, that shameless indifference to the protection of the dignity of women as images of God, stands out in shocking contrast to the high ideals announced at the beginning of this war...Condoned immorality is no aid to army morale."49

Catholics were by no means the only creed in the chaplain corps who objected to this practice and the condoning of prostitution by the military establishment. However, Catholics had a forceful and courageous defender in Vicar General O'Hara at the Military Ordinariate. Even prior to America's entry into the war, O'Hara protested to the War Department over the fact that in some camps soldiers were required to carry contraceptives when they left the post. The General Staff informed him that such regulations were not countenanced by them. O'Hara communicated to his chaplains that they were to tell their soldiers to refuse these orders. O'Hara worked amicably with Navy Chief of Chaplains Robert D.

Workman and Army Chief William R. Arnold and even Gen. George Marshall, who considered him to have a special status in regard to the army.50 But O'Hara was crystal clear on where the Ordinariate stood on this issue and he backed up his chaplains in the face of intense government pressure where a weaker man would concede. Nevertheless each chaplain would have to face down his commanding officer if the matter reared its ugly head.

Foley slept the sleep of the just and on the next day he vested for Mass and prepared to deliver the sermon of his life. He said two Masses and a general service as usual on a Sunday. At all of the services he talked about sexual relationships and the responsibility of single and married men. He used St. Paul for ammunition and then let loose:

> Men, if anybody speaks differently, counsels differently, makes it easier to act differently, makes temptation easier by putting in your path the means of avoiding the consequences of misdeeds, no matter who that man is, whether he is low or high, whether seaman second class or whether wearing two stripes of gold braid, or four, or an admiral's, that man is going against God's law. Have nothing to do with him or his doctrine which is hot from Hell.51

There are no secrets on warships. Every man aboard already knew about the confrontation between the captain and the chaplain the day before, and Foley was scarcely circumspect in his reference to naval authority. Furthermore, the captain avoided the church services that day. Just before noon, Dr. Walker came into Foley's room and told him he was pleased with the sermon and that he was disgusted with the way some of the officers carried on. "It took courage to deliver that sermon. I admire you for it." Foley answered, "My obligation to deliver it, Doctor."52

That night a few of the officers were in Dr. Walker's room and Foley was the talk of the town. Navigation Officer Paul Myers said he went by the captain's emergency cabin the day before, saw the look of amazement on his face and wondered what was going on. "Straightening him up on his morals", said Foley. Myers continued, "You are the first man who has talked up to him. He came into the chart room after you left, highly indignant and remarked, 'The chaplain is opposed to the prophylactic box on the quarter deck. I wanted to throw him out of my room. Said it was opposed to his beliefs.'" Foley replied, "Opposed to my beliefs, which are God's also. They were God's before they were mine." Myers continued, "He'll be glad to see you leave the ship." Foley said, "I told him that if the President contemplated such action he would have to be opposed."53 Despite the obvious challenge to Farrar's authority as captain of the ship, Farrar did not attempt to discipline Foley. Perhaps he understood that Foley was the type to endure red hot pincers rather than back down on principle, or perhaps he figured that his time was short and the next chaplain would be more submissive.

The battle of the captain and the chaplain settled down into a Cold War status. Back in New Zealand on February 7. Foley went about making arrangements for another dance for the men though Captain Farrar prohibited corsages this time. Foley also made his usual rounds bringing the sacraments to other ships tied up with the *Clymer* such as the *Fomalhaut*. He extricated a drunken crewman from a breaking-and-entering charge and he visited his sister friends at their convent and had dinner with various religious orders around Wellington. The night of the dance, the captain, obviously still smarting from the incident with Foley, brought it up again. Foley recorded the latest exchange:

> Dance again tonight, just as pleasant as last night, no untoward incident of any kind, thank heavens. Management and men and officers enjoyed themselves. Captain at his table, "Chaplain it does my heart good to hear the men say to me, 'Good Evening,

Captain.'" "I love all those men," he says "They don't know it yet, but they will some one of these days."

Poor man doesn't know how they love him. Reminds me of the Rector, Gomez, wrote to St. Francis Xavier. He was head of the Seminary at Goa, a sprig of a lad brought out from Portugal to head it. Thought St. Francis a bit on the slow side not new enough in his methods, etc. Ruled with an iron hand, had to be censured by Xavier. Gomez wrote back, "I'm not interested in learning that you love the men, but in finding out whether or not the men love you."

If the Captain only knew !!! Some of the men of the 1st division managed to obtain hold of his gin bottles. They emptied them of three quarters of their contents and poured water back in!!

Man sidled up and said to the Captain, "Great guy, Chaplain, now we are losing him. Never get another like him."

Captain, "Nonsense, son we'll get another and he will be a lot better." Good thing I'm not sensitive! I smiled and answered "I sincerely hope so, Captain,—for sake of the men."

He is still smarting from the interview of February 5th about venereal disease. After he had a couple of drinks he stopped me as I was maneuvering around the officers table and said, "Chaplain, when we had that talk, I was thinking of the fighting efficiency of the ship." I said nothing, but gave him a noncommittal smile. That was no place to reopen the discussion. If he wants to see me later aboard ship about it, fine, "Barcus is willing."54

The *Clymer* had another week in New Zealand before going back to her regular duties. Foley expected his orders to come through any day so he wanted to clean up his desk and finish any business left undone. He did not want to leave any of the men hanging when he was transferred so he went through the insurance policies and other papers that the new man would inherit. He had marriage documents concerning two men who wanted to marry two New Zealand girls, very lady-like cousins. The papers made him think of another sailor who found the girl of his dreams in every port and he came to Foley to marry every one. Each time Foley told him, "No, no, no way." The sailor was so young and some unscrupulous women married servicemen for the allotment or even the insurance, hoping he would get killed. With some difficulty, Foley dissuaded him from his multiple matrimonial plans.55

After landing in Noumea on February 27, Foley got to meet another of the august personages displaced by the war. Most Rev. Thomas S. Wade was Bishop of the Northern Solomons and Vicar-Delegate for the South and Central Pacific when the Japanese occupied Kieta in July 1942. Wade was visiting his Tunuru mission station at the time and the Japanese Commanding Officer ordered him to turn himself in at Kieta. He was kept prisoner in his own rectory until the Japanese evacuated on August 6 to meet the American landing. Wade took to the mountain trails aided by his loyal natives and continued his work as best he could. Soon after, he learned that the Japanese had ordered all missionaries to be captured and treated as spies, which meant summary execution. He used a short wave transmitter to contact Admiral Halsey who had some of his missionaries evacuated.56

Bishop Wade himself elected to stay on Bougainville with a few of his men: Fathers Albert Lebel, Henry Hebert and Roland Dionne, all of Maine, and James McConville and Richard O'Sullivan of Ireland and Australia, respectively. The band acted as guerrilla missionaries, tending to their people, always on the run just one heartbeat ahead of the Japanese. Their mission reluctantly ended when some Australian officers showed up and demanded that Wade's party leave with them or else. They were taken by submarine to Guadalcanal and then sent to New Caledonia where the priests acted as auxiliary army chaplains. Wade was named Vicar Delegate of the American Catholic forces in the Southwest Pacific representing Archbishop Spellman.57

When Foley was brought to the bishop's residence he expected to see a man in broken health like his counterpart Bishop Aubin who had suffered so on Guadalcanal. Wade looked well physically, if still bowed by responsibilities. Foley got to speak to him for a few minutes and asked him if he could deliver a message to Bishop Richard J. Cushing of Boston, the patron of the missions. Wade said to ask Cushing if there were anything he could do to end his exile. He wanted to return to Bougainville to his flock, but he could not secure permission from the authorities. He had spoken to Halsey who demurred on the grounds of military necessity. Wade asserted that the Australians were the ones who wanted to keep him from returning to Bougainville. The island was under an Australian mandate and the government resented the good works the missionaries did for the natives, whom the Aussies treated like slaves.58

Foley had seen and heard all of this before, wherever he had journeyed in the Pacific. A Dutch priest once told him that the Japanese could scarcely treat the Javanese worse than his own people and Foley had seen with his own eyes Frenchmen whipping natives like dogs. The English, French, Australian, and Dutch regimes were all the same, and he hoped the day was soon coming when this brutal European colonialism ended. Foley promised to visit Bishop Cushing when he got back to Boston though he doubted even the indefatigable bishop held any sway against the entrenched powers of imperialism. Foley would soon be in a position to make good his promise.

On March 14, Foley's relief came aboard the U.S.S. *George Clymer*, Chaplain Winfred Woolard, a "Disciples of Christ" from Texas. Foley wished him good luck. With Murvale T. Farrar as skipper, he would need it. The next morning at 0630, Foley said his last Mass aboard the ship. In wartime, twenty-one months is a very long time and it was not easy for him, a sentimental man, to say good-bye to "his boys." More than one of the sailors approached him with tears in their eyes. Foley was pretty choked up too. At dinner, Kip Morey and the other officers gave him a little send off. As the boat pulled away from the APA heading toward the dock at Tulagi, Foley gave a final blessing and Godspeed to the ship and the crew, good and bad, who manned her.59

On Tulagi, Foley ran into Navy pilot Joe Costigan, B.C. '40, from Sachem St. in Roxbury. After almost two years in the Pacific, Foley had learned that the area was a satellite campus of Chestnut Hill. He rarely pulled into a port or base that did not have either a fellow Jesuit or a few alumni from the Hill. Occasionally however, he would have to settle for company from Holy Cross. This day Costigan took him up in an SBD—Douglas Dive bomber and they traversed the island searching for a plane that disappeared two days earlier. They could not find the wreck, so the pilot did crash dives, buzzing the ships in the harbor, including the *Clymer.* The "flying padre" had the thrill of his life.60

The U.S.S. *Tryon* brought Foley to Noumea where he was glad to spend a few more days with his brother Ed. On April 1, he boarded the *David Shanks,* an army transport headed west. On April 17, the vessel passed under the Golden Gate Bridge which made the passengers, many of them psychotic cases, hysterical with excitement. After a nine day stopover, Foley left Oakland for Chicago on a Pullman. He even said a Mass in the club car. He got to Chicago on April 29.61 Two days later he was home with his joyous mother and siblings. It had been an exciting and horrific tour of duty. Now he had the whole month of May to relax and forget about the war, safe at home. But he could not forget it. The war was still not done with him, nor he with it.

Notes: Chapter 8

1 Foley diary, October 15, 1943.

2 Rentz, *Bougainville and the Northern Solomons,* passim.

3 Ibid.

4 Foley diary, October 15, 1943; Michael G. Lemish, *War Dogs: Canines in Combat* (Washington, D.C.: Brassey's, 1996), 97, 98. Though men have used dogs in war for various tasks since the advent of the institution, the

United States military traditionally lagged behind her European counterparts in this regard. Both the Allied and Central powers used huge numbers of dogs in the First World War but when America became involved in the Second, there was no War Dog program in place. The Dogs for Defense plan, slapped together with less than precise thought, had several false starts before some dogs were successfully trained and utilized.

5 Foley diary, October 16, 1943.

6 Foley interview, March 10, 1995.

7 Copy of Foley's letter, author's collection.

8 Foley interview, March 10, 1995; Foley diary, October 20, 1943.

9 Foley diary, October 20, 1943; Halsey and Bryan, *Admiral Halsey's Story,* 174, 175.

10 Foley diary, October 21, 1943; Rentz, *Bougainville and the Northern Solomons,* 18.

11 Foley diary, October 24, 1943. As the invasion and battle transpired, the War Dogs proved their worth on the Bougainville jungle. During the three month campaign dogs provided security and messenger service and often flushed out Japanese from their holes. Caesar and Jack, both German Shepherds, were wounded by sniper fire but survived. Andy and Jack, Dobermans, performed well as did other Dobermans, however all six bitches in the group were too skittish and could not be worked. Two dogs were killed in Bougainville, one by mortar fragments, the other by gunshot. Both Generals Geiger and Turnage praised the War Dog Platoon in an after-action report. Lemish, *War Dogs,* 97–103. After the war Chesty Puller at Camp Lejune was ordered to detrain the dogs for their integration back into civilian life. Again the War Dog program was to be abandoned in peacetime though Commandant Vandergrift asked Puller his opinion on the most suitable breeds for future consideration. Puller recommended the German Shepherd and Boxer and advised against Dobermans which he thought were too nervous to stand artillery and mortar fire. His report was not warmly received by the Doberman society. Davis, *Marine,* 234, 235. Considering the performance of the dogs on

Bougainville as an example, noise problems seemed to be based upon sex rather than breed.

12 Foley diary, October 26, 1943.

13 Foley diary, October 29, 1943.

14 Foley diary, October 30, 1943. Telephone interview with Mr. William F. Draper, February 1997. Draper's Aleutians and Bougainville paintings were published in the *National Geographic* in August 1943 and April 1944 issues respectively.

15 The painting, entitled "Divine Services" is held by the Navy Art Collection in Bldg 67 at the Washington Navy Yard. Draper's caption reads, "Aboard the flagship of the invasion force, Marines and the ship's company gather for Divine Service the day before the invasion and landing. It is Sunday morning, but more than an ordinary one, for the landing will be made at dawn Monday. These services, held quietly and unostentatiously on the forward deck, will be remembered by Marines and sailors who attended long after other Sunday mornings are forgotten. This same scene, men in jungle suits for jungle warfare, gear piled high in every nook and cranny is being repeated throughout the convoy." Draper told me that he "thought it would be good." He went on to become a successful artist back in the civilian world. Marine Richard M. Gibney, another World War II combat artist and man of considerable talent himself, told me that, "Draper was one of the best." The painting and its subject, John Foley, would meet at a much later date.

16 Foley diary, October 31, 1943; Rentz, *Bougainville and the Northern Solomons,* 22, 23.

17 Foley diary, October 31, 1943; Foley interview, March 6, 1995.

18 Foley diary, November 1, 1943.

19 Foley interview, March 3, 1995.

20 Foley diary, November 1, 1943; Rentz, *Bougainville and the Northern Solomons,* 24–26.

21 Foley diary, November 1, 1943; Rentz, *Bougainville and the Northern Solomons,* 25, 27; Aurthur and Cohlmia, *The Third Marine Division,* 58, 59.

22 Foley diary, November 1, 1943; Rentz, *Bougainville and the Northern Solomons,* 31.

23 Foley diary, November 1, 2, 1943; Foley interview, March 3, 1995.

24 Foley diary, November 1, 3, 1943. Hannon was a Maryknoller who rose to the rank of commander before being released from the navy in 1946. See Drury, *The History of the Chaplain Corps United States Navy,* vol. III, 117.

25 Foley diary, November 3, 1943; Rentz, *Bougainville and the Northern Solomons,* 38, 39; Halsey and Bryan, *Admiral Halsey's Story,* 177, 180.

26 Fahey, *Pacific War Diary,* 66.

27 Foley diary, November 11, 1943; Rentz, *Bougainville and the Northern Solomons,* 52, 53.

28 Foley diary, November 12 , 1943.

29 Foley diary, November 13, 14, 1943. The *Denver* suffered nineteen dead from this attack.

30 Foley diary, November 15, 1943.

31 Foley diary, November 19, 1943.

32 Foley diary, November 25, 1943.

33 Foley interview, March 3, 1995.

34 Ibid. Soon after, Father Minton was transferred to the Naval Advanced Base on Guadalcanal. When Foley saw him again only three months later he had lost forty pounds. Even as a garrison base, Guadalcanal remained a hell-hole.

35 Ibid.

36 Joseph H. Fichter, S.J. *James Laynez Jesuit,* (St. Louis: B. Herder Book Co., 1944), 276, 277. Laynez was the outstanding theologian at the Council of Trent and became the Second General of the Society of Jesus. Before these tasks, however, he served as a chaplain for Christian forces

fighting African pirates in 1550. Laynez ran the hospital, demanded provisions for the sick and mixed his own ointments and unguents. He heard
the confessions of the dying, absolved apostate monks, baptized infidel
children, reconverted renegade Catholics and preached the good word. He
was so occupied that he ate and slept little and was deeply affected by the
trust of the soldiers who would give him their money and other valuables
to hold prior to battle. He refused to take any pay for his service. See
Fichter, *James Laynez Jesuit,* 92, 95 and James Brodrick, S.J., *The Origin of
the Jesuits* (London: Longman's, Green, 1940; reprint ed., Chicago: Loyola
Press, 1997), 226, 227.

37 Foley diary, December 12, 1943; Foley interview, March 6, 1995.

38 Foley diary, December 17, 19, 22, 25, 1943.

39 Foley diary, December 31, 1943, January 4, 1944. Muehrcke,
Orchids in the Mud, 206, 214; Foley interview, March 3, 1995.

40 Foley diary, January 5, 1944.

41 Foley diary, January 9, 1944. The seeming miracles performed by
the Naval Construction Battalion "Seabees" in the Pacific theater never
ceased to amaze all who beheld them. See *Building the Navy's Bases in
World War II,* 2 vols, (Washington, D.C.: United States Government
Printing Office, 1947).

42 Foley diary, January 9, 1944.

43 Foley diary, January 10, 1944.

44 Foley diary, January 11, February 2, 3, 1944.

45 Foley diary, February 5, 1944.

46 Ibid.

47 Ibid.

48 Ibid.

49 "Army Morale," *America* (February 28, 1943): 574.

50 McAvoy, *Father O'Hara of Notre Dame,* 221, 226–228, 251.

51 Foley diary, February 6, 1944.

52 Ibid.

53 Ibid. Bishop John J. McNamara of the Merrimack Region of the Archdiocese of Boston was the Navy Chief of Chaplains between 1983–1988. During his service days he had more than a few conflicts with superior officers over moral questions and he offered another theory about why they would sometimes concede the chaplain's point. Most career military and naval officers, unlike reservists, are always looking to the next promotion and try to avoid controversies. In one instance, McNamara preached a fiery sermon against the Roe v. Wade decision a week after it was announced and his C.O. was furious that he dared to criticize the goverment. The meeting was unpleasant but the officer understood that McNamara was not going to change and "if push came to shove, the chaplain is paid to interpret to his people…the Gospel." Interview Most Rev. John J. McNamara 15 October 1996, Lawrence, MA.

54 Foley diary, February 17, 1944.

55 Foley diary, February 29, 1944; Foley interview, March 6, 1995. Reminiscing about the sailor fifty years after the war, Foley chuckled, "That's my major achievement, having him give up each girl. I'm sure he was grateful to me…eventually."

56 Foley diary, March 2, 1944; Decker, *Saving the Solomons,* 103, 104.

57 Decker, *Saving the Solomons,* 104.

58 Foley diary, March 2, 1944.

59 Foley diary, March 14, 15, 1944; Drury, *The History of the Chaplain Corps United States Navy,* vol. III, 302.

60 Foley diary, March 16, 1944. Interestingly, Father Riedel was surveyed for also taking a brief flight.

61 Foley diary, March 22, April 1, 1944.

CHAPTER 9

▼

"DRIVE TO THE EMPEROR'S PALACE"

As Foley rode the train to New York he contemplated his new assignment. The only job he wanted in the navy was to chaplain a fighting vessel. Instead, he was to be shorebound at Bethesda, the National Naval Medical Center just outside of Washington, D.C. Others would have figured it to be an easy berth. All Foley could think of was that there was some ship going in harm's way that rated a chaplain but had not gotten one. Hospital chaplain work would be fulfilling surely, yet couldn't he be doing more with young men again, in the line of fire? He resolved to do his best at the hospital. After all, Ignatius, Francis Xavier, and the other founders of the Jesuit order tended to the sickest of the sick outcasts whom nobody would touch. Apparently this was what the Lord wanted of him for now. Meanwhile, however, there was no harm in asking for a warship in his prayers.

Foley started his tour of duty at Bethesda on Memorial Day, May 30, 1944. He was suitably impressed by the edifice, a new modernistic building of nineteen decks with a three-decker building forming an "H" behind it. "Large territory this", he thought as he toured the place. He met one of his fellow chaplains, John Wesley Weise, a Methodist from Pennsylvania. There was another minister and another priest assigned there as well. Nevertheless, there was plenty of work to go around. He was told that personnel numbered around five thousand, with approximately two hundred doctors and two hundred dentists, most of them young and in training. Because of the war, the hospital was filled to capacity and the chaplains had to find their own accommodations. Foley got a room with a family for $48 a month, high rent indeed, but not unusual for the overcrowded Washington area in wartime.1

The next day Foley started dealing with the patients. Apart from a few entries, he also abandoned the diary that he had kept from the day he boarded the *George Clymer*. Whatever work that was to be done at the hospital, he obviously did not regard it the stuff of his combat chronicle. For the most part, Bethesda was to prove not very different from peacetime work. His first case was a sailor who wanted to legally change his name. After that, the "clients" came fast and furious. A doctor asked him to baptize a baby. A WAVE wanted to make a confession. An MP wanted him to get him released from the hospital. A sailor need a lift home and thought the chaplain could pull some strings. Another WAVE wanted to talk about a dream concerning her grandfather.2

Weeks and months passed. In August, Foley was joined by Fr. John Burke, an alumnus of Holy Cross and before the war Dean of men at Notre Dame, a job roughly equivalent to Foley's at Boston College. Foley found the facilities appreciably different from those on the APA. He said Mass in the large auditorium for the young women training to be Corps WAVES. Attendance was always good. They had three hundred new girls every three months. He had a standard talk for each incoming batch which concerned the sexual pitfalls of navy life. He warned them that there would be bad guys, nice guys, and in-betweeners, and that eternal vigilance was the watchword. In essence, his advice was "Don't listen to sweet talk." Foley saw at first hand the results of mistakes and the only solution was to try to get to them before they went astray. One day he was asked to talk to a WAVE who had threatened suicide. She told him she had fallen for a shorebased sailor who was wonderful in every way. When he got aboard ship he wrote her that he had a wife and three children somewhere and the WAVE also discovered that he had infected her with a venereal disease.3 The girl felt that her life was over and Foley tried to cheer her up. On top of everything else she was treated as a pariah by the other WAVES in sick bay who were there for appendix operations or other minor maladies.

More than once he came to the rescue of service personnel having problems with their sex life, or problems with doctors interested in their sex life. He was approached by a Marine who smashed a psychiatrist in the face and was going to face charges. Foley asked what it was all about and it turned out the psychiatrist was grilling him with questions about sex. The Marine had had enough and struck him. Foley went to the chief psychiatrist and told him that he would have reacted the same way, "massacred him verbally, no fisticuffs" if anyone invaded his sexuality with a lot of questions. The chief psychiatrist agreed and said that there had been a lot of trouble with that particular individual and would see to it that no charges would be leveled against the Marine.4

Because of the location and nature of the hospital, Foley sometimes met politicians and celebrities undergoing treatment. When Secretary of State Cordell Hull checked in, the head nurse asked Foley to go up and visit him on the fifteenth deck, even though the Secretary was not Catholic. Hull's wife was there and greeted him with genuine southern courtesy. Foley and Hull talked politics for awhile and found accord on their opinion of the press. The press's role in the war was a long standing sore spot with Foley, and Hull referred to reporters as "polecats" who spewed their venom on him from their trees. The genteel Mrs. Hull interjected that her husband sometimes used strong language.5

The admiral who ran the Bethesda Naval Hospital had tremendous responsibilities, overseeing thousands of personnel. Foley admired him greatly, knowing from experience what difficulties administrators faced. His relationship with the admiral took a different turn when the man told him he wanted to convert to Catholicism. His wife and two sons were Catholic and the boys were studying for the priesthood, one of them in the Jesuit order. The admiral went through all of the instructions but found he could not accept the real presence of the Lord in the Eucharist. When he told Foley this, Foley understood his doubts and tried to hammer home the essential element of faith in the matter. He said,

> To be perfectly honest you are keeping company with some of the disciples of Our Lord, who walked out on him. "How can we accept this?" and they walked out on him. And these were men who had worked miracles when he sent them out, raised the dead to life and gave sight to the blind. They walked out on him. It is one of the key truths of our Catholic faith and your wife and two boys accept it otherwise they wouldn't be studying for the priesthood. Also one of the early fathers of the Church said we are accused of being cannibals but we are not. Christ is really present in the consecrated forms of bread and wine.6

The admiral could not be convinced to take the final step. He could only say, "Father, I appreciate all you have done for me." When Foley left Bethesda, he still had not come around, but Foley hoped that someday he could accept the body and blood in his mind and in his soul.7

After several months at the hospital Foley was informed that he was to be transferred again. He was anxious to learn of his new assignment and hoped that his prayers had been answered. Though he had given up the diary earlier he did make a few notes about his time at Bethesda:

EXPERIENCES IN NAVAL MEDICAL CENTER
1. Killed the call for PhM1/c Independent Duty.
2. Sick WAVE reading "Song of Bernadette." When I asked her if she liked the book, "Yes, if it didn't pay so much attention to Mary. Like you Catholics, you overrate her!" Reply— "If introduced to your mother, then I deliberately put her on the shelf, would you like it? You'd want to do the same with the mother of Christ. Yet you can't separate them. Go to Bethlehem, they are together, at Nazareth, the same. On Calvary, the same, even when He is dead He is in her arms as when first born." After that, each time I visit the girl, ask her, "How is the girl with a grudge against the Mother of God?" Still a staunch Methodist when she left and not on speaking terms with the mother of God.
3. Gus Sunnerberg—victim of leukemia, former heavyweight wrestling champion of the world. Finally found out the value of prayer. "Tell it to these young corpsmen here but they say that I am getting soft. I guess they will have to learn the hard way, same as I did."
4. Remark of Protestant—"Some of my best friends are Catholics. not just one day a week, but seven."
5. Apgar—Wounded aboard the bridge of the USS *Texas* off the Normandy Coast, lost one leg below the knee, other in a bad way also. Asked him how many blood transfusions he had, "Wish I never had any."
6. Jensen—dying of cancer of the bronchial tubes, listed as a Catholic. Asked if he wanted to go to Confession and Communion. Puzzled expression, said he wasn't a Catholic, checked with mother -mixed marriage, that boy brought up

by an uncle, a Lutheran. Remorse written indelibly on that mother's face. Son going before Christ whom he didn't know because of her neglect. Trying to catch the last word—hardly strength to whisper message—"Give my best to everybody."

7. Russian member of Soviet Embassy broke neck swimming. Introduced self as a priest, I inquired what he was. Although he understood and spoke English up to that point, answer, "Sorry, I do not understand." Same of two of his friends whom I met in passageway.

8.WAVE loaned $166 to two sailors for liberty, and to one who wanted "to buy flowers for his wife's grave."8

When Foley learned of his new assignment he was stunned. He was slated to be assigned to the chaplain school, which had been relocated to the College of William and Mary at Williamsburg, Virginia in March 1943. It was a practice to reassign combat veterans to the school as faculty members so that chaplains in training would get an unvarnished account of what they could expect. The executive officer of the school from October 1943—March 1944 was Fr. J.F. Robinson, a linchpin of the institution since its founding at Norfolk. On a Catholic Hour broadcast on the NBC network he explained the reasoning in assigning chaplains who had had combat duty. "These men do not pretend to be pedagogues. They were ordered to the School because each has a story to tell and these combined experiences present a fairly composite picture of the 1943 Navy chaplain."9

In June 1944 Robinson was reassigned to become the Assistant Director to the Chief of Chaplains, in essence the executive officer of the Chaplains Division. It was to Father Robinson that Foley appealed for a ship. He had prayed earnestly for sea duty, yet a Jesuit was not a monk and Foley was not content to simply let navy bureaucracy decide his fate. Often, action was called for and his philosophy was similar to the old chestnut, "trust in the Lord but keep your powder dry." Strictly speaking, neither the Chief of Chaplains nor the Assistant Director were in charge of assignments. Since the huge wartime expansion of the Corps, that duty had been delegated to the detail officer who in turn had several assistants to help him with the work.10

Nevertheless Foley asked Jack Robinson to pull some strings. He understood an assignment to the chaplain school was meant to be a compliment. After all, he was a professor and understood that only highly recommended men were assigned to the school. Foley wanted no part of it, however, and considered the prospect of being trapped in a classroom while the guns were still sounding to be harsh punishment for his sins. Robinson could not say no to a man so desperate to return to the fray. While all men approved for the Chaplain Corps were supposed to be eligible and prepared for sea duty, in reality an appreciable number were not fit in one way or another. Some men were considered simply too old for the strenuous routine of ships in hazardous waters including calls to General Quarters twenty-four hours a day and the prospect of going in the water from a sinking ship. Many of the non-Catholics had families and were not enthused about leaving the states, especially if there was a chance that they would not be coming back. Still others could not stand the attendant loneliness of a chaplain aboard ship, even though surrounded by a crew.

Furthermore, a combat chaplain needed to be a man of considerable personal fortitude. Perhaps apart from the captain, no man aboard ship was expected to be steadier than the chaplain. If, under fire or when a ship was damaged the chaplain lost control or showed any signs of cowardice, he could cause a general panic and breakdown in confidence in authority. The captain got paid to be stoical, but if the man of God feared dying, why should enlisted men obey orders from a secular source? And in the end the issue of assigning men to ship or shore came down to one of the supply and demand. The Chaplain Corps never made its official allotment of one chaplain for every 1,250 naval personnel so it would be the height of folly to deny a man a ship who was begging to be shot at. It so happened that a new vessel was nearing completion and a chaplain had not yet been assigned. Robinson told Foley, "Sure I can get you a ship. How about an aircraft carrier?"11

John Foley's duty at Bethesda Naval Hospital ended officially on January 15, 1945. He was to report to Puget Sound by January 27 to go aboard his new ship, the *Commencement Bay* -class escort carrier U.S.S. *Vella Gulf* (CVE-111). Escort or "jeep" carriers were a new departure for the navy. Early in the war a few merchant vessels were equipped with short flight decks and otherwise modified to become the prototypes of the escort carrier. Initially the vessels were meant to supply minimal air cover for convoys and anti-submarine work. Jury-rigged vessels never perform well and major problems were immediately apparent, though a start had been made. Experiments continued and *Bogue* and *Sangamon* -class escorts were introduced, the latter type converted oilers. The CVEs saw limited action in the North African and Solomons campaigns. The *Bogue* -class vessels became aircraft transports when the *Casablanca* -class type were introduced.12

In early 1943 a final type of escort carrier was approved, based largely on the *Sangamon* -class rather than the *Casablancas*. Main improvements included the placement and performance of the engines and a vastly strengthened anti-aircraft defense in the form of thirty-six 40 mm guns. The weapons were introduced to bolster the 20mm and .50 caliber guns ordinarily emplaced for anti-aircraft duty. It was evident even by that point in the war that the main threat to surface ships, particularly carriers, would come from the skies, and kamikazes needed to be shot to pieces before they came within striking distance. Jeep carriers were still far more vulnerable than full-sized flattops which were faster and carried more planes and defensive firepower.

The *Vella Gulf* was the seventh of the *Commencement Bay* escort carri-ers. Constructed by the Todd-Pacific Shipyards at Tacoma, Washington, she was launched October 19, 1944 and commissioned April 9, 1945 with Capt. Robert W. Morse commanding.13 The vessel's chaplain, Lt.

senior grade John Foley, acclimated himself to the new vessel. It felt good to be back aboard a warship after being shorebound for so long. The escape from the chaplain school assignment had been a close call, and nothing in the course of the Pacific War indicated that the conflagration was coming to an end. Foley hoped that he could be of service to the fighting men until the last shot was fired. To ensure that his battle chronicle had an epilogue, he began to keep his daily diary again as well.

Almost from his first day aboard the *Vella Gulf*, Foley became aware that the executive officer was distinctly hostile to him. Captain Morse, on the other hand, was a gentleman in every way. As events transpired, Episcopalian Morse seemed to go out of his way to give Foley anything he wanted. Foley figured two decent captains out of four was pretty good.14 The exec's behavior puzzled him until he learned that he was another ex-Catholic nursing unnamed grudges against the Church. Though Foley made it a point from day one to check out who was listed in sick bay as a Catholic, he never hunted down men or officers who did not attend the sacraments. Aboard the *Clymer* and now on the *Vella Gulf* he knew there were some officers who avoided him because he reminded them of what they once were. He simply prayed that they would come back to where they belonged. If he could catch them on the rebound, fine. If they returned in thirty years that would still be a blessing, but he was not about to blackjack anyone back into the Church.

The trouble between the exec and the chaplain began when the *Vella Gulf* sailed from Puget Sound to San Diego in early May to embark a detail of her assigned air group and conduct shakedown exercises. It was clear that the vessel was very soon heading for the Pacific and as always at such times the chaplain was deluged with requests for compassion leave. Though a great advocate of the lowly swabbie, Foley's evaluation of each case was reached after great discernment. His previous conflicts with superior officers were based upon what he considered intolerable moral transgressions, not over issues of naval discipline or arbitrary dislikes. His typical advice to sailors with some minor problem (even if it seemed to be a major one) was to accept whatever came. That meant that men should take punishment details, transfers, and petty annoyances and "offer them up" without complaint. The less a man crossed swords with an officer in any way the better off he would be.

There were legitimate reasons for compassion leave which concerned serious difficulties at home and so Foley went to the executive officer for approval of fourteen cases. When Foley went to see him, there was a junior officer present. After Foley explained the cases, the exec snapped, "Chaplain, do you think all I have to do is to grant what you bring in to me?" Foley knew what the man was doing. He wanted to humiliate him in front of the young officer, which was a grievous violation of navy etiquette. Foley already knew that there was much more behind this. He replied, "Commander, I don't bring in everything that is requested of me to represent to you, and in fact there are far more men who have seen me with this request than these fourteen you have." The exec glowered and said nothing. Later Foley discovered that all fourteen leaves had been granted.15

The air group would not be composed of navy fliers, but Marine Corps airmen. The Marines had long been clamoring for more effective carrier-based air support for ground troops. Problems with coordination between Marine and navy components were evident at the battle of Tarawa and in the summer of 1944 General Vandergrift convinced Admiral Nimitz on the idea of Marine carrier air groups (MCVG) which would be composed of an eighteen-plane fighter squadron (VMF) and a twelve-plane torpedo bomber squadron (VMTB). Though six squadrons were envisioned only four were ultimately organized before the war ended. Fighters were to be a mix of Hellcats and Corsairs, which caused a degree of logistical confusion. The vessels chosen for the Marine mission were the new CVEs *Block Island, Gilbert Islands, Cape Gloucester,* and the *Vella Gulf.* The commander of the *Vella Gulf* Marine air group, designated MCVG-3 was Lt. Col. Royce W. Coln.16

Even as the *Vella Gulf* was taking aboard her Marine contingent and gearing up for shakedown runs, the war against the Nazis in Europe had finally come to an end. On V-E Day, May 8, Foley addressed the *Vella Gulf's* company concerning the great day:

> This is Fr. Foley; ship's Chaplain speaking. This morning official confirmation was received that the war in Europe is over. In accordance with the wishes of our Commander-in-Chief, President Harry S. Truman and in prayerful union with millions of our fellow Americans ashore, we stop for a few minutes in our busy lives aboard ship to thank God for the victory that has crowned our arms.
>
> First we shall say a prayer, then pause for a minute of respectful silence in tribute to the men who have died ashore and afloat in the Army and Navy and end with a blessing.
>
> In the name of the Father and of the Son, and of the Holy Ghost.
>
> Almighty and everlasting God, Lord of battles, mercifully hear the prayers of us. Thy servants, who turn to Thee in gratitude in this hour of victory for our arms in Europe.
>
> We thank Thee that the scourge of war, the blood the sweat and the tears will no longer rack and agonize Thy people and our brothers in arms in that part of the world.
>
> Grant that we, who have stern tasks ahead, whose duties call to the fighting line in another theatre, may be strengthened by Thy grace for their courageous execution.
>
> May we continue to place our trust in Thee, mindful of The words, "In vain do they build unless the Lord build with them."
>
> Finally we ask, O Lord of Mercy, to remember the souls of those who made this victory possible by pouring out the red sweet wine of their youth on the altar of our country's freedom, that others may live.

> Eternal rest grant to them, O Lord, and May the perpetual
> light shine upon them, through Jesus Christ our Lord,
> Amen.17

Sailors and Marines aboard the *Vella Gulf* could hardly be overwhelmed
with relief. The Pacific war had always been a different breed of cat, the
Japanese an unfathomable foe. The war in the east was a naval war and by
1945 its fury was intensifying, not diminishing . The apocalyptic battle of
Iwo Jima and other God-forsaken Japanese outposts seized in the winter
and spring had been paid for in rivers of blood. An invasion of Okinawa,
only 350 miles from the homeland had commenced in April and the
fighting was even now reaching new heights in the level of ferocity.
Kamikazes, at first an intermittent or circumstantial threat, now fell on the
American fleet like enormous fiery hail. Ships were stripped of superfluous
deck impediments to cram on additional 40mm mounts, more valuable to
a great vessel's survival than columns of 16" naval guns. It was at Okinawa
that the *Franklin* was gored by two direct bomb hits and Father
O'Callahan became the war's sole Congressional Medal of Honor chaplain. Only through superhuman effort was the *Franklin* salvaged. Others
went to the bottom dragging their human missile with them.

Thus the mood of ships heading for the whirlwind in the Pacific was
less than euphoric. It appeared that the Japanese would have to be crushed
in Tokyo and in every primitive hamlet in the home islands. The *Vella
Gulf* continued to ready herself to play her part in the finale of the epic
tragedy. She operated in the waters around San Diego conducting drills
and exercises. Foley got to know the Marine flyers of the ship's fighter
squadron VMF 513 and torpedo bomber men of VMTB 234. It seemed
to Foley that the Marine Corps was at least 75% Catholic. The figure is
high but it is certainly true that Catholics were drastically overrepresented
in the World War II Corps. Many of the Marine flyers and maintenance
crews were serious Catholics and together with the ship's complement of
1,500 Foley was kept hopping.18

The ship anchored at San Diego for a few days and the crew dispersed, some to the navy's unofficial brothels, in the stinking border town of Tijuana, half an hour to the south. Others just walked around as tourists but Foley knew the recreation of a sailor was not that of a seminarian.19 The sailors needed to get a special pass to go south of the border. Foley's yeoman aboard the *Vella Gulf* was a young man from Pittsburgh, Abraham Lincoln Dibacco, who had a fair sense of humor. While in San Diego Foley told Dibacco to get him a pass to go to Tijuana. The yeoman replied, "Not you, too Father!" Foley did poke around the town for a few hours and bought a cheap souvenir for his mother in Somerville. On the way back to the ship he turned it over and saw that it was made in New York City.20

There were some lighthearted moments but the war continued to claim young lives even stateside. On May 12, the fliers practiced catapult take-offs in their F4Us. Foley watched the fascinating movements of the aerial ballet. The deck crew swarmed around the planes, each man's duty identified by the color of his cloth helmet and jersey. The chaplain could not yet distinguish what the red, green, yellow, white, blue, and brown helmets indicated but he would soon learn. The first two planes were rocketed aloft with no difficulty. The next one would not be so fortunate.

Foley observed the entire sequence of events:

> Plane number three is jockeyed into position on the cata-
> pult, the flight officer director goes through his gestures, she
> spins down to the edge of the flight deck rears up like a charg-
> ing horse, turns over, lands with a crash right side up and
> then drifts by within 15 feet of the port side forward sponson,
> where I am. She is slowly sinking with the cockpit half under-
> water, the pilot lumped over and blood staining the water
> round the area."21

Foley instinctively strained toward the flooding plane and called out absolution as the carrier churned past the iron coffin. A destroyer raced over but it was too late. The plane and the pilot 2nd Lt. Edward Groves, USMC were gone.22

Later the officers watched a film of the fatal takeoff. It was evident that the pilot's head smashed into the dashboard when the plane bucked, sealing his fate. The exec came to Foley and told him that the captain wanted a memorial service for the pilot. Foley said that although Groves was not Catholic the best thing the he could do was to say a Mass for him. The officer hesitated then just uttered, "I see." The Mass was held on the hangar deck with a plane directly behind the celebrant. A chair was left empty for the dead pilot.23

About a week later the officer came to Foley again and told him that the captain wanted an account of the accident placed in the ship's newspaper. The tension between them was palpable so Foley decided to have it out. He said, "By the way, will you forget that you're a commander and I'm just a lieutenant, senior grade?" The exec said, "What are you after?" Foley replied, "Now at the Mass that we had for the pilot we lost last week you sat in the front row and you looked most uncomfortable." He said, "I thought you might single me out." Foley responded, "For what? I could have singled you out. You're listed down in sick bay as a Catholic and you haven't been to Mass once since you've been aboard ship." The exec said, "Oh I gave all that up. Gave it all up." "Well suppose our carrier is hit now by the Jap bombers and I'm not wounded and I'm kneeling over you to give you the sacraments of the sick, would you want them?" The officer shook his head, "No, no, not at all. You die like a dog." Foley pressed him, "Well suppose you go before God, you're one of those killed and you meet Christ Our Lord and you give that weakest of all excuses, 'I gave it up.' Don't you think you'd be embarrassed?" He replied, "Oh, a little magic might help." This was the wrong thing to say. Foley told him, "Oh no, I won't give it to you unless you say you're sorry there. I won't give it to you! Because it is not magic. It is a God-given right."24

Nothing was resolved at that juncture and the strain between the two men continued until Foley left the ship. Despite this barrier, Foley respected the officer as a courageous man because he had been in on the initial stages of the Guadalcanal campaign and had gone through hell there. Foley never believed in the slogan "no atheists in fox holes" since he had met unbelievers who acted bravely in extremely hazardous situations. More to the point was the hope that such people could be brought back to the Church on a mature level at some time in the future. "Foxhole" religion, induced by fear of physical danger, was hardly the basis for serious spiritual commitment.

At the end of May the ship went into the Naval Repair Base at San Diego for a fourteen day yard overhaul. On June 17, the escort carrier *Vella Gulf* finally got underway for Pearl Harbor. The night before, Foley had gone to confession at the San Diego Cathedral. As he walked the streets afterwards, he drank in the sight of the buildings and storefronts and looked hard at the faces of passersby, trying to impress their images upon his memory. He knew that the last act was about to be played out in the east. Whether the *Vella Gulf* would acquit herself well or go to the bottom a blazing hulk, only God knew.25

Steaming toward the Hawaiian islands, some of the Marine personnel wanted to talk. Seiss, one of the TBM pilots, told Foley that he had been training stateside for this for three years. He had never married and worried about being responsible for his radioman and gunner, but all three were prepared to do whatever needed to be done. About five o'clock on June 25 Diamond Head came into view. Later the vessel entered the channel off of Ford Island. The *Arizona* was visible, like an enormous grave marker, an eternal tomb for her crew. Foley thought of Father Schmitt, the first chaplain killed in the war aboard the *Oklahoma* on December 7, 1941.26 He had died so that other men would live. He could have saved himself but chose to drown while helping sailors escape. Could any chaplain have a better model and inspiration? *Requiem et pacis!*

Pearl Harbor was jam packed with shipping, and when Foley hit shore the next day he knew that he would meet some old friends. He dropped in on Fr. Jack Twiss, a diocesan priest from Boston, and also saw Father Sheehy, formerly of the *Saratoga* and now, like Twiss, assigned to the 14th Naval District. That night he attended a farewell dinner for Sheehy, who was heading back to the states. Father McQuade was there, he who had been so horribly burned and blinded when the cruiser *Minneapolis* was torpedoed in the 1942 Solomons campaign. Foley also saw Fr. Bill Babb, another native Bostonian who was a professor at Loyola prior to enlisting in the navy.27

Foley got to do a little sightseeing and found Honolulu to be a deppressing place, with Hawaiians, Chinese, and Japanese crammed in together in poor housing. The Royal Hawaiian Hotel was a different story. It had been converted into a recreation center for submarine crews, who enjoyed the lovely accommodations and beautiful beach in front. He also went aboard the *Tranquillity* , a hospital ship to see two of his old Bethesda graduates, now nurses aboard the vessel. When Foley returned to the *Vella Gulf* , he was given the bad news that another pilot had been seriously injured while practicing night landings. Lt. William R. Winn from Georgia hung precariously to life while life aboard the baby flattop went on.28

The ship headed from Pearl to continue practicing plane drills. Foley watched the exercises on deck late in the evening to be there just in case there were more mishaps and injuries. He wrote in his diary:

> Night carrier landings at midnight, eerie setting. Landing signal officers are dressed in luminous outfits that reflect back in orange, green and black colors. Paddles in hands which they wave on or off the pilots, also luminous. Planes coming in look like giant bugs with purple flames leaping in angry snortings from exhausts on both sides of the engines, much like two eyes on a giant bug.

Then wing lights of green, red, and tail of blue light up
the plane for all to see. Long, slender pencils of light from
little fountain pens along the deck help the pilots to make
the hazardous landings. Fortunately we have no accidents
as they fly on and off all night until dawn. Sleep, naturally,
was intermittent.29

While watching the landings Foley was informed that Lt. Winn had
died. The chaplain prepared to perform a memorial service.30

After returning to Pearl again the crew had a few days before finally
heading out for battle operations. The officers socialized at the Royal
Hawaiian, the enlisted men had their own joints of varying seediness
downtown. Foley's pursuits were more pedestrian. He was watching a
movie topside on one of the beautiful summer nights when he got the
word that he was needed to attend to an injured man. Usually there was a
chain up along the hangar deck elevator but somehow one of the sailors
fell straight down the elevator to the deck below and was severely broken
up. Foley knew him well. He was one of the oldest men aboard, well into
his forties, and had begged the chaplain to get him off the ship. Foley had
made a pitch but transfers were not up to him and the man stayed aboard.
On the way to the hospital at Pearl, Foley tried to get a simple act of contrition out of him though he was not Catholic. The man was adamant.
Foley said, "You haven't been perfect all your life have you?" "No I haven't
been, chaplain." Foley replied, "There are some things you are sorry for
just tell God you're sorry." The sailor snapped, "I WON'T! If he had been
as _ _ good to me as I had been to him, I wouldn't be in this pickle!"31

At the hospital Foley talked to the Catholic chaplain about the sailor
and told him that if he could not get anywhere with him, perhaps the
Protestant chaplain could. Foley was troubled because there was more to
the story. The injured sailor had divorced his wife by mail and hooked up
with another woman in San Diego. The chaplain figured that the woman's
interest in the sailor was strictly pecuniary and if he died she would have

hit the jackpot in the form of his $10,000 insurance. Foley would never know the outcome of this case because the *Vella Gulf* was ready to shove off.32

On July 9, the carrier was steaming toward Eniwetok in Micronesia. The vessel anchored in the atoll lagoon on the 16th and then shoved off again toward Guam. At Apra Harbor on Guam Foley was glad to see his much-traveled brother Ed who was still doing medical work. That Sunday, Foley got to say Mass on three carriers, the *Vella Gulf, Manila Bay ,* and *Suanee.* The next day, July 23, the *Vella Gulf* shoved off to strike the Pagans in the Marianas group, north of Saipan and Tinian.33 A wave of excitement and anticipation shot through the entire complement of the vessel including the chaplain. Foley loved life aboard ship, particularly the frenetic activity of this flattop. He enjoyed the feeling of being on deck in rolling seas and had learned the significance of the brightly colored helmets and jerseys of the deck crews. His heart skipped a beat every time a plane took off and landed and he even found the staccato bark of the 40mm antiaircraft guns to be hypnotically soothing in a terrible way:

> Aboard a carrier you have what other ships lack, the intimate contact with the offensive blow, the conversations with the pilots and air crew before and after the strike, you hear the thunderous, climatic roar of the engines in the grey dawn, you see them quivering with tremendous power as they strain to get airborne.
>
> Then too, you experience the constant heavy apprehension over the fate of each pilot and you participate in the daily routine of flight preparations.34

Foley knew he would miss this life if God allowed him to return home unscathed. He would return to his dean's seat at Boston College to push papers around and succor upset parents of lax freshmen. He would mothball his blues and khakis, throw his superfluous ties in the trash and once again don his first uniform, a black habit. He would leave behind the rules, regulations, and traditions of the U.S. Navy and pick up where he left off in a much bigger and older organization, one he regarded as the cornerstone of western culture. No longer would he sail the deep sea on APAs and carriers. After the war he would resume his work as crew member on the bark of Peter.

The day before the strike on Pagan Island, Foley and other extras such as four newspaper reporters were in on the briefing in the pilot's ready room. Foley recounted the scene in his diary that night:

Mr. Royce, Combat Intelligence Officer, takes over for a few minutes with remarks on a slide map that he shows of the island to be hit, Pagan, pointing out some features of the terrain. When he steps down, men relax in the leather-upholstered chairs, lighting up their cigarettes for awhile. Then all are galvanized into attention by Lt. Koln. "We've got the pictures, boys. Here they are." Lights are dimmed again, and photos are flashed on the screen.

He talks quietly, like a college prof. as he points out each target for the six strikes.

"Strike Able has a juicy white building here on the tip of this jetty. First four fighters will go in strafing bombs. When you do that there shouldn't be much left."

"Strike Baker, two big white houses sitting up on the top of this cliff. No scruples about hitting them, for natives don't live in houses like that.

Remarks that he will be sitting up there with them. I'll drop smoke on two of the targets to mark them, "so you fellows can do your stuff."

"By the way, on these two positions here, make one pass and then go rendezvous for altitude and advantage then make a second pass, if you haven't met with much fire on the first pass. If you have, forget the second pass, pick out some other target for what you have left."

Questions asked are answered about strafing shipping answer negative, may be our B-29 men being helped by natives. All ships will be our own.

Somber reminder that trip is not a pleasure venture, by Lt. picking up mike, instructing men, "Remember, fellows, leave your wallets behind and all identification; you won't need any of that."35

The next day the *Vella Gulf* launched twenty-four sorties against Japanese positions on Pagan. Anti-aircraft fire was light and all of her planes returned safely albeit a few with bullet and shrapnel damage. The pilots were giddy with excitement after this first raid and were eager to engage the enemy again. They got their chance on the 26th against Rota, situated between Saipan and Guam. Twenty-one sorties were launched and again all came home though some planes had gone in so low that they were damaged by fragments of their own bombs. On deck that night Foley watched much larger and destructive war birds overhead, a fleet of B-29s heading toward the home islands of Japan. He thought the Japanese leaders were insane to continue to subject their people to the awesome destruction that the glistening silver behemoths could impose. He blessed each plane crew as they passed over and were swallowed up by the sky.36

The *Vella Gulf* then made for Tanapoag, Saipan, 150 miles north of Guam. Saipan, like other islands that had seen horrific, almost apocalyptic battles, was now a way station for ships gathering for the final showdown. The plan was in place. Operation DOWNFALL would commence with an invasion of Kyushu in early autumn. Casualties of ground troops were expected to be astronomical, and if the example of Okinawa was any indication, losses to the invasion fleet due to kamikazes and other defensive tactics could be mind boggling. When the landing was made, the *Vella Gulf* would surely be one of the invasion flotilla.

On Saipan, Foley had the opportunity to celebrate Mass aboard the *St. Olaf,* an army hospital ship. He found a Jesuit army chaplain already aboard, Fr. John Halloran of the Missouri Province. The long black line was everywhere it seemed. Halloran told Foley that two of his fellow Jesuits from New England were ashore on Saipan, Frs. Jimmy McLaughlin with the 121st Seabees and Jimmy Dolan with the 751st AAA. After Mass Foley found McLaughlin still sound asleep in his sack at the Seabee base. McLaughlin was roused to find Foley looming over him, a face he had not seen for four years. He had been on Tinian and had just recently moved with his outfit to Saipan. McLaughlin showed Foley the little chapel he had had made out of scrap wood. One thing about Seabee chaplains, they always had lovely improvised chapels put up by their "Can Do" boys.37

After leaving Saipan, Foley's carrier steamed off again toward Guam. At sea she continued flight qualifications with a number of navy pilots. One touched down on deck, took off again, and instead of gaining altitude, went into the water and sank like a stone. Foley gave the pilot absolution. It was all there was to do as the plane went to the bottom with its occupant securely strapped into the cockpit. Back at Guam, Foley went aboard one of the *Vella Gulf*'s sister ships, the CVE *Block Island* to say Mass on Sunday August 5. After Mass he was approached by Marine pilots who were Boston College grads. It turned out that Guam had its own Boston College and Holy Cross clubs guided by the mottoes *In Hoc Signo Vinces* and *Ever to Excel.* Once more Foley thought that the war seemed to be an extended field trip for both the faculty and the student body of the Jesuit schools.38

Back in Foley's home town, Boston College was in a perilous financial situation by the time the war was coming to an end. It had been so denuded of teachers and students that there was some consideration given to closing up shop until the boys came home. In February 1944 there were 306 students in Arts and Sciences. By April the figure was down to 236. A desperate War Fund Drive was initiated to raise $250,000, chiefly from alumni and local businessmen. William Cardinal O'Connell put up the

first $5,000 only a few months before he died in April 1944. The sub-
scription was more than fulfilled by September, but by that time the
Heights was a ghost town. The government had no complaints about the
patriotism of all-male Catholic colleges, which tended to be outstandingly
zealous in their service to the state. This stemmed from a long standing
need for Catholics to "prove" their loyalty and Americanism in the face of
the insistent charges of bigots who questioned their allegiance to America
because of their devotion to a "foreign potentate." In fact the cost of this
uncritical nationalism of American Catholics has been very high. Of the
5,052 Boston College students who served in the war, 155 never returned.
In small compensation, they won 560 decorations and 40 citations. Apart
from the students and Jesuit faculty chaplains, 123 other priests who were
graduates of B.C. served as chaplains, mostly from the Boston
Archdiocese.39

There was once source of outside income that proved to be a steady if
minor supplement to B.C.'s dwindling finances. The chaplains in both the
navy and the army had their pay sent directly home to the Province treasurer. The Jesuits at that time did not receive a salary in religious life, and
were glad to be able to send money home. Foley's navy pay as lieutenant
senior grade amounted to over $400 per month. He had also gotten
involved in a stock-share pool with a group of officers which paid off to
the tune of about $200 a month. He sent this cash directly to Fr. William
Murphy, the college president, throughout the war years.40

August 6, 1945, dawned early as usual aboard the *Vella Gulf* with
General Quarters. The chaplain of the vessel went about his standard
duties that day, but soon found that he had two visitors who were in need
of his services. A Marine, Stan Glowacki, came to him to talk religion.
Foley never tired of shop talk and found the young man to be very serious
about the important things. Glowacki told Foley that he wanted to
become a lay brother when the war was over, and the chaplain felt that he
seemed to be ready for that important step, young as he was. Some people,

whether because of solid upbringings or the mysterious call of a vocation knew where they were going from the start.41

Not long afterward, Lt. Bill Massey asked Foley for a few minutes. He too had been pondering spiritual questions and had come to some different conclusions. He was puzzled by what seemed to be the "meaningless universe" in which human beings lived. He wanted some assurance from the priest that the truths of religion were not just manufactured by an overheated imagination. There was nothing unusual in this. Foley had talked to countless young men and women who had seen too much in this war. Foley had to give them the very difficult explanation that

> ...all of the evil in the world had to be laid at the doorstep of human beings. God was not responsible for it and there would be no trouble in the world if people were puppets without free will. The temptation when tragedy came into one's life was to say if God is all powerful why did he do this to me, if he is all loving why didn't he step in. The biggest problems are prayer, faith and suffering in anybody's life and the supreme test is death. It is a test of faith, a tragedy in capital letters, to find whether the faith has no roots or the roots of an oak tree.42

Only hours before Foley was having these deep theological discussions, a B-29 Superfortress dropped a single atomic bomb on the city of Hiroshima, Japan, destroying most of the city and approximately 100,000 people. The *Vella Gulf* did not get word of this event until August 9, when the ship had dropped anchor at Buckner Bay, Okinawa. The officers discussed the unexpected turn of events. One pilot said he would not want that responsibility even if he were carrying out orders. That same day the city of Nagasaki was hit with a second atomic device, killing about 35,000.43

Hiroshima was a likely bombing target, being Japan's eighth largest city, headquarters of the 2nd General Army and a major military embarkation point. The fact that it had not already received much attention from American bombers should have been highly suspicious. The destruction of Nagasaki, however, still remains inexplicable. Though there were some armaments factories in the area, Nagasaki was the most westernized and Christian area in Japan. Converted by Jesuits in the 16th century, the Japanese Catholics were brutally suppressed for decades but retained the faith, even combating the troops of the central government in a three month battle until being exterminated. At the time of the Second World War the city was the site of the Urakami cathedral and had a thriving Catholic populace of native faithful and clergy as well as a number of foreign priests. Of Nagasaki's 20,000 Catholics, at least 10,000 were wiped out by the atomic blast. There had been a conscious decision on the part of American war planners not to target for atomic destruction Kyoto, the traditional religious center of Japan. Apparently there was not a second thought given to obliterating a city of highly westernized Catholic Japanese.44

At 2140 on Friday August 10 the *Vella Gulf* was called to General Quarters, in response to an outburst of gunfire from the ships in the immediate area. No one knew whether or not they were under attack, or whether the Japanese were making a last-ditch effort to sink the fleet at Okinawa. It took several hours for word to go around that the firing was unauthorized celebrating due to scuttlebutt that the war was over. Six men were killed and another thirty wounded by the display, particularly senseless considering that the war had not yet ended officially. The carrier remained on alert and steamed back toward Guam on August 11 with a load of sixty planes to be serviced there. Rumors continued to fly. A Japanese hospital ship returning from Wake was stopped by an American destroyer and inspected. Its evacuated garrison, bypassed by the war, resembled skeletons. On August 15 the *Vella Gulf* approached the harbor in Guam. While still preparing to dock, the P.A. system crackled to life, calling the crew to stand by for a special announcement. Foley dropped what he was doing. Could this be the announcement that they had been waiting for for years? It was the Feast of Our Lady's Assumption. Was she interceding here? Suddenly the word came through. Secretary of the Navy James Forrestal had announced officially that the Japanese had surrendered. The war was over.45

The first thing Foley did was to seek out the executive officer on the bridge. He said, "Commander, I'd like to make a short prayer of thanksgiving that the war is over and we only lost one pilot." The exec turned toward another officer and sneered, "The chaplain wants to say a prayer. Huh." He turned back to Foley and said, "Go ask the captain." Foley did just that. He found Captain Morse and asked his permission. Morse responded, "Go right ahead, Father." Foley returned to the exec, gave him a textbook salute and said, "I got permission from the captain, *sir*, to say a prayer." The officer was speechless.46

> This is the Chaplain, Fr. Foley speaking. You have just heard the official pronouncement in the form of an ALNAV from the Secretary of the Navy that the war is over. It is only appropriate that the arrival of this moment which has been the object of so many prayers should be commemorated by an act of thanksgiving to Almighty God for the blessing of victory. So we stop for a minute in the shipboard routine to pray.
>
> O Almighty and everlasting God, Father of mercies. Whose treasures and goodness are infinite, we raise our minds and hearts to Thee in thanksgiving that this day the nations of the world are no longer locked in deadly strife and that Thou hast crowned our arms with victory.
>
> Grant we beseech Thee, that in our moment of victory, we may not forget to walk in the way of Thy Commandments and so merit Thy blessing upon ourselves and our great country in the days of peace that are ahead.

We ask Thee, in Thy mercy to be mindful of our comrades in arms, who made this victory possible, the Marines and soldiers who reddened the beaches from Casablanca to Iwo Jima, and the sailors and pilots who fought their ships and planes to a flaming end. To them, O Lord, and to all who place their trust in Thee, grant a place of refreshment, light, and peace, through Our Lord and Savior, Jesus Christ, Amen.47

The next day the ship received a message from CINCPAC Admiral Halsey regarding future conduct dealing with the Japanese. Foley and some of the others read it with great amusement. Halsey's order against "insulting epithets" and "abuse and vituperation" was in laughable contrast to his sign on Tulagi which shrieked "Kill Japs Kill Japs Kill More Japs!" The first casualty of war, the chaplain noted, is always the truth.48

Though hostilities had officially ceased, routine aboard the carrier went on as usual. There was an understandable fear that some Japanese would continue fighting, either because they had not gotten the word or out of sheer fanaticism. Combat air patrols continued to fly off the *Vella Gulf* in order to intercept any Japanese pilots looking to make a grand gesture at the twelfth hour. The ship steamed north, destination unknown to most of the crew. A meeting of the officers was held in which the captain and executive officer extolled the virtues of staying in the regular navy. When the captain asked for a show of hands of reservists who planned to stay on, not one went up.49

Foley knew how they felt. Most of these men had been willing to do their part in the war, perhaps even lay down their lives if necessary, but the navy was not their life. They had families at home and hopefully would get their old jobs back in the civilian world. Foley did not have a family, but he had his community, the Jesuit brotherhood, and he was anxious to return to Boston College. Some of the reservists, to their great displeasure, would be called back to duty in a far less popular war in another five years.

By August 22, the *Vella Gulf* was heading into the infamous typhoon which put a number of ships on the bottom. Since he had gotten his sea legs on the rougher Atlantic the turbulence did not bother him. Other sailors who had spent all of their time in the Pacific, however, were seasick for days. Planes were grounded and lashed securely to the deck with steel cables. The ship was now part of an armada of over fifty vessels heading toward Yokohama.50

September 22 was V-J Day. The crew of the *Vella Gulf* heard the proceedings over the radio. Ten of the officers clustered in the wardroom eagerly absorbing every word. President Truman spoke, then General MacArthur, who talked of remembrance for the sailors who were buried at sea. One of the officers who had survived the sinking of the *Yorktown* wiped tears from his eyes. Many of his friends had gone down with the ship. Admiral Nimitz read a list of names of men buried in the cemetery near his Guam headquarters. They represented seemingly every nationality of people who called themselves American. Foley knew the cemetery well and had stopped to pray there for the interred. Relief at the end of the war was mixed with grief that had been bottled up for years. Nor was the danger yet passed. One of the vessel's planes spun in upon landing and breaths were held until the pilot could be seen swimming away from the sinking plane.51

The ships continued on a course toward Yokohama. Gradually the feeling sunk in that the maelstrom was indeed over. On September 5, for the first time since the war started, ships were lit up like Christmas trees at night. Men stood on deck to see the unfamiliar sight, a blaze of red and green running lights. Foley noted in his dairy that censorship regulations had been lifted and added with no apparent irony that "we can now tell everything about where we have been and what we have been doing."52 Foley had recorded in meticulous detail everywhere he and his two ships had gone for more than three years, on an almost daily basis in his diary. While Foley was a mere lieutenant and there was little chance of this document ever falling into the hands of the enemy, it was as blatant a violation of censorship rules as could be conceived. His memoir was filled with the names of officers and enlisted men, destinations, ports of call, and dissension aboard ship.

Around 0800 on September 8, the *Vella Gulf* and fourteen other ships dropped anchor in Sagami Bay off Yokohama. Foley thought the terrain very similar to that of the New England coastline, with a long beach and densely treed area in the background. A trolley car with brown sides, yellow trimmed windows, and silver roof clattered along the shoreline, reminding him of a like contraption that plied the ways on Revere Beach, north of Boston. Along the cliffs, gun positions could be seen and someone voiced the universal opinion that he was glad they did not have to fight their way ashore at this piece of real estate. Overhead, C-54s, B-17s, B-24s, and B-29s rumbled back and forth, many ferrying released prisoners of war to freedom.53

The *Vella Gulf* moved on later that day and arrived in Tokyo Harbor under the shadow of 12,000 ft. high Mount Fujiyama. The vessels joined an American armada already anchored, a fleet composed of every conceivable ship from tugs to battlewagons and flattops. Foley surveyed the awesome scene. Three forts guarding the entrance to the harbor had been reduced to rubble. On one side of the harbor a stranded Japanese destroyer lay on a bank while a battleship gutted by fire kept it company. Foley thought it a fitting day for him to be sailing into the heart of Japan. September 10 was the anniversary of Blessed Charles Spinola, an Italian Jesuit who labored twenty years in the islands and was killed in the mass execution of Jesuits and their Christian followers in Nagasaki in 1622.54

The crew anxiously awaited permission for liberty. Everyone wanted to see the faces of the enemy and view the much-vaunted destruction of his homeland by the B-29 raids. On September 13 liberty was granted and the chaplain hopped into a landing craft with the rest of the men going ashore for the city of Yokohama. He brought along some yen and thirty packs of cigarettes. He figured he could find someone who would appreciate them. Upon landing Foley and his companions found the dock area to be slightly damaged and not very different than any other seaport. The talk was that the B-29s had "written the city off the map." The group of American naval officers thought as usual the air force was exaggerating things until they turned a sharp corner. "Then a landscape of utter desolation met our eyes. We were on the edge of the business section of Yokohama. That area about four square miles was completely destroyed. Acre after acre was leveled to the ground. As if to point out the devastation, here and there by some quirk of fate a building would be left partially standing, a melancholy survivor of the holocaust that consumed its neighbors."55

Out of the rubble they glimpsed three white women, obviously English by their dress, who told them that the devastation had all been effected on one day, May 28, and two of the structures that survived were the Catholic church and a Catholic hospital. One of the women insisted on bringing Foley to the hospital which was run by a nursing order of nuns. Though untouched by the bombing it was an empty shell, having been seized by the Japanese Navy during the war. When they left they stole everything except the walls. They left the elevators in only because they could not get them out. The nuns could not say when they would be able to begin functioning as a hospital again. At the church the French pastor who had been in Japan for twenty-two years gave Foley some advice for the Americans in dealing with the Japanese. First, the military class must be driven out of public life and second the emperor's divinity must be taken from him. Foley found the church to be quite attractive, reminding him of a couple back home in Massachusetts. The familiar statues of Our Lady and the Little Flower were there, along with St. Stanislaus, who had a curious Japanese cast to his eyes. "But it was a Catholic church and a Catholic felt at home immediately in it."56

On his way back to the ship Foley got to see the true effects of the "big day" back in May. Water and gas lines had still not been repaired and the Japanese he saw were clad in rags and starving. Occasionally a trolley car clattered by, but here and there burned-out trolleys were lying on their sides cluttering up the streets. The B-29s had indeed wiped Yokohama off the map. Traditional business went on as usual, however. When Foley and three of the ship's pilots passed a brothel the youngest pilot said, "Father go over there and let me take a picture of you with one of the girls!" Foley said, "Oh no, I know what you would do. You would send it to my big boss the New England Provincial."57

When the war ended Archbishop Spellman, the Military Vicar, had cabled to Admiral Halsey indicating that he would like to tour the recently liberated areas in the Philippines and Japan. He arrived in Manila on August 27 then went on to Okinawa and Tokyo. On the 15th there was a meeting aboard the *South Dakota* with all of the available Catholic chaplains in the area. Foley knew Spellman from his days in the Boston Archdiocese and he greeted him graciously. There were about one thousand men at the Mass that Spellman celebrated, and afterward the archbishop waded into the crowd shaking hands and even recalling the names of individuals he had previously met all over the world. At that time Halsey was living on the battleship and the admiral and the prelate got along famously.58

Two days later Foley and the *Vella Gulf* crew were given liberty again, this time to visit Tokyo itself. The train from Yokohama to Tokyo had a coach marked "Reserved for the U.S. Army" and the navy had no qualms about taking these conquerors' privileges. The cars reminded Foley of Boston's "El" sardine cans except the Boston variety had some limit to their capacity. The Japanese were crammed into these cars to bursting. On the way to Tokyo proper Foley saw mile upon mile of destruction "where there had been factories, there was only chimney after chimney that stood against the skyline, like giant cement pencils that had been frozen in the act of writing some message across the sky. Where the factories had not been leveled, their walls stood at crazy angles, ready to topple, it seemed with the slightest breeze." Hovels with miserable peasants in front continued right into Tokyo.59

Foley's destination was the Jesuit University Sancta Sophia run by Father Bitter, S.J., a German, whom Foley knew from his days at Heythrop College in England years before. He was told by Fr. Sam Hill

Ray, one of the chaplains at the Spellman meeting, that Bitter was still alive. Ray had already made it to the university in the company of two other Jesuit chaplains, Fr. Charles Robinson and Fr. Paul O'Connor, who had relieved Robinson as chaplain of the *Missouri*. When the war ended Robinson was detached to act as interpreter on Admiral Badger's staff and was in fact instrumental in discovering the whereabouts of American POWs held in Japan. He had taught at the Catholic University in Tokyo in the early twenties and spoke the language like a native. In overseas cap and deck jacket, grey-haired Robinson passed easily through checkpoints, resembling as he did a grizzled admiral rather than a lowly chaplain. Robinson and the others brought some food to the starving Jesuits at the university but their situation was still desperate.60

Foley knew it would be difficult to get to the university. He only had a few hours ashore, knew no Japanese, and had no transportation. He went into a bank and found a manager who spoke English and provided him with a detailed map. Foley paid for the information with a pack of Luckies and the Japanese went wild with glee at receiving such a valued prize. After studying the map, however, he realized that he could never make the school and get back in time for his launch. At the train station again he bumped into some flyers. Another group on the opposite landing told them they were on the wrong platform so Foley and the flyers jumped the tracks. Shades of North Station.61

Further liberties were canceled until the 19th due to the terrific winds blown up by the latest typhoon. Foley did go ashore at the first opportunity at attend a chaplains' meeting at an officer's club concerning the issue of prostitution. The chaplains had earlier complained because initially the military authorities had allowed the brothels to remain open. Foley noticed many of them, usually displaying signs in pidgin English such as the "Welcome House," "Geisha Girls House" and "For Naval, Flyers and Miyatary." Another said "Business For Closed." Foley also toured the Yokosuka navy yard and noticed that much of the equipment had been furnished by T.E. Smith and Co., Glasgow. These machines had produced ships and weapons that had killed many British and American boys. He ruminated that greed and vice knew no distinctions between nations.62

The *Vella Gulf* was slated to leave Japan on the 21st for Okinawa, and Foley wanted one last chance to get some supplies to Father Bitter at the university. He was told that the Jesuits and their community were starving, and that Father Bitter, who was once nearly 170 pounds was now less than 120. Foley had grabbed items with two hands and stuffed them in a bag including a dozen filet mignons, half a dozen cans of corn and beets, a jar of jelly, peanut butter, beef broth, cartons of cigarettes and more. Once again he had left the ship with a bag of provisions, this time the landing craft brought the liberty group right to the dock in Tokyo. Foley's problem remained, however, as he had no idea where the university was located except that it was in the "vicinity of the Imperial Palace."63 That was not much help considering that the city was a blasted wasteland.

As soon as Foley hit the deck he saw an American sailor fooling with a Japanese truck. He yelled out, "Whose truck?" The sailor, Samuel Malfo of San Francisco replied, "I don't know." "Where did you get it?" "Right here on the dock." "Ever driven one of these before?" "No sir." "Well you'll learn. Drive to the Emperor's palace." Foley hopped in the passenger side, yelled "All aboard" and a conglomeration of officers and men piled into the back. The driver tore off through the streets swerving past roadblocks of debris and wreckage everywhere. Most of the men were dumped off at the Ginza shopping district but Foley, the driver, and a few hardy souls took off again looking for the palace. They had been driving for half an hour when Foley asked, "How much gas do we have?" Malfo replied, "I don't know. Gauge is broken. Let's keep going until we stop."64

After attempting to get directions from several people and becoming more hopelessly lost, Foley climbed to the top of a six story building and spied the Imperial grounds surrounded by a moat. They headed in that direction and saw that the entrances were guarded by American MPs, the only ones they saw in the city. The Japanese, ever submissive to authority, were the essence of courtesy and the Americans never felt that they were in

danger. Some boys directed them to a Japanese man who turned out to be
a Marist priest with some command of French. The multi-lingual chaplain could *parlez-vouz* well enough and the Marist piled into the passenger
side of the truck while Foley hung on the running board. The group traveled another twenty minutes through the rubble and finally sped into the
driveway of a big brown building. Father Bitter and six of the community
greeted Foley and his strange band.65

Foley dropped off his horde of loot but only had ten minutes to visit
because he was due back at the ship. The Jesuits told him that their old
building was destroyed by fire though the new ones were only slightly
damaged. They also told him that Hirohito was responsible for the decision to surrender, regardless of the wishes of the militarists. There was
even some talk that the emperor himself might someday become Catholic!
At that the truckload of Yanks headed back toward the liberty dock. As
they neared their destination the engine began to sputter. Foley told the
driver to coast it as far as possible and then pull over to the sidewalk. He
did and stopped by smashing into another truck.66 Their joyride over, the
group off-loaded and bolted for the dock. Foley bade *adieu* forever to
Japan as the boat pulled away.

The next morning September 21 the *Vella Gulf* shoved off for
Okinawa. Now that the killing and dying was over, Foley wanted to get
back to Boston College as soon as possible. He had already gotten a letter
from his superior, New England Provincial Father James H. Dolan, ordering him to come home as soon as the war was over. Foley received the letter more than six weeks after it was sent. Foley answered the letter but
soon received another one from Dolan demanding to know why he had
not answered the first one. The magisterial Dolan wrote in an appropriate
style, beginning his letter with, "By virtue of my authority as the
Provincial of New England and also as one of my subjects..." Though
Foley spent a great deal of time overseas he was not at the top of the point-
step system and did not expect any special treatment to get home early.
Nevertheless, so that he could answer Dolan truthfully, he went to

Captain Morse to explain the situation. Morse laughed and said, "Your big boss, Father, doesn't know how the navy runs."67

At Buckner Bay, Okinawa, the *Vella Gulf* loaded a passenger complement of 656 men for passage back to the states after one last stop at Pearl Harbor. On October 5, as the vessel approached Hawaii Foley was informed that he had been promoted to lieutenant commander. The rank meant nothing to him. He would have to spend a few more months in the navy before his turn for rotation came up, but with the war ended his reason for being there was gone. The carrier arrived at Pearl on the evening of October 6. In the morning chaplain Foley awoke and went up to the flight deck to view the beautiful sunrise, the lush green of the pineapple fields, and the imposing mountains.68 Pearl, where the murder had all begun four years earlier, and now it was truly over.

Notes: Chapter 9

1 Foley interview, March 17, 1995.

2 Foley diary, May 31, 1944.

3 Drury, *History of the Chaplain Corps United States Navy*, vol. III, 42; Foley interview, March 6, 1995.

4 Foley interview, March 6, 1995.

5 Foley interview, Marcy 17, 1995.

6 Ibid.

7 Ibid. Foley never did learn how the admiral made out but for the rest of his long life he wondered about it and how the man felt the day his sons were ordained.

8 Foley diary, no date.

9 Drury, *History of the Chaplain Corps United States Navy*, vol. II, 61.

10 Ibid., 94.

11 Ibid., 95. In fact there were few incidences of chaplain cowardice in the face of the enemy and most men who were involved in actual combat performed in an exemplary manner. The case of Father O'Callahan

aboard the stricken *Franklin* was the most famous but certainly no solitary example of a chaplain whose moral authority and personal courage averted a disaster even when line officers themselves had panicked. Captain Gehres gave him much of the credit for saving the ship. Father Robinson, who had been instrumental in the smooth operation of the wartime Chaplain Corps died in a plane crash February 23, 1945, his faith in God unshaken.

12 William T. Y'Blood, *The Little Giants: U.S. Escort Carriers Against Japan* (Annapolis: Naval Institute Press, 1987), passim.

13 *Dictionary of American Naval Fighting Ships,* vol. III, 475.

14 Foley interview, March 10, 1995.

15 Foley interview, March 6, 1995.

16 Y'Blood, *The Little Giants,* 392, 393; Robert Sherrod, *History of Marine Corps Aviation in World War II* (Washington, D.C.: Combat Forces Press, 1952), 330, 331, 397; John Pomeroy Condon, *Corsairs and Flattops* (Annapolis: Naval Institute Press, 1998), 87–90, 114. Two other carriers with navy fliers were to round out Carrier Division 27 which never actually operated as a unit before the war ended and in fact the four jeeps with Marine fliers were not used for close air support after all. Sherrod believed that the Marine CVEs were poorly used because the commander of the escorts at Okinawa, Rear Adm. Calvin T. Durgin frowned on overspecialization and felt the Marine units expected preferential treatment. Sherrod maintained that the admiral was overruled in the post-war period and that the concept of Marine fliers supporting Marine ground troops worked well in Korea. Sherrod however, was definitely a Marine Corps partisan and it can hardly be denied that the Corps is perpetually seeking special missions to avoid being defunded or considered superfluous.

17 Foley diary, May 8, 1945.

18 Foley diary, May 9, 11, 1945; Foley interview, March 3, 1995.

19 The Jesuits' long experience with fighting men gave them a realistic attitude. When Francis Xavier went to Malacca in 1545 he found the

Portuguese there to be as debauched and pagan as the natives. He brought them back by persuasion. Men who worked with Xavier noted, "Very often he used to join men at their games and diversions, showing a keen interest in the play. If, out of respect for him, they desisted, he would very agreeably invite them to continue, saying that they were soldiers and had no need to live like monks...So easy was his manner in every company that with soldiers he seemed to be a soldier and with merchants a merchant." Brodrick, *The Origin of the Jesuits*, 127, 128.

20 Foley interview, March 6, 1995.

21 Foley diary, Mary 12, 1945.

22 Ibid; Foley interview, April 13, 1995.

23 Foley interview, March 6, 1995, April 13, 1995.

24 Foley interview, March 6, 1995.

25 Foley diary, June 17, 1945.

26 Foley diary, June 25, 1945. Schmitt was awarded a Navy and Marine Corps medal posthumously but some *Oklahoma* sailors have always considered it a disgrace that their heroic chaplain was not decorated with the Medal of Honor considering that no man could have done more above and beyond the call of duty. A copy of the Navy and Marine Corps citation can be found in Stephen Bower Young, *Trapped at Pearl Harbor: Escape from the Battleship Oklahoma* (Annapolis: Naval Institute Press, 1991).

27 Foley diary, June 26, 1945.

28 Foley diary, June 27, 1945.

29 Foley diary, June 28, 1945.

30 Ibid.

31 Foley interview, March 6, 1995.

32 Ibid.

33 Foley diary, July 16, 20, 22, 1945.

34 Foley diary, July 22, 1945.

35 Foley diary, July 23, 1945.

36 Foley diary, July 26, 1945.

37 Foley diary, July 28, 1945. Fr. James Dolan was decorated with the Bronze Star for his service on Saipan. See Giblin, *Jesuits as Chaplains,* 50, 76, 123.

38 Foley diary, August 5, 1945.

39 Dunigan, *A History of Boston College,* 300, 301, 313, 314. Even the wartime yearbooks are reduced in dimensions.

40 Foley interview, March 17, 1995.

41 Foley diary, August 6, 1945.

42 Foley diary, August 6, 1945; Foley interview, March 17, 1995.

43 Foley diary, August 9, 1945.

44 John Toland, *The Rising Sun: The Decline and Fall of the Japanese Empire 1936–1945.* 2 vols. (New York: Random House, 1970), 992. See also Takashi Nagai, *The Bells of Nagasaki* (Tokyo: Kodan Sha International 1984). This is a story of a Catholic Japanese doctor who worded feverishly to save lives in the aftermath of the blast. In Hiroshima the dazed Japanese who found their way to the Jesuit novitiate in Nagatsuka, two and a half miles from the center of the city were well cared for. The rector of the novitiate, Pedro Arrupe, S.J., had studied medicine prior to becoming a Jesuit and along with the other Jesuits was responsible for saving many lives. Several of the Society were injured in the blast, others succumbed to radiation poisoning. See Pedro Arrupe, S.J., "Hiroshima," *Catholic Digest* (April 1946): 69–72; John B. Siemes, S.J., "Report from Hiroshima," *Jesuit Missions* (March 1946): 30–32.

45 Foley diary, August 10, 11, 12, 13, 15, 1945.

46 Foley diary, August 15, 1945; Foley interview, March 6, 1995. There was one footnote to the antagonistic relationship between Foley and the officer. After the war Foley was given copies of his fitness reports. The exec had recommended that Foley be given a commission in the regular navy. Foley believed that he must have respected his sticking to his guns. In the years ahead, Foley often wondered if the man ever came back to the Church, noting that the Lord never exiles people completely. "Twixt the stirrup and the ground the mercies sought and the mercies

found…I'd be very happy to see him in heaven…if I get there. There is no guarantee."

47 Foley diary, August 15, 1945.

48 Foley diary, August 16, 1945. Samuel Eliot Morison, who could never be accused of being overly critical of his ex-boss, fairly gushes over the sign in his history. His Brahmin sensibilities likened the war to "Indian fighting" and he "cheered when the Japs were dying." Morison, *Struggle for Guadalcanal,* 187.

49 Foley diary, August 21, 1945; Foley interview, March 17, 1995. When the Korean War broke out Foley was at his post as dean of admissions and dean of freshmen and sophomores. He was not recalled to service though as usual there was a dearth of chaplains in both army and navy. He gave a talk to the men who were going in, primarily about what to expect in the service. He noted that the men who had been drafted were not all that keen about the Korean "police action." Foley interview, April 13, 1995.

50 Foley diary, August 22, 24, 1945.

51 Foley diary, September 2, 1945.

52 Foley diary, September 5, 1945.

53 Foley diary, September 8, 9, 1945.

54 Foley diary, September 10, 1945.

55 Foley diary, September 13, 1945.

56 Ibid.

57 Foley diary, September 13, 1945; Foley interview, March 6, 1945.

58 Foley diary, September 15, 1945; Ray, *A Chaplain Afloat and Ashore,* 102. Ray was a Jesuit from the New Orleans Province who served aboard the seaplane tender U.S.S. *Hamlin* (AV-15).

59 Foley diary, September 17, 1995.

60 All three of the Jesuit chaplains left an account of their trip to the university. See Lt. Charles A. Robinson, "Report from Japan," *Jesuit Missions* (January 1946): 2,3; Paul L. O'Connor, S.J., "Letters from Tokyo" *Woodsock Letters* vol. 74, 1945: 323–326. Ray, *A Chaplain Afloat*

and Ashore, 91–99. Robinson returned to Japan to do missionary work after being released by the navy.

61 Foley diary, September 17, 1945. North Station is the subway stop on Causeway Street in Boston that serviced the old Boston Garden. Jumping into the pit and crossing the tracks was common though it was wise to avoid the electrified third rail.

62 Foley diary, September 19, 1945.

63 Foley diary, September 20, 1945.

64 Ibid.

65 Ibid.

66 Ibid.

67 Foley interview, April 13, 1995. After Foley was back at Boston College for some time Dolan came around for his annual interview of all of his priests. Foley asked him if he had sent a letter to all of the chaplains like the one he sent him. Dolan said someone told him to write the letter. Foley later recalled, "I said it wasn't good advice. He didn't know I wasn't at the top."

68 Foley diary, October 5, 6, 1945.

CONCLUSION

John Foley returned to the United States aboard the *Vella Gulf*. She arrived in San Francisco on October 12 and he left the ship less than a month later on November 10. He was officially released from service on January 14, 1946. He returned to Boston College and immediately resumed his duties as Dean of Admissions and Dean of Freshmen and Sophomores. Fr. Michael Pierce, who had kept the seat warm for him during the war years gladly relinquished the titles and responsibility. The rest of the many New England Jesuit chaplains filtered back to the school within the year. Though the men who had gone off to war sometimes swapped stories among themselves, there was a tacit understanding that it was time to get back to the order's work.

And Foley did just that. He was extremely organized and methodical and had a pleasant demeanor that served him in good stead in positions where diplomacy was needed. (A demeanor that masked an iron will, as both his naval and ecclesiastical superiors sometimes discovered.) In 1951 he went to Boston College High School as principal and oversaw some of the school's expansion. That same year he was removed from the naval reserve list. Though the country was again at war, he was not called up to return to active duty and so his chaplain days were definitely over.

Now categorized as a high school administrator, Foley next served as rector at Cheverus High School in Portland, Maine from 1955–1961. Like most veterans in the post-war period his day-to-day work kept him too busy to think much about the war. Occasionally, something would bring back old times. Reading about the deaths of Halsey or Spruance or Wilkinson would take him back, as would dates such as October 23. He recalled that was the day they heaved up the chain on the *Clymer* and set out for the invasion of North Africa. The memories were pleasant for the most part except when he recalled taking care of sailors and Marines who were dying.

But he was in for the shock of his life one day while walking in downtown Portland. Passing by a navy recruiter's office he noticed a series of oil paintings so he stopped to admire them. The scenes were very familiar. A couple of paintings depicted Japanese planes being shot down, executed from the perspective of a ship's gun crew. Others showed Marines climbing down nets into landing craft and running ashore while explosions went off in the water. The landing craft had PA27 painted on them in large white characters. The last image was a group of sailors and Marines kneeling on the deck of a ship behind a priest in alb and chasuble, bowing to the consecrated Lord. John Foley had come face to face with his past self in Draper's painting, done right before the Bougainville invasion.

Foley did not say anything but somehow a captain at the Brunswick naval airbase was told that the priest in the painting was still alive and rector of a local high school. Realizing that there was publicity potential there, the captain arranged for Foley to receive a copy of the painting at a presentation in New York City. He and a Catholic officer flew in a small plane to New York where he was given a fine dinner and then presented with the copy. When he returned home he gave it to his mother, the woman who predicted while she was ironing that she would never live to see his ordination. It was now almost forty years later.

Between 1961–1968 he worked as rector at another Jesuit high school, Xavier in Concord, Massachusetts. The timing for the opening of a new

Catholic school could not have been worse. By the mid-1960s the Church was in turmoil due to the jumble of changes introduced by the Second Vatican Council. Xavier, like other schools, experienced dwindling applications, teacher walk-outs and general demoralization. Foley left in 1968 and the school closed a few years later.

He then went to the Immaculate Conception rectory in the South End of Boston to serve as retreat director, a post he enjoyed until the end of his long life. He traveled all over America, Canada, Ireland, England, Scotland, Malta, and Rome giving retreats for the clergy.

His sonorous voice, which he deemed "appropriately lugubrious" for retreat work, never failed him. In the spring of 1995, Foley was diagnosed with inoperable stomach cancer. He understood that death was near and refused extraordinary treatment. At the same time this writer contacted him and he agreed to a series of interviews relating his wartime experiences. At one of these meetings he came ambling down a perpetually darkened hall at St. Mary's, the Jesuit residence at Boston College, with a sizable box under one arm and said, "I'm listing to port today. Every so often you slide back into the old talk."

The box contained a poorly typed copy of a diary of over 500 pages. When Foley got back from the war he gave his original notes to his three secretaries who transcribed them in fits and starts in their spare time. He had never attempted to get it published and knew that at the final hour he would have to trust his story to someone else. He pushed the box across the massive oak table and said, "So everything is in there from beginning to end. And you take sacred care of it…"

John Patrick Foley of the Society of Jesus died October 21, 1995. In assessing his wartime chaplaincy he was emphatic. "I came into the navy to be in with our men when they were fighting and dying. To be a priest for them. That was it."

Foley's time as a naval chaplain was really a brief interlude in a long career as a priest. However, he considered these years as among the most rewarding. Like so many Americans of his generation, World War II was a watershed in his life, and after the war he would see it as a defining point in his priesthood. Unlike many people, the horrific scenes he witnessed did not shake his faith nor did he for one moment question his theology. Instead, the war made him firmer in his beliefs that evil was the result of fallen human nature. On the other hand he was continually delighted by the faith he saw manifested in so many of the young men and women he ministered to. Some disappointed him, but Foley ascribed that to the foolishness and indiscretion of youth. His parish was composed almost exclusively of teenagers and men in their early twenties. He knew the war would season them, if they survived it. And there was plenty for a priest to be satisfied by in that era. Attendance at Mass was high and devotions such as the rosary and Eucharistic adoration were popular.

Foley's chaplain experiences were typical in some ways. The single most gratifying discovery was that he finally observed the Church universal in action. While the Roman Church had always claimed to be catholic, it took a voyage to the far ends of the earth to drive home the reality of this concept. He saw firsthand the fruits of a handful of incredibly dedicated missionaries; priests and nuns who had voluntarily banished themselves to brutal, deadly environments, all to raise their people out of paganism. Foley did what he could for missionaries, almost all of whom were displaced when their property was destroyed by the warring factions. If he had to steal sacks of food from his ship's larder to keep a group of nuns and children from going hungry, so be it. He would take the chance on how that would look on his own personal ledger sheet. He thought that a few Americans, at least, would not mind some of their tax dollars going for food and not just bombs. In this, he was not alone. Many of the chaplains assigned to the Pacific Theater attempted to aid the missionaries either through direct contributions or with "midnight requisitions." The help was desperately needed. On Guadalcanal, for example, neither the Japanese nor the American governments ever paid the missionaries for their property that was destroyed.

It was the Church universal that Foley saw in jungle chapels, where dark-skinned, semi-naked natives attended Mass side by side with camouflage-clad Marines. It was the same familiar Church deep into enemy territory where priests and servicemen from Boston or Witchita or San Francisco could go and pray, even if St. Stanislaus appeared to be Oriental. It was the same ritual, performed in the "dead" language that preserved its integrity that comforted those wayfarers 10,000 miles from home. The Catholics themselves were not the only ones to understand this. On Guadalcanal, a non-Catholic soldier said to Fr. Thomas Reardon, "The Catholic Church is like the Standard Oil Company. It has stations wherever you go."

Foley was fairly illustrative of an average priest of the day as well, albeit one with superior powers of observation and discernment. While Catholics in general tended to be intensely patriotic, many priests in the services understood that there was a line to be drawn separating a man's duty to God from devotion to the State. Thus Foley, like many other Catholic chaplains, had no qualms at bucking the authority of their superiors if they felt orders were detrimental to the men's moral well-being. Regarding sexual matters, the chaplains' saw the specious reasoning behind the military's relativistic argument, "Don't do it, but if you do, don't get caught." The thesis was unsound and individuals such as Foley were more than willing to face court martial rather than compromise their principles. In this sense, the chaplains represented an annoyance to some commanders. Others considered the chaplains essential for the men's morale. Foley served under two men whom he regarded with the greatest respect. The other two he believed to be unprincipled careerists. In any case, he always considered that his primary responsibility was to be of service to the enlisted men. Whether or not he was sufficiently deferential to authority was a trivial matter. And he loathed hypocrisy and injustice. He was disgusted by the creatures who administered the European imperial regimes and felt the same about the stateside warhawks who preached race hatred and genocide.

Another facet of many of the Catholic chaplains' service was the opportunity for evangelizing both non-Catholics and lax Catholics. It was not Foley's style to wield a Bible and shout "hallelujah." If he were to bring in coverts to the Church it would not be with histrionics and harangues but with equal measures of faith and reason. Foley and many other Catholic chaplains were often approached by black men seeking instruction in the faith. This was delightful duty. The men were looking for answers to questions that no one else would address. If the Church provided anything, it was answers to every question. Often the answers were hard to take, and some, like the sincere admiral at Bethesda, could not accept them. But many others did, and throughout the war conversions were high, mostly attributable to the good example of the Catholic chaplains.

Even those who did not convert often experienced a change of attitude. The drunken pharmacist's mate from the South aboard the *Clymer* had heard all manner of invective about priests and the Church, but living with John Foley on a day to day basis showed him that Jesuits did not have horns and tails and that others had deceived him. Some of Foley's most devoted admirers were Protestants who retained their fondness and respect for him long after the war was over. In fact, goodwill toward the Catholic Church, never great in America, was comparatively strong in the post-war period up until the 1960s. This was primarily due to Catholics' performance in the war, exemplified by servicemen in general and chaplains in particular.

The chaplains often had to deal with the thornier problem of antagonistic ex-Catholics. Again, Foley's method was rarely confrontational except when he was pushed to the wall. The only real conflicts Foley had along these lines were with the *Clymer* crewman who deliberately flooded the deck during Mass and clashes with the executive officer on the carrier. He always believed that such men were bearing a heavy load of guilt for walking away from the Church and felt sorry for them. He did not believe that disputation would bring them back but that they would have to change their attitudes on their own after serious reflection.

As for the war itself, Foley considered it a disaster beyond compare and though he thoroughly enjoyed most of his work, dealing with young men who had been killed or blinded or disfigured was heartbreaking. He could not hate the Japanese but there was no question in his mind that they would have fought to the last man, woman, and child if the atomic bombings did not force them to yield. Some chaplains, deeply affected by their experiences, became pacifists in the post-war era. Not John Foley. He had seen kamikazes dive on American ships even after the armistice and he observed the murderous terrain on the Japanese mainland upon which Marines and soldiers would have had to sacrifice themselves. He never believed the Japanese could have been starved into submission. Revisionist theories about the political use of the atom bomb never swayed him. Having been in the eye of the storm when it blew fiercest, Foley believed that anything that ended it was a blessing. When asked in 1995 if he ever had problems adjusting, the ninety-one-year-old Jesuit replied, "I was just very grateful to God that he brought me back. But thank God I was never disturbed psychologically…maybe later."

BIBLIOGRAPHY

I. PRIMARY SOURCES

Manuscript Sources

Diary of John Patrick Foley, S.J. Copy in Author's Collection.

Dowling, S.J., Richard J. "Father Joseph Timothy O'Callahan, S.J." O'Callahan Papers, Archives of the College of the Holy Cross.

Foley, S.J., John P. "An Essay on Herodotus—The Forgotten and Libelled Historian." Archives of the New England Province, Society of Jesus. *Golden Jubilee in the Society of Jesus 1923–1973*. No pagination. Archives of the New England Province, Society of Jesus.

Letter from Ben F. Carson, dated December 26, 1998. Author's Collection.

Letter from Fr. Charles Riedel, C.S.V. to Bishop O'Hara, August 19, 1943. Archives of Clerics of St. Viator, Arlington Heights, IL.

Letter from Fr. Charles Riedel, C.S.V to Father French, September 12, 1944. Archives of Clerics of St. Viator.

Letter from John Patrick Foley to his mother. Copy in Author's Collection.

Pfab, S.M., Charles Borromeo. "American Hospital Chaplains During the Civil War 1861–1865." Ph.D. dissertation, Catholic University of America Library, 1955.

Statement of Fr. Charles Riedel, C.S.V. Archives of Clerics of St. Viator.

Suver, Charles. "Iwo Jima." Unpublished Manuscript. Suver Papers, Archives of the Oregon Province of the Society of Jesus.

Suver, Charles. Speech at 47th Anniversary Reunion of Iwo Jima Veterans." February 20–23, Biloxi, MI. Suver Papers, Archives of the Oregon Province of the Society of Jesus.

Vital Statistics Data Sheet, O'Callahan Papers, Archives of the College of the Holy Cross.

Personal Interviews

Cartier, SMSM, Sister Mary Theresa. Waltham, Massachusetts. Interviews, July 2, 9, 1997.

Draper, Mr. William. Telephone Interview, February 1997.

Foley, S.J. John Patrick. Boston College, Chestnut Hill, Massachusetts. Interviews, March 3, 6, 10, 17, April 13, 1995.

Jones, Mr. Leonard. Telephone Interview, January 10, 1998.

Leonard, S.J., William J. Boston College, Chestnut Hill, Massachusetts. Interviews, September 27, October 4, 1995, September 1996.

McNamara, Most Reverend, John J. Auxiliary Bishop of Boston, Merrimack Region. Lawrence, Massachusetts. Interview, October 15, 1996.

Published Primary Sources

Arnold, Brig. Gen. William R. "We are Strong in Spirit." *Faith of Our Fighters.* Edited by Ellwood C. Nance. St. Louis: Bethany Press, 1944.

Arrupe, S.J., Pedro. "Hiroshima." *Catholic Digest* (April 1946): 69–72. Cartier, SMSM, Sister Mary Theresa. "Horrors Start As Yellow Men Strike." Pictorial Review. *Boston Sunday Advertiser,* June 27, 1943.

Corby, C.S.C., William. *Memoirs of Chaplain Life: Three Years with the Irish Brigade in the Army of the Potomac.* Chicago: La Monte, O'Donnell, Printers, 1893; reprint ed., Edited by Lawrence Frederick Kohl. New York: Fordham University Press, 1992.

Curtis, Samuel Ryan. *Mexico Under Fire: Being the Diary of Samuel Ryan Curtis 3rd Ohio Volunteer Regiment During the American Military Occupation of Northern Mexico 1846–1847.* Edited by Joseph E. Chance. Fort Worth: Texas Christian University Press, 1994.

Cushing, Bishop Richard. "An Open Letter to Friends of the Missions." *The Boston Pilot,* March 6, 1943.

_____.*The Missions in War and Peace.* Boston: The Society for the Propagation of the Faith, n.d.

Doenitz, Admiral Karl. *Memoirs: Ten Years and Twenty Days.* Cleveland: The World Publishing Company, 1959.

Duffy, Francis P. *Father Duffy's Story: A Tale of Humor and Heroism, of Life and Death with the Fighting Sixty-Ninth.* New York: George H. Doran Co., 1919.

Ellis, John Tracy, ed. *Documents of American Catholic History.* Milwaukee: The Bruce Publishing Co., 1956

Fahey, James T. *Pacific War Diary 1942–1945.* Boston: Houghton, Mifflin Co., 1963.

Fisk, James. E. "Mass on a Volcano." *Catholic World* (January 1949): 312-316.

Foss, Joe and Foss, Diana. *A Proud American: The Autobiography of Joe Foss.* New York: Pocket, 1992.

Gehring, C.M., Frederic P. *A Child of Miracles: The Story of Patsy Li.* New York: Funk & Wagnalls Co., Inc., 1962.

Halsey, William F. and Halsey, III, Bryan J. *Admiral Halsey's Story.* New York: McGraw-Hill Books, Co., 1947.

Hubbard, S.J., Bernard R. *Father Hubbard's report on the need for Jesuit relief and recontruction in Europe.* Chicago: National Jesuit Fund, 1945.

Kilmer, Joyce. "Prayer of a Soldier in France." in *The World's Great Catholic Poetry.* Edited by Thomas Walsh. New York: The MacMillan Co., 1947.

King, Arthur G. *Vignettes of the South Pacific: The Lighter Side of World War II.* Cincinnati, Ohio: Arthur G. King, M.D., 1991.

Leonard, S.J., William J. *Where Thousands Fell.* Kansas City: Sheed & Ward, 1995.

Moens, John. " Marine Raider in the Pacific." Interview of John Apergis. *Military History* (August 1998): 42-48.

Morriss, Mack. *South Pacific Diary 1942–1943.* Lexington, Kentucky: The University Press of Kentucky, 1996.

Nagai, Takashi. *The Bells of Nagasaki.* Tokyo: Kodan Sha International, 1984.

Muehrcke, Robert C. *Orchids in the Mud: Personal Accounts by Veterans of the 132nd Infantry Regiment.* Chicago: J.S. Printing, 1985.

O'Callahan, Joseph T. *I Was Chaplain on the Franklin.* New York: The MacMillan Co., 1956.

O'Connor,S.J. Paul L. "Letters from Tokyo." *Woodstock Letters.* 74 (1945): 323–326.

Polk, James K. *The Diary of James K. Polk During His Presidency, 1845–1849.* Edited by Milo Milton Quaife. Chicago: A.C. McClurg & Co., 1910.

Ray, S.J., Samuel Hill. *A Chaplain Afloat and Ashore.* Salado, Texas: The Anson Jones Press, 1962.

Robinson, Lt. Charles A. "Report from Japan." *Jesuit Missions* (January 1946).

Siemes, S.J., John B. "Report from Hiroshima." *Jesuit Missions* (March 1946): 30–32.

Stilwell, Joseph W. *The Stilwell Papers.* Edited by Theodore White. New York: William Sloane Associates, Inc., 1948.

Vandergrift, Lt. Gen A.A. "Religion on Guadalcanal." *Faith of Our Fighters.* Edited by Ellwood C. Nance. St. Louis: Bethany Press, 1944.

Welsh, Peter. *Irish Green and Union Blue: The Civil War Letters of Peter Welsh.* Edited by Lawrence F. Kohl with Margaret Cosse Richard. New York: Fordham University Press, 1986.

Young, Stephen Bower. *Trapped at Pearl Harbor: Escape from Battleship Oklahoma.* Annapolis: Naval Institute Press, 1991.

II. SECONDARY SOURCES

America (January 9, 1943).

America (November 7, 1942).

"Analecta." *Ecclesiastical Review.* 107 (July 1942).

Anderson, S.J., George M. "Bernadine Wiget, S.J. and the St. Aloysius Civil War Hospital in Washington, D.C." *Catholic Historical Review* 76 (October 1990): 734–764.

"Aren't All Catholic Chaplains from Boston?" *The Pilot* (October 27, 1995).

"Army Morale." *America* (February 28, 1943).

Aurthur, Robert A. and Cohlmia, Kenneth. *The Third Marine Division.* Edited by Robert T. Vance. Washington, D.C.: Infantry Journal Press, 1948.

Bangert, S.J., William V. *A History of the Society of Jesus.* St. Louis: The Institute of Jesuit Sources, 1986.

A Brief History of the Catholic Chaplaincy and the Archdiocese For the Military Services. Washington, D.C.: Archives of the Archdiocese for the Military Services, n.d.

Bauer, Jack. *The Mexican War 1846–1848.* New York: Macmillan Publishing Co., 1974.

Beaudot, William J.K. and Herdegen, Lance J. *An Irishman in the Iron Brigade.* New York: Fordham University Press, 1993.

Becker, S.J., Joseph M. *The Re-Formed Jesuits: A History of Changes in Jesuit Formation During the Decade 1965–1975.* San Francisco: Ignatius Press, 1992.

Belloc, Hilaire. *The Crusades: The World's Debate.* Milwaukee: The Bruce Publishing Co., 1937.

Billington, Ray Allen. *The Protestant Crusade 1800–1860: A Study of the Origins of American Nativism.* New York: Macmillan Co., 1938; reprint ed., Chicago: Quadrangle Books, 1964.

Blakely, S.J., Paul L. "A Father's Letter That Will Live." *America* (November 21, 1942).

Blair, Clay. *Hitler's U-Boat War: The Hunters 1939–1942.* New York: Random House, 1996.

Blankfort, Michael. *The Big Yankee: The Life of Carlson of the Raiders.* Boston: Little, Brown and Co., 1947.

Boyle, Esmerelda. *Father John McElroy: The Irish Priest.* n.c.: Thomas McGill & Co., 1878.

Brodrick, S.J., James. *The Origin of the Jesuits.* London: Longman's, Green, 1940; reprint ed, Chicago: Loyola Press, 1997.

Building the Navy's Bases in World War II. 2 Vols. Washington, D.C.: United States Government Printing Office, 1947.

Burke, S.J., James L. *Jesuit Province of New England: The Formative Years.* Boston: New England   Province of the Society of Jesus, 1976.

Campbell, S.J., T.J. *Pioneer Priests of North America 1642–1710.* 3 Vols. New York: The America Press,   1914.

Cook, Harry T. *"Remember the Maine!" An Historical Narrative of the Battleship Maine as told by its Chaplain The Right Reverend Monsignor John P. Chidwick.* Winchester, VA: Winchester Printers and Stationers, 1935.

Condon, John Pomeroy, *Corsairs and Flattops.* Annapolis: Naval Institute Press, 1998.

Costello, John. *The Pacific War.* New York: Rawson, Wade Publishers, Inc., 1981.

Davis, Burke. *Marine! The Life of Lt. Gen. Lewis B. (Chesty) Puller, USMC (Ret).* Boston: Little, Brown and Co., 1962.

Decker, S.M., Rev. Charles F. ed. *Saving the Solomons: From the Diary Account of Rev. Mother Mary Rose, S.M.* Bedford, Massachusetts: The Marist Missions, 1948.

Donovan, S.J., Charles F. "First Light." *Boston College Magazine* (Fall 1994).

_____. *A History of Boston College from the Beginnings to 1990.* Chestnut Hill: The University Press of Boston College, 1990.

Dower, John W. *War Without Mercy: Race and Power in the Pacific War.* New York: Pantheon Books, 1986.

Drury, Clifford M. *The History of the Chaplain Corps United States Navy* 3 Vols. Washington, D.C.: U.S. Government Printing Office Bureau of Naval Personnel, 1950.

Dudon, S.J., Pere Paul. *St. Ignatius of Loyola.* Milwaukee: The Bruce Publishing Co., 1949.

Dugan, S.J., John J. "Life Under the Japs: From Bataan's Fall to Miraculous Rescue at Cabanatuan by Yanks." *Boston Sunday Globe* (April 1, 1945).

Dunigan, S.J., David R. *A History of Boston College.* Milwaukee: The Bruce Publishing Co., 1947.

Durkin, S.J., Joseph T. *Journal of Father Adam Marshall 1824–1825.* Scranton: University of Scranton Press, 1943.

Egan, Maurice Francis and Kennedy, John B. *The Knights of Columbus in Peace and War.* 2 Vols. New Haven: Knights of Columbus, 1920.

Ellis, John Tracy. *Catholics in Colonial America.* Baltimore: Helicon Press, 1965.

Ettinger, Albert M. and Ettinger, A. Churchill. *A Doughboy with the Fighting Sixty-Ninth.* Shippensburg, Pennsylvania: White Mane Publishing Co., 1992.

Finley, C.S.P., James F. *James Gillis, Paulist.* Garden City, New York: Hanover House, 1958.

Fitchner, S.J., Joseph H. *James Laynez Jesuit .* St. Louis: B.Herder Book Co., 1944.

"For the Record." *Jesuit Missions* (November 1945).

Frank, Arthur Layton. *The Politics of Torch.* Lawrence: The University Press of Kansas, 1974.

Frank, Richard B. *Guadalcanal.* New York: Random House, 1990.

"Fr. Jim Hennessy 1905–1942." pamphlet printed for private circulation by the Mission Academia of St. John's Seminary, 1950.

Fujita, Neil S. *Japan's Encounter with Christianity.* Mahwah, New Jersey: Paulist Press, 1991.

Fulop-Miller, Rene. *The Jesuits: A History of the Society of Jesus.* New York: Capricorn Books, 1963.

Gaustad, Edwin Scott. *A Religious History of America.* New York: Harper & Row, 1966.

Gannon, Michael. *Operation Drumbeat.* New York: Harper & Row, 1990.

Gannon, S.J., Robert I. *The Cardinal Spellman Story.* Garden City, N.Y.: Doubleday & Co., Inc., 1962.

Gelb, Norman. *Desperate Venture.* New York: William Morrow and Co., 1992.

Germain, Dom Aidan Henry. *Catholic Military and Naval Chaplains 1776–1917.* Washington, D.C.: Catholic University, 1929.

Giblin, S.J., Gerard F. *Jesuits as Chaplains in the Armed Forces 1917–1960.* Woodstock, Maryland: Woodstock College Press, 1961.

Glines, Carroll V. *The Doolittle Raid: America's Daring First Strike Against Japan.* New York: Orion Books, 1988.

Grant, Dorothy Fremont. *War Is My Parish.* Milwaukee: The Bruce Publishing Co., 1944.

Guadalcanal Echoes. "From Secnav to Alnav: Regarding Personal Diaries." (August/September 1997).

Guadalcanal Echoes. "Chaplain of the 132nd Dies." Reverend Francis Gorman. (May/June 1998).

Hamilton, O.S.U., Jeanne. "The Nunnery As Menace: The Burning of the Charlestown Convent, 1834." *U.S. Catholic Historian* 14 (Winter 1996): 35–65.

Handlin, Oscar. *Boston's Immigrants.* New York: Athenaeum, 1975.

Haring, Bernard. *Embattled Witness: Memories of a Time of War.* New York: The Seabury Press, 1976.

Hennesey, James. *American Catholics: A History of the Roman Catholic Community in the United States.* New York: Oxford University Press, 1981.

Higham, John. *Strangers in the Land: Patterns of American Nativism 1860–1925.* New York: Athenaeum, 1955; reprint ed., Westport, Connecticut: Greenwood Press, 1981.

"History of U.S.S. George Clymer (APA-27)." Office of Naval Records and History, Ship's History Section, Navy Department.

Holy Bible: The Old Testament Douay Version and The New Testament Confraternity Version. New York: P.J. Kenedy & Sons, 1961.

Honeywell, Roy J. *Chaplains of the United States.* Washington, D.C.: U.S. Printing Office, 1958.

Hume, Edgar Erskine. *The Medical Works of the Knights Hospitallers of Saint John of Jersualem.* Baltimore: The Johns Hopkins Press, 1940.

Jenkins, Burris. *Father Meany and The Fighting 69th.* New York: Frederick Fell, Inc., 1944.

Johnstone, Tom and Hagerty, James. *The Cross on the Sword: Catholic Chaplains in the Forces.* London: Geoffrey Chapman, 1996.

Jolly, Ellen Ryan. *Nuns of the Battlefield.* Providence: The Providence Vistor Press, 1927.

Karig, Walter and Kelley, Welbourn. *Battle Report: Pearl Harbor to Coral Sea.* New York: Farrar &   Rinehart, Inc., 1944..

Kenny, S.J., Michael. *The Romance of the Floridas: The Finding and the Founding.* New York: The Bruce Publishing Co., 1934.

Kinneen, S.J., Joseph S. ed. *Holy Cross College Service Record War of 1917.* Worcester: Harrigan Press, 1920.

Lapomarda, Vincent. A. *The Jesuit Heritage in New England.* Worcester: The Jesuits of Holy Cross College, 1977.

Leatherneck (September 1997).

Leckie, Robert. *American and Catholic: A Narrative of their Role in American History.* New York: Doubleday & Co., 1970.

Lee, Gerard A. "The Military and Hospitaller Order of St. Lazarus of Jerusalem." *Irish Ecclesiastical Record* CX (1968): 372-380

Lemish, Michael G. *War Dogs: Canines in Combat.* Washington, D.C.: Brassey's, 1996.

Lord, Robert H.; Sexton, John E.; and Harrington, Edward T. *History of the Archdiocese of Boston in the Various States of its Development: 1604–1943.* 3 Vols. New York: Sheed and Ward, 1944.

Loxton, Bruce. *The Shame of Savo.* Annapolis: Naval Institute Press, 1994.

MacNamara, Paul. "Father Gehring" *Catholic Digest* (January 1945): 45–48.

Maguire, William A. *The Captain Wears a Cross.* New York: The MacMillan Co., 1943.

Maher, Sister Mary Denis. *To Bind Up the Wounds: Catholic Sister Nurses in the U.S. Civil War.* Westport, Connecticut: Greenwood Press, 1989.

McAleer, John. *Rex Stout: A Biography.* Boston, Little, Brown and Co., 1977.

McAvoy, C.S.C., Thomas T. *Father O'Hara of Notre Dame: The Cardinal Archbishop of Philadelphia.* Notre Dame, Indiana: University of Notre Dame Press, 1967.

McEniry, Sister Blanche Marie. *American Catholics in the War with Mexico.* Washington, D.C.: Catholic University Press, 1937.

"Military Faculties, laid down by the Sacred Consistorial Congregation for the Military Ordinariate of the United States of America." *Ecclesiastical Review* 107 (July 1942): 29–45

Miller, Robert Ryal. *Shamrock and Sword: The Saint Patrick's Battalion in the U.S.-Mexican War.* Norman, Oklahoma: University of Oklahoma Press, 1989.

Morison, Samuel Eliot. *Operations in North African Waters October 1942—June 1943.* Boston: Little Brown and Co., 1947.

_____.*The Struggle for Guadalcanal August 1942–February 1943.* Boston: Little, Brown and Co., 1951.

_____. *The Two-Ocean War: A Short History of the United States Navy in the Second World War.* Boston: Little, Brown and Co., 1963.

Morris, Eric. *Corregidor: The End of the Line.* New York: Military Heritage Press, 1982.

New York Times. "Obituaries", Frederic P. Gehring, (May 3, 1998).

O'Brien, Charles. "John F. O'Hara, C.S.C. Military Delegate (1939–1945)." *Records of the Catholic Historical Society of Philadelphia.* LXIV (1953).

O'Brien, Steve. "' Perhaps We'll Land on Friday':The Catholic Chaplain in World War II Films." Paper delivered at the "World War II: A Dual Perspective" Conference, Siena College, Loudonville, New York, June 4–5, 1998.

O'Connor, Thomas H. *Boston Catholics: A History of the Church and Its People.* Boston: Northeastern University Press, 1998.

O'Connell, James H. *History of the Diocese of Hartford.* Boston: D.H.Hived Co., 1900.

Official Guide to the Army Air Forces. New York: Simon and Schuster, 1944.

Office of the Chief of Chaplains. *American Army Chaplaincy.* Washington, D.C.: The Chaplain's Association, 1946.

Office of Naval Operations. *Dictionary of American Naval Fighting Ships.* Washington, D.C.: Navy History Division, 1968.

O'Malley, S.J., John W. *The First Jesuits.* Cambridge: Harvard University Press, 1993.

O'Neill, S.J., Charles A. "The 1st Invasion." *Jesuit Missions* (November 1945).

Ordinariate of Army and Navy Chaplains. *United States Catholic Chaplains in the World War.* New York: The Chauncey Holt Co., 1924.

"Pearl Harbor blame hurts admiral's kin." *The Boston Sunday Globe.* (December 7, 1997): A-40.

Petillo, Carol Morris. *Douglas MacArthur: The Philippine Years.* Bloomington, Indiana: Indiana University Press, 1981.

Pogue, Forrest C. *George C. Marshall: Ordeal and Hope.* New York: The Viking Press, 1966.

The Priest Goes to War. New York: The Society for the Propagation of the Faith, 1945.

Quimby, Rollin W. "The Chaplains' Predicament." *Civil War History* 8 (1962): 26–27.

_____. "Congress and the Civil War Chaplaincy." *Civil War History* 10 (1964): 249–250.

Rentz, *Bougainville and the Northern Solomons.* n.c.: Historical Section Division of Public Information Headquarters U.S. Marine Corps, 1948.

Reynolds,S.J., Edward D. *Jesuits for the Negro* . New York: The America Press, 1949.

Royster, Charles. *A Revolutionary People at War: The Continental Army and American Character, 1775–1783.* New York: W.W. Norton & Co., 1979.

Schurhammer, George. *Francis Xavier: His Life, His Time.* 4 Vols. Loyola University Press, 1973–1982.

Scott, Otto J. *The Creative Ordeal: The Story of Raytheon.* New York: Athenaeum, 1974.

Seward, Desmond. *The Monks of War: The Military Religious Orders.* London: Penguin Books, 1972.

Sexton, John E. and Riley, Arthur J. *History of St. John's Seminary.* Boston: Roman Catholic Archbishop of Boston, 1945.

Shannon, James P. ed. "Archbishop Ireland's Experiences as a Civil War Chaplain." *Catholic Historical R Review* XXXIX (October 1953): 298–305.

Shaw, Richard. *Dagger John: The Unquiet Life and Times of Archbishop John Hughes of New York.* New York: Paulist Press, 1977.

Sherrod, Robert. *History of Marine Corps Aviation in World War II.* Washington, D.C.: Combat Forces Press, 1952.

Smith, John Mortimer. *The Military Ordinariate of the United States of America, Canon Law Studies # 443.* Washington, D.C.: The Catholic University of America, 1966.

Solari, Giovanna R. *The House of Farnese* . Garden City: Doubleday & Co., 1968.

Spector, Ronald H. *Eagle Against the Sun: The American War with Japan.* New York: Vintage Books, 1985.

Tanaka, Yuki. *Hidden Horrors: Japanese War Crimes in World War II.* Boulder: Westview Press, 1996.

Time (December 7, 1942).

Thwaites, Reuben Gold. *Jesuit Relations and Allied Documents.* 73 Vols.

Toland, John. *The Rising Sun: The Decline and Fall of the Japanese Empire 1936–1945.* 2 Vols. New York: Random House, 1970

Tregaskis, Richard. *Guadalcanal Diary.* New York: Random House, 1943.

The War of the Rebellion—Official Records of the Union and Confederate Armies. Series III. Vol 1.

Watt, Mary Caroline. *St. Martin of Tours.* London: Sands & Co., 1928.

Weinberg, Gerhard L. *A World at Arms: A Global History of World War II.* New York: Cambridge University Press, 1994.

Wiley, Bell Irvin. "Holy Joes of the Sixties: A Study of Civil War Chaplains." *Huntington Library Quarterly* Vol. 1. (1953): 287–304.

Williams, Michael. *American Catholics in the War: National Catholic War Council, 1917–1921.* New York: The MacMillan Co., 1921.

Woodstock Letters: A Record of Current Events and Historical Notes Connected with the Colleges and Missions of the Society of Jesus.

Wyant, William K. *Sandy Patch: A Biography of Lt. Gen. Alexander M. Patch.* New York: Praeger, 1991.

Y'Blood, William T. *The Little Giants: U.S. Escort Carriers Against Japan.* Annapolis: Naval Institute Press, 1987.

0-595-22694-9